CHILDREN IN
CLASSROOMS

DANIEL SOLOMON
ARTHUR J. KENDALL

CHILDREN IN
CLASSROOMS

An Investigation of
Person-Environment
Interaction

 PRAEGER PUBLISHERS
Praeger Special Studies

New York • London • Sydney • Toronto

PRAEGER PUBLISHERS
PRAEGER SPECIAL STUDIES
383 Madison Avenue, New York, N.Y. 10017, U.S.A.

Published in the United States of America in 1979
by Praeger Publishers,
A Division of Holt, Rinehart and Winston, CBS, Inc.

9   038   987654321

Library of Congress Card Number: 79-62899

Printed in the United States of America

LB
3013
.S6
1979

ACKNOWLEDGMENTS

A large number of people have been involved in this project, in one way or another. We would like to express our sincere appreciation to the many children (and their parents), teachers, principals, assistant principals, and school secretaries who generously cooperated with us and tolerated the demands of the project, to the several area assistant superintendents, directors of instruction, pupil services supervisors, school psychologists, and other area personnel who gave assistance and advice at various phases, and to those central office administrators who helped the project through its initial stages. The strong and continual support, encouragement, and advocacy of Dr. Raphael Minsky, Supervisor of Psychological Services in the Montgomery County Public Schools during the period of this research, was of particular importance.

This project benefited from having the services of an exceptionally able and diligent group of research assistants. Those involved in the pilot study data collection were Nancy Allgire, Rod Fujii, David Goldstein, Henry Crabbe, Steven Koppel, Andrea Weiss, and Kathy Pearce. Kathy Pearce and Janet Chap coded the pilot study creativity and inquiry data. The classroom observers for the main study were Nancy Allgire, Henry Crabbe, Bruce Goodro, Ruth Hannon, Jennie Forehand, Margaret Geckos, Elaine Murphy, June Padrutt, and Kathy Pearce. The same people also administered the questionnaires and tests, with the addition of Sue Brennan, David Goldstein, Jim Goldstein, John Davey, Rod Fujii, Virginia Hodge, Pat McClure, and Robert Walker. Coding of the main study data was done by Ruth Hannon, Margaret Geckos, Elaine Murphy, June Padrutt, Nancy Allgire, and Kathy Pearce. Kathy Pearce also did much of the class visit scheduling (and rescheduling) and helped to coordinate and organize various phases of the research. Librarians in the school system's Educational Materials Laboratory were very helpful with several computer literature searches. A number of other people helped us with key punching and occasional computer programming services, and facilitated our work with the computer systems at the Catholic University of America and the Montgomery County Public Schools. Various project reports and papers were ably typed by Mrs. Doris Peddicord. Additional help has been provided by Pat Bulman and Jean Solomon. A project advisory committee (chaired by Dr. Sarah Edwards), made useful suggestions regarding several phases of this research. Dr. Barak Rosenshine made a number of very helpful comments and suggestions regarding an earlier version of this mono-graph. To all of these people we are very grateful.

The research project described in this book was supported by a grant from the Spencer Foundation, Chicago, Illinois, and was con-ducted under the auspices of the Montgomery County Public Schools, Rockville, Maryland.

CONTENTS

Page

ACKNOWLEDGMENTS   v

LIST OF TABLES   xii

LIST OF FIGURES   xviii

Chapter

1   PERSONS AND ENVIRONMENTS   1

Interactional and Noninteractional Approaches
to the Study of Human Behavior   1
Generality-Specificity of Behavior   3
Similarity between Situations as a Mediator of
Behavioral Consistency   5
Investigations of Person-Situation Interactions   9
Components-of-Variance Analyses   9
Interactions between Specific Variables   11
Interactional Theories and Approaches   13
Characterizing the Situation   17

2   STUDENTS AND CLASSROOMS   19

Noninteractional Research in Education   20
Studies of Teaching   21
Studies of Classroom "Climates" and Instructional
Programs   32
Comparison of "Follow Through" Models   33
Comparison of "Open" and "Traditional"
Approaches   34
Studies of Interactions between Student and
Treatment Characteristics   36
Studies Involving Open Education   36
Other Research on Student-Treatment Inter-
actions   38
Rationale for This Research   41

Chapter		Page
3	THE PILOT STUDY	46
4	THE MAIN STUDY: GENERAL PLAN AND DATA COLLECTION PROCEDURES	53
	General Plan	53
	Design	53
	Data Analyses	54
	Recruitment of Classrooms and Children	55
	Classroom Observations	57
	Teacher Descriptions of Classroom Activities	58
	Measures of Attitudes, Values, and Self-Assessments	59
	Measures of Inquiry Skill, Writing Quality, and Creativity	63
	Measures of School Achievement and Socioeconomic Status	66
	Teachers' Ratings of Students' Classroom Behavior	66
	Measures of Preferences, Orientations, and Motives	67
5	DERIVING DIMENSIONS OF CLASSROOM ENVIRONMENT	71
	Instrument Reliability and Refinement	71
	Factor Analyses of Classroom Observations and Descriptions	72
	Observation Form Cover Sheet	72
	General Organization and Activities Section of Observation Form	75
	Teacher Activities Section of Observation Form	77
	Student Activities Section of Observation Form	81
	Student Ratings Section of Observation Form	85
	Classroom Ratings Section of Observation Form	88
	Teacher Ratings Section of Observation Form	88
	Teacher Questionnaire	91
	Second-Order Analysis of Classroom Factors	100
6	DERIVING DIMENSIONS OF CHILD CHARACTERISTICS AND EDUCATIONAL OUTCOMES	107
	Preference, Orientation, and Motive Scales	107
	Item Analyses and Reliability	107
	Factor Analysis	108
	Factor Analyses of Achievement Tests	112

Chapter   Page

Creativity and Inquiry-Skill Measures   113
    Reliability   113
    Factor Analyses   117
Attitude and Value Scales   118
    Item Analyses and Reliability   118
    Factor Analyses   118
Factor Analyses of Student Class and Self-
    Evaluations and of Teachers' Ratings of Students   121
    Student Class and Self-Evaluations   121
    Teachers' Ratings of Students   123
Some Data on Convergent Validity   124
List of Factors and Indexes Representing Classroom
    Characteristics, Child Characteristics, and
    Educational Outcomes   125

7   IDENTIFYING CLASSROOM "TYPES" AND
     CHILD "TYPES"   128

Cluster Analysis of Classrooms   129
    Cluster One   134
    Cluster Two   134
    Cluster Three   135
    Cluster Four   135
    Cluster Five   135
    Cluster Six   136
Cluster Analysis of Children   138
    Cluster One   139
    Cluster Two   142
    Cluster Three   142

8   EFFECTS OF CLASSROOM "TYPES" AND
     CHILD "TYPES" ON OUTCOMES   145

Cluster and Sex Main Effects   150
Interactions   157
Summary of Interactions Involving Child Clusters
    and Classroom Clusters   168

9   EFFECTS OF CLASSROOM "DIMENSIONS" AND
     CHILD "DIMENSIONS" ON OUTCOMES   171

Classroom and Child-Dimension Main Effects   171

Chapter   Page

    Classroom Dimension by Child Dimension Inter-
      actions   183
      Interactions with Classroom Warmth   184
      Interactions with Control/Orderliness   193
      Interactions with Commonality Versus Variety
        of Activities   202
      Interactions with Individualized Teacher-Student
        Contact   206
      Interactions with Verbal (Academic) Participation   208
      Interactions with Emphasis on Student Expressive-
        ness   219
    Summary of Dimension-by-Dimension Interactions   227

10   SUMMARY, CONCLUSIONS, AND IMPLICATIONS   231

    General Summary   231
      Main Effects   235
      Cluster-by-Cluster Interactions   236
      Dimension-by-Dimension Interactions   241
    General Conclusions   246
      Interactions   246
      Main Effects of Classroom Variables   251
      Clusters and Dimensions   253
    Implications   254
      Practical Implications   254
      Theoretical Implications   256

Appendixes

A   ANALYSES OF CLUSTER-DIMENSION INTER-
    ACTIONS AND OF INTERACTIONS INVOLVING
    PRIOR ACHIEVEMENT LEVELS   258

    Investigations of Cluster-by-Dimension Inter-
      actions   258
      Interactions between Child Factors and Class-
        room Clusters   258
      Interactions between Child Clusters and Class-
        room Factors   265
    Summary of Cluster-by-Dimension Interactions   271
      Child Dimension by Classroom Cluster Inter-
        actions   271
      Classroom Dimension by Child Cluster Inter-
        actions   272

Appendix   Page

    Investigations of Interactions Involving Children's
    Initial Status on Selected Achievement-Related
    Measures   274
    Summary of Interactions Involving Children's Prior
    Status on Cognitive Measures   284

B   SUPPLEMENTARY TABLES   286

BIBLIOGRAPHY   301

ABOUT THE AUTHORS   317

LIST OF TABLES

Table   Page

5.1   Factor Analysis of Observation Form Cover
Sheet Data   73

5.2   Factor Analysis of Observation Form General
Organization and Activities Items   76

5.3   Factor Analysis of Observation Form Teacher
Activities Items   78

5.4   Factor Analysis of Observation Form Student
Activities Items   82

5.5   Factor Analysis of Observation Form Student
Ratings   86

5.6   Factor Analysis of Observation Form Class
Ratings   89

5.7   Factor Analysis of Observation Form Teacher
Ratings   92

5.8   Factor Analysis of Teacher Questionnaire   95

5.9   Second-Order Factor Analysis of Classroom
Measures   101

6.1   Factor Analysis of Preference, Orientation,
and Motive Scales   109

6.2   Factor Analysis of Third Grade Cognitive
Abilities and Achievement Tests   112

6.3   Factor Analysis of Fourth Grade Achievement
Tests   113

6.4   Intercoder Correlations for Selected Subsample
of Protocols (N = 98–101): Creativity, Inquiry
Skill, and Writing Quality   114

6.5   Factor Analyses of Pre- and Posttest Creativity
and Inquiry Scores   115

Table		Page
6.6	Factor Analyses of Pre- and Posttest Attitude Scales	119
6.7	Factor Analysis of Student Class and Self-Evaluations	122
6.8	Factor Analysis of Teacher Ratings of Students	124
7.1	Classroom Clusters: Means, Standard Deviations, and F-Ratios for Cluster Components (classroom factor scores)	130
7.2	Child Clusters: Means, Standard Deviations, and F Ratios for Cluster Components (child factor scores)	140
8.1	Distribution of Children by Sex within Child Clusters	147
8.2	Distribution of Children by Sex within Classroom Clusters	147
8.3	Distribution of Boys in Child Cluster by Class Cluster Combinations	148
8.4	Distribution of Girls in Child Cluster by Class Cluster Combinations	148
8.5	Distribution of All Children in Child Cluster by Class Cluster Combinations	149
8.6	Means for Classroom Cluster Main Effects on All Dependent Variables	151
8.7	Means for Child-Cluster Main Effects on All Dependent Variables	156
8.8	Means for Sex Main Effects on All Dependent Variables (based on class means)	157
8.9	Means for Significant Two-Way Interactions between Sex and Classroom Clusters	158

Table		Page
8.10	Means for Significant Two-Way Interactions between Sex and Child Clusters	159
8.11	Means for Significant Two-Way Interactions between Child Clusters and Classroom Clusters	161
8.12	Means for Significant Three-Way Interactions among Child Clusters, Sex of Child, and Classroom Clusters	164
9.1	Correlations between Class Means on Individual Variables (Orientations and SES) and Second-Order Classroom Factor Scores	173
9.2	Regression Coefficients (Betas) and Multiple Regression Coefficients from Multiple Regression Analyses Showing Class-Level Main Effects on Cognitive Skills and Self-Esteem	176
9.3	Regression Coefficients (Betas) and Multiple Regression Coefficients from Multiple Regression Analyses Showing Class-Level Main Effects on Residual Attitudes and Values	180
9.4	Regression Coefficients (Betas) and Multiple Regression Coefficients from Multiple Regression Analyses Showing Class-Level Main Effects on Student- and Teacher-Rating Outcomes	182
9.5	Means for Significant Two-Way Interactions between Child Factors (plus SES) and the Class Factor, "Warmth and Friendliness Versus Coldness"	185
9.6	Means for Significant Three-Way Interactions among Child Factors (plus SES), Sex, and the Class Factor, "Warmth and Friendliness Versus Coldness"	186
9.7	Means for Significant Two-Way Interactions between Child Factors (plus SES) and the Class Factor, "Control and Orderliness Versus Lack of Control"	194

Table   Page

9.8   Means for Significant Three-Way Interactions
        among Child Factors (plus SES), Sex, and the
        Class Factor, "Control and Orderliness Versus
        Lack of Control"   196

9.9   Means for Significant Two-Way Interactions
        between Child Factors (plus SES) and the Class
        Factor, "Commonality Versus Variety of
        Activities"   203

9.10   Means for Significant Three-Way Interactions
        among Child Factors (plus SES), Sex, and the
        Class Factor, "Commonality Versus Variety
        of Activities"   205

9.11   Means for Significant Two-Way Interactions
        between Child Factors (plus SES) and the Class
        Factor, "Nonindividualized Versus Individual-
        ized Teacher-Student Interaction"   207

9.12   Means for Significant Three-Way Interactions
        among Child Factors (plus SES), Sex, and the
        Class Factor, "Nonindividualized Versus
        Individualized Teacher-Student Interaction"   209

9.13   Means for Significant Two-Way Interactions
        between Child Factors (plus SES) and the Class
        Factor, "Energetic Encouragement of Verbal
        (Academic) Participation"   212

9.14   Means for Significant Three-Way Interactions
        among Child Factors (plus SES), Sex, and the
        Class Factor, "Energetic Encouragement of
        Verbal (Academic) Participation"   215

9.15   Means for Significant Two-Way Interactions
        between Child Factors (plus SES) and the
        Class Factor, "Emphasis on Student Expressive-
        ness"   220

9.16   Means for Significant Three-Way Interactions
        among Child Factors (plus SES), Sex, and the
        Class Factor, "Emphasis on Student Expressive-
        ness"   222

Table   Page

10.1   Summary of Significant Cluster-by-Cluster
        Interaction Effects, Showing Outcome Measures
        which Obtained Highest Scores for Different
        Combinations   237

10.2   Summary of Significant Dimension-by-Dimension
        Interaction Effects, Indicating Relationship
        Directions Obtained with Different Outcomes   242

A.1   Means for Significant Two-Way Interactions
        between Child Factors and Classroom Clusters   259

A.2   Means for Significant Three-Way Interactions
        among Child Factors, Sex, and Classroom
        Clusters   263

A.3   Means for Significant Two-Way Interactions
        between Child Clusters and Classroom Factors   266

A.4   Means for Significant Three-Way Interactions
        among Child Clusters, Sex, and Classroom
        Factors   268

A.5   Fourth Grade Reading Comprehension Means
        for Interaction between Classroom Clusters
        and Prior Reading Level   276

A.6   Means for Significant Two-Way Interactions
        between Classroom Factors and Specific Prior
        Status Measures on Parallel Outcome Measures   277

A.7   Means for Significant Three-Way Interactions
        among Classroom Factors, Sex, and Specific
        Prior Status Measures on Parallel Outcome
        Measures   281

B.1   New Achievement Motivation Scales: Item-Total
        and Interscale Correlations   286

B.2   Class Preference Scales: Item-Total and
        Interscale Correlations   288

Table   Page

B.3   Correlations between Individual-Level Factors,
       Outcome Residuals, and Miscellaneous Measures   290

B.4   Cutting Points for Trichotomized Variables Used
       in Analyses of Variance (Other than Factors)   300

LIST OF FIGURES

Figure		Page
7.1	Factor Score Profiles of Classroom Clusters	132
7.2	Factor Score Profiles of Child Clusters	141
8.1	Mean Scores for Class Clusters on Selected Dependent Variables	153
8.2	Interaction Effect of Child Clusters and Class Clusters on Creativity	162
8.3	Interaction Effect of Child Clusters, Sex, and Class Clusters on Perseverance/Social Maturity	166
9.1	Main Effects (Betas) of Class Factors on Cognitive Skills and Self-Esteem	178
9.2	Interaction Effect of SES, Sex, and Class Warmth on Achievement-Test Performance	190
9.3	Interaction Effect of Preference for Class with Autonomy, Sex, and Control-Orderliness on Achievement-Test Performance	200
9.4	Interaction Effect of Personal Control and Commonality of Activities on Creativity	204
9.5	Interaction Effect of Achievement Motivation, Sex, and Nonindividualized Teacher-Student Interaction on Writing Quality	210
9.6	Interaction Effect of Personal Control, Sex, and Expressiveness Emphasis on Creativity	224
10.1	Cluster-Cluster Interaction Cells Showing High Scores on Outcome Measures	240
10.2	Dimension-Dimension Interaction Cells Showing Positive and Negative Trends	244
A.1	Interaction Effect of Prior Reading and Control-Orderliness on Reading Comprehension	278

1 PERSONS AND ENVIRONMENTS

The research described in this monograph is concerned specifically with students in educational settings, yet it deals with a number of issues that have been of central concern to social science in general, and not just to the field of education. These issues center around the relative impact of human behavior of person characteristics, environmental (or situational) characteristics, and the interaction between the two. In order to place the research into its appropriate theoretical, empirical, and methodological contexts, the relevant social science literature as well as the educational research literature will be discussed, respectively, in this chapter and in Chapter 2.

INTERACTIONAL AND NONINTERACTIONAL APPROACHES TO THE STUDY OF HUMAN BEHAVIOR

Ekehammar (1974) has distinguished three general approaches to personality conceptualization: "personologism," "situationism," and "interactionism." The three approaches differ in the types of factors which they identify as being primary determinants of behavioral variation: For personologists, the primary determinants are "stable intraorganismic constructs" (for example, traits, psychic structures, or internal dispositions); for situationists, they are environmental or situational factors. For interactionists, however, neither set of factors is seen as primary; it is the interaction between the two which is postulated as the prime source of behavioral variation. These designations need not be limited to personality theories. Much of classical learning theory, and experimental psychology in general, for example, can be characterized as a search for those situational factors or contingencies which produce or account for variations in behavior. Much of the theorizing and research in sociology and anthropology could be similarly characterized, although, of course, the specific situational-environmental factors which are

1

studied, and the behaviors which are predicted, are quite different between these areas.

Ekehammar points out that although interactionist theories were proposed as long ago as the twenties they have not been part of the mainstream of social science and have generated relatively little research. However, he feels that this situation has changed in the last decade or so with the development of more appropriate statistical methodologies.

Critiques of noninteractionist approaches have appeared from time to time. These have evoked agreement and nods of recognition, but seem to have directly generated relatively little research. Thus, Wrong (1961) criticized sociology for assuming complete social determinism, for seeing persons as completely internalizing and conforming to the norms, role obligations, and standards set down by cultures and social systems. Bauer (1964) similarly criticized communications research for concentrating on the intended effects of communicators and substantially ignoring the contributions made to communicative transactions by the audience. The implicit model of human behavior to which he was objecting in this research might be characterized as passive and reactive. In a discussion of person-environment interaction in organizational settings, Levinson characterized two non-interactionist positions in the following way:

> I have used the term "mirage" theory for the view,
> frequently held or implied in the psychoanalytic litera-
> ture, that ideologies, role-conceptions, and behavior
> are mere epiphenomena or by-products of unconscious
> fantasies and defenses. Similarly, the term "sponge"
> theory characterizes the view, commonly forwarded
> in the sociological literature, in which man is merely
> a passive, mechanical absorber of the prevailing
> structural demands (Levinson 1959: 178).

Cronbach discussed the division of psychologists into two camps, each with its own theories, assumptions and methodologies, and with little knowledge of, or interest in, the other's territory. He called these camps "correlationists" and "experimentalists." The correlationists examine relationships between different individual characteristics and assume that behavioral dispositions tend to generalize across situations. When behavioral variation among situations or interactions with situational characteristics (or both) are found, they are considered to represent "noise" which, if possible, should be avoided or ignored. The experimentalists manipulate situational parameters and attempt to identify effects which hold for all individuals. Situational effects which are influenced or moderated by individual differences are discounted as not contributing to the development of general laws. Cronbach called for an effort to integrate these two approaches—to develop an interactional psychology which would "permit us to predict . . . the behavior of organism-in-situation" (1957).

These critiques probably apply more clearly to the actual research undertaken in these various fields than to the formal statements of theories. Even in the most unideterministic theories there can often be found, in some corner, a statement that the factors of concern may interact with factors on other levels in some situations. Yet, if one considers what are the major emphases of these theories and, even more, the actual research generated or inspired by them, the critiques appear to hold up. Indeed, if one looks at the research that has been influenced, either directly or indirectly, by such an explicitly interactionist theory as that of Murray (1938), it becomes evident that the bulk of that research has selected specific variables from the "person" side of the theory (for example, the need for achievement), but has not investigated them in relation to (or interaction with) the parallel variables from the "situation" side.

GENERALITY-SPECIFICITY OF BEHAVIOR

Mischel, in the course of an extensive critique of "trait" theories of personality, reviewed and discussed a large amount of research concerning the degree to which behavior or traits generalize (1968). Since trait theories generally assume at least some degree of consistency of behaviors or behavioral styles across different situations, this research evidence could constitute an important element in assessing their basic validity or tenability. Mischel's review included cognitive and intellectual measures as well as measures of personality variables. He concluded that the level of correlation of personality measures across settings was generally low. This was true for such variables as attitudes toward authority and peers, moral behavior, sexual identification, dependency, aggression, rigidity, tolerance for ambiguity, and cognitive avoidance. Different methods were used to assess generality for different variables. The generality of attitude toward authority, rigidity, tolerance for ambiguity, and cognitive avoidance were assessed by correlating different measures of the same construct. Generality data concerning moral behavior, sexual identification, dependency, and aggression were derived from observations of behavior in different situations. Although the logic of the two approaches is somewhat different, the results and conclusions were similar: there was little evidence for generality, either across situations or across measurement instruments (which, in a sense, can also be considered to represent different "situations").

Mischel's review showed greater generality for intellectual and cognitive variables. Ability measures, in particular, tend to be highly correlated; while comparisons of striving behavior across situations show modest correlations. Research on cognitive styles (field independence, leveling-sharpening, reflectivity-impulsivity) showed moderate correlations between parallel measures and, in some cases, for the same measure across tasks. Investigations of stability across time, assessed in longitudinal investigations, showed parallel results: correlations tended to be fairly high for measures related to intellectual and cognitive processes, and relatively low for personality-related measures. Mischel's conclusion from this review was that "behavior tends to be extremely variable and unstable except when stimulus conditions and response-reinforcement relations are highly similar and consistent (1968: 178).

Other evidence, not cited by Mischel (most of it being more recent) is consistent with this conclusion. "Achievement behavior" was measured for children in different "skill areas" by Crandall (1965) and Crandall and Battle (1970). The correlations tended to be low, providing little evidence for generality. Solomon (1969) obtained observations of children's "achievement-related behavior" in several types of tasks, and also found relatively low correlations across tasks. Sermat (1970) compared competitive and cooperative individual behaviors in two experimental games ("chicken," "prisoner's dilemma") with those produced in two other tasks (a paddle game and a dyadic picture interpretation task). Consistency of behaviors across situations was relatively slight. Slovic (1972) compared risk-taking behavior between tasks differing in the required mode of response. The between-task correlations ranged from .30 to .64; Slovic felt that these were low, considering that the tasks were identical except for the mode of response (choosing a preferred bet versus setting selling prices for bets).

Cross-situational consistency of behaviors related to introversion-extroversion was examined by Newcomb (1929) in an observational study of boys at a summer camp. Specific behaviors related to these traits were observed in 30 different situations. Correlations were examined between the behaviors making up a given trait, and for the same behaviors across situations. Little evidence for consistency was found, with either type of comparison.

Nelson, Grinder, and Mutterer (1969) partially replicated the classic Hartshorne and May (1928) study which had investigated the consistency of moral behavior across different "temptation situations," and was one of the first studies to explore this issue. In the Nelson study, several different methodologies were applied to moral behavior data obtained in different situations. First, a series of zero-order correlations were examined, and these showed, as did the original

Hartshorne and May data, generally low correlations of moral behavior across situations. A principal components analysis was also performed, parallel to one done by Burton (1963) in a reanalysis of the original Hartshorne and May data. Nelson et al. found, as did Burton, a first general factor which accounted for about 40 percent of the total variance in the correlation matrix. They also found a stable second factor which seemed to reflect responses to academic achievement cues, while the first factor appeared to represent achievement-related but nonacademic cues. The factor analysis results led Burton to affirm (and Nelson et al. to agree with) the notion that there is "an underlying trait of honesty." Other analyses, however, led Nelson et al. to conclude that this trait contributed a relatively small amount of the variance in predicting moral behavior, that situational variations also contributed a relatively small amount, and that a person-by-situation interaction appeared to contribute the largest portion. It is worth mentioning, however, that all of these sources were significantly involved, indicating that all three—the person, the situation, and the interaction between them—were required for the most complete and accurate prediction of behavior.

SIMILARITY BETWEEN SITUATIONS AS A MEDIATOR OF BEHAVIORAL CONSISTENCY

In discussing the results of his reanalysis of the Hartshorne and May data, Burton concluded that individuals may differ in the range of situations to which their "honesty" trait applies, as a result of prior experiences in these situations (1963). He also proposed that generalization across situations may be mediated by cognitive factors. Other writers have suggested that individuals' perceptions of similarities among situations may function to mediate the generalization of particular behaviors across those situations. Allport (1967) proposed that individuals' subjective perceptions of similarity among the "fields" that confront them determine generalization and the transfer of behavior across those fields. Mischel also holds that generalization occurs according to similarity among situations as perceived by individuals. He further suggests that "the person's expectancies mediate the degree to which his behavior shows cross-situational consistency or discriminativeness. When the expected consequences for the performance of responses across situations are not highly correlated, the responses themselves should not covary strongly" (1973: 272). These expectancies and situational perceptions develop out of, and reflect, the idiosyncratic history of the individual. Solomon (1977) has also suggested that the generalization of behavior across situations is mediated by subjective perceptions of similarity,

and that individuals develop categories and dimensions for characterizing situations which may be used to order situations in terms of
the degree of their similarity.

Some studies have provided evidence that objectively-defined
similarity mediates behavioral consistency across tasks. In the study
of children's achievement-related behavior mentioned above, Solomon
(1969) identified two task dimensions (convergence-divergence and
verbalness-nonverbalness) on which six tasks varied. Correlations
of student behavior measures across tasks were then ordered in terms
of the number of common dimensions between each pair of tasks (2, 1,
or 0). Correlations between variables from the same task were also
included as the highest possible level of similarity (identity). For
boys, the average intertask correlation increased as the number of
common dimensions increased; the same did not occur for girls.
In the same study, performance data for several learning tasks,
reported by Stevenson and Odom (1965), were reanalyzed in terms
of the same task dimensions (convergence-divergence and verbalness-
nonverbalness). Between-task correlations were again organized in
terms of the number of similar task dimensions, and average correlations were compared. The predicted progression was found for
both sexes. For example, the average correlation for boys was .50
when the tasks had two common dimensions, .23 when they had one
common dimension, and .08 when they had no common dimensions.
If objectively-defined similarity can show such a clear influence on
across-task behavioral similarity, it seems reasonable to expect that
subjectively-defined similarity would show it even more clearly. Yet
this apparently has not yet been investigated.

Several methods for assessing similarity among situations have
been proposed. One, used in the study just described, is to relate
tasks in terms of a priori designated dimensions of response requirements. More complex categorical representations of situations are,
of course, also possible, and could lead to more finely differentiated
gradients of similarity. Rotter (1955) has suggested methods for
assessing similarity among situations which seem primarily objective,
but at least some of these could probably be developed into subjective
methods. Situations can be considered similar if they arouse similar
expectations of reinforcement, if they actually demonstrate similar
patterns of reinforcement, and if behavior generalizes from one to
the other situation (to the extent of the generalization). The last
criterion is probably not appropriate for the purpose under discussion,
since it seems to assume the relationship between situational similarity and behavioral consistency which in our view needs to be tested.

Price and Bouffard (1974) have suggested an interesting method
for assessing situational similarity. They developed an instrument
which paired each of 15 situations (for example, "in class," "on a

bus") with each of 15 behaviors ("run," "read," "shout"). Subjects
rated the degree of appropriateness of each behavior in each situation,
on a ten-point scale. The authors suggest that an index of similarity
could be derived by comparing the behavioral appropriateness ratings
between various pairs of situations. Although this is essentially a
subjective method, it could be made into a quasi-objective method by
using mean scores derived from a large sample of subjects. A more
direct subjective method was used by Solomon (1977). Subjects were
given booklets with all possible pairings of 12 tasks (one pair to a
page) and simply asked to rate the degree of similarity between them
on a six-point scale (ranging from "about as <u>similar</u> as two different
things <u>can</u> be" to "about as <u>dissimilar</u> as two things can be"). Parallel
methods have been used widely in studies of perceived stimulus similarity.

Three recent studies have applied to the generality-specificity
issue, an approach which considers the degree of an individual's
cross-situational consistency in behavior as itself an individual difference variable. Campus (1974) described her study as an investigation
of the moderator effect of trans-situational consistency. Male under-
graduates told stories about themselves in response to TAT (thematic
apperception test) cards, and rated themselves on a list of adjectives
(representing needs) for each story. They also rated the same needs
on a self-description questionnaire, and responded to other instruments measuring anxiety, extraversion, and field independence.
The trans-situational consistency index was derived from a "within-
persons" analysis of variance (needs by situations), and consisted
of the square root of the proportion of variance of need scores
accounted for by mean needs (across the stories). It was found, as
predicted, that correlations between the same need scores assessed
by different instruments was higher for the more consistent subjects.
Consistency was also found to relate negatively with anxiety and with
a need factor related to hostility, and positively with extraversion
and with need factors related to conformity and mastery over the
environment.

In a study by Bem and Allen (1974), data on subjects' friendliness and conscientiousness were derived from several sources: they
were asked to rate their own general level and variability for each
of these traits, and also to rate their behavior on each in several
specific hypothetical situations; ratings from friends and parents
were also obtained; and the subjects were observed in two situations.
Within-subject standard deviations across all the measures of each
trait constituted one index of variability. Self-rated variability was
correlated with this derived index of variability. Subjects who, by
self-rating, were consistent with respect to friendliness showed
higher correlations between different measures of the same trait

than those who rated themselves as variable. The same analysis did
not work as well for conscientiousness, except when variability was
operationalized as intra-individual variance across items of a conscientiousness scale.

In the study by Solomon (1977), cross-situational consistency
was defined as the within-subject standard deviation of the ratings of
liking for 12 hypothetical tasks. This consistency measure was correlated with the average similarity score assigned to each paired comparison of tasks. The correlation for the total sample was -.35,
indicating that those whose task preferences were more varied saw
the tasks as less similar than those whose task preferences were
relatively homogeneous. This seemed quite consistent with the notion
that perceptions of similarity may perform a mediating function in
cross-situational generality, insofar as stated preferences for tasks
are concerned. In an additional analysis, subjects were divided at
the median on the consistency measure, with above-median individuals
considered "specifiers" and below-median individuals, "generalizers."
Multidimensional scaling solutions were then calculated for each group,
using the matrix of between-task, similarity-score paired comparisons. For boys (but not girls) it was found that the same amount of
similarity matrix variance was accounted for by fewer dimensions
for the generalizers than the specifiers. This was interpreted as
meaning that the specifiers had a more complex cognitive structure
with regard to this domain of tasks. It was suggested that these
results indicate that theories which assume cross-situational generality and those which assume specificity may both be correct—but only
for some individuals—and that further efforts toward the identification
of important mediating and moderating variables was needed.

From the results of all three of these studies, it seems reasonable to conclude that the concept of traits may after all still be a
viable one, but that individuals may vary greatly in the range of situations to which a given trait may apply. One person may wish to strive
and excel in most life situations, another may do so only in academic
situations, and still another in academic and athletic situations. Bem
and Allen (1974) suggested that differences in generality may be
accounted for by differences in individuals' perceptions of the relevance of particular situations to particular traits. A judgment of
trait relevance could, of course, be one criterion for determining
whether two situations are similar. Other cognitive factors which
can be used to describe situations (and thereby to determine their
similarity) have also been suggested by various writers. Mischel
(1973) cited several cognitive social learning variables (including
cognitive competencies, encoding and categorization of events,
expectancies and subjective values) which in his view help determine
individuals' behaviors in specific situations. Coutu (1949) discussed

the subjective "meaning" of situations and "personic selectors" as internal factors determining the reactions of individuals to situations. Kelly (1955) dealt with "personal constructs" in a similar manner, emphasizing individuals' development of coherent, but idiosyncratic, views of social reality. Solomon (1963, 1966b) suggested that individuals make judgments of the "appropriateness" of particular behaviors to particular situations, and that such judgments may serve as cueing factors, activating particular needs or motives, indicating to the individual that the situation is suitable for the attempted fulfillment or expression of these needs or motives. It was also suggested that such judgments may vary from individual to individual, depending on their specific prior experiences in situations which are perceived as similar.

Although some of the earlier correlational studies on the generality-specificity issue seemed impelled by a "situationist" perspective, the results of the three studies described above (Campus 1974, Bem and Allen 1974, Solomon, 1977) are most consistent with the "interactionist" perspective. If the results are conceptualized in a "persons-by-situations" framework, it is evident that there are some individuals whose behavior is predominantly determined by the "persons" factor (the "generalizers") and some whose behavior is predominantly determined by the "situations" factor (the "specifiers"). For the group as a whole, this would constitute a persons-by-situations interaction.

INVESTIGATIONS OF PERSON-SITUATION
INTERACTIONS

Components-of-Variance Analyses

Ekehammar (1974) felt that interactionist theories have made little headway in the past because, until recently, an appropriate methodology for testing them did not exist. Recent studies employing a "components-of-variance" approach have been used to make judgments about the relative contributions to behavior of "persons," "situations," and the interaction between them. This literature is described in detail by Ekehammar (1974) and Bowers (1973). Here we will examine a few exemplary studies.

Endler and Hunt (1968, 1969) developed questionnaires concerning "anxiousness" and "hostility" in which subjects were asked to describe their behavior with respect to different modes of response in a variety of different situations. Repeated-measures analyses of variance were used to analyze the results, with persons, situations, and modes of response as separate independent variables. Over several studies with different samples of subjects and with different forms of the questionnaires (sampling different sets of situations and modes of response), they found a fairly stable pattern of results: persons generally contributed from 4 to 6 percent of the variance, situations from 4 to 8 percent, modes of response from 14 to 27 percent, various two-way interactions about 10 percent each, and the three-way interaction (persons by situations by modes of response) up to 33 percent. They concluded that the various interactions were more important to the prediction of anxiety and hostility than any (or all) of the main effects. These results led them to conclude, in one study, that "anxiety is idiosyncratically organized in each individual" (1969: 20).

Nelson, Grinder, and Mutterer (1969) also conducted a components-of-variance analysis of the behavioral responses to various temptation situations. They found from 13 to 15 percent of the variance attributable to differences among situations, from 15 to 26 percent (depending on the particular analytic model and item scale used) attributable to differences among persons, and from 60 to 70 percent attributable to the combination of the person-by-situation interaction and error variance (the two were confounded since there was only one observation per situation per person). It seemed reasonable to believe that a large part of this latter variance was in fact due to the interaction.

A components of variance analysis was also applied to the data on preferences for striving tasks in Solomon's study (1977). For the total sample, the persons effect contributed 17 percent of the variance; the tasks effect, 3 percent; and the interaction, 17 percent. (Within-sex analyses produced slightly different results: the persons and tasks effects were somewhat stronger for girls, the interaction effect substantially stronger for boys.)

In the Price and Bouffard (1974) study of appropriateness judgments of different behaviors in different situations, a three-way repeated-measures analysis of variance produced results indicating that persons contributed 6 percent of the variance; situations, 17 percent; behaviors, 18 percent; the persons-by-situations interaction, 6 percent; the persons-by-behaviors interaction, 8 percent; the situations-by-behaviors interaction, 15 percent; and the combination of the three-way interaction and error variance, 31 percent.

This approach to the analysis of the relative contributions by different sources to total behavioral variance has been criticized on the grounds of artificiality. It has been suggested that the proportion of variance attributed to situations or to interactions with situations is heavily dependent on the range and distinctiveness of the situations selected as stimuli. The greater the range and extremeness of situations represented, the greater the proportion of variance they will be found to contribute. That this is true has been demonstrated empirically in a study by Cartwright (1975). He abbreviated the Endler and Hunt anxiety inventory, limiting it to modes of response which subjects had rated as reflecting anxiousness, and to situations having a "definite but not extreme likelihood of producing anxiety." Results with this abbreviated scale indicated from 15 to 21 percent of the variance attributable to situations, from 33 to 59 percent attributable to persons, and the remainder to a combination of the interaction and error variance. Of course, it is possible to argue that the restriction of situational and interactional variance in this study was as artificial as the possible expansion of it in the other studies. Perhaps the only way to arrive at a generally valid decision as to the relative contributions of persons, situations, and interactions would be to sample broadly and randomly both from persons and from natural (not experimental) situations. The importance of the "ecological validity" of the situations investigated, and the value of sampling situations as carefully and broadly as subjects in psychological research has been stressed by Brunswik (1956) and Hammond (1954) but has not been widely implemented. Still, with regard to the issue at hand, it seems likely that person-by-situation interactions do have an important role in human behavior, even if the exact magnitude of that role may be undetermined. The fact that so many studies—encompassing such a broad range of behaviors, domains of situations, types of instruments, and types of dependent variables—have consistently found substantial contributions of person-situation interactions suggests fairly clearly that they are truly present.

Interactions between Specific Variables

The above studies have been useful in demonstrating the probable existence of person-by-situation interactions. However, they give little information about the specific contents of these interactions. Studies of a different sort, which investigate the effects of joint variations of particular person variables and particular situation variables, are necessary to provide this kind of information. Several of these studies have been reported, and a number of them are reviewed by Endler and Magnusson (1976b).

In some of these studies, situational factors which lead to the minimization or maximization of personality effects on outcomes have been investigated. For example, Terhune (1968) manipulated the degree of situational "threat" in different series of experimental "prisoner's dilemma" games. Subjects selected for the experiment were dominant in either achievement, affiliation, or power motives. It was found that behavioral differences between subjects who were dominant in different motives were minimized in the most threatening games. Related results were obtained by Mischel, Ebbesen, and Zeiss (1973) in a different type of study. They experimentally manipulated success and failure through feedback provided to subjects about their performance on a test of "intellectual attainment." In a control condition, no such feedback was provided. Subjects' "repression-sensitization" scores were also obtained. Subjects were provided with lists of information about their "strengths" and "weaknesses," and the length of time each subject spent attending to each list was monitored. Although there was a general tendency for "repressors" to spend more time attending to strengths, and "sensitizers" more time attending to weaknesses, this effect was strongest in the control condition. The authors suggest that this indicates that personality factors are most potent when situational factors are weakest, a conclusion which also can be applied to the results of the Terhune study.

Thus, there appear to be situational factors which can maximize and minimize the effects of personality. There also appear to be personality factors which reflect greater and lesser sensitivity to situational variation. In part, this was demonstrated by the studies cited earlier which investigated individual differences in cross-situational consistency, but it has been looked at in other ways as well. Wilson (1976) used a sentence-completion test to identify "safety-oriented" and "esteem-oriented" subjects. Each type of subject participated in three experimental conditions in a study of altruism. In one condition, the subject was alone, in a second, the subject was with two "passive confederates," and in a third condition, the subject was in a group with a "helping model" and a "passive bystander." During a waiting period, subjects heard crashes and screams from the next room, followed by silence. A strong interaction effect was found: The helping behavior of esteem-oriented subjects was not significantly differentiated across conditions, while that of safety-oriented subjects was. The safety-oriented subjects helped significantly less when with the passive bystander than in any of the other conditions.

Snyder and Monson (1975) measured the conformity of subjects who differed in their tendency to be "self-monitoring" and in "neuroticism" in group discussions under "public" (observed by a television monitor) and "private" (not observed) conditions. Subjects who scored high on the self-monitoring measure, and those low in neuroticism, were more likely to conform to (or agree with) their group's "risk preferences" in the public than the private condition. Those who were low in self-monitoring, and those high in neuroticism, did not differ between conditions.

Other studies have found effects whereby the direction of differences between experimental conditions is reversed for subjects of different personality types. Some of these have involved the personality measure, "locus of control." Baron et al. (1974) conducted two experiments—one investigating "form discrimination" of lower-class black children, the other, "concept attainment" in college students. Two experimental conditions were involved in each study: a "self-discovery of success" condition (involving intrinsic feedback) and an "unverifiable verbal praise" condition (involving extrinsic feedback). In each study, internals performed better on the task in the "self-discovery of success" condition, and externals in the "unverifiable verbal praise" condition.

Similar person-situation interactions have been obtained in studies concerning anxiety, leadership, achievement motivation (see Endler and Magnusson 1976b). Additional research of this sort, dealing more explicitly with educational settings, will be discussed in the next chapter. It seems clear that, although the empirical search for specific person-situation interactions is relatively recent, there is already sufficient evidence to indicate that explorations in this area should continue.

INTERACTIONAL THEORIES AND APPROACHES

Lewin (1935, 1951) developed an explicitly interactionist theory which stressed subjective perceptions (the "life space"). In his view, it is necessary to consider all relevant aspects of the impinging environment ("forces") and all aspects of the psychological field (including goals, values, needs, and perceptions) as it exists for the individual. He emphasized the importance of examining the total field, not isolated or abstracted elements, and of examining behaviors and "psychological events" by considering both the state of the person and that of the environment: "To understand or to predict behavior, the person and his environment have to be considered as one constellation of interdependent factors" (1951: 239-40). He also felt that it was important to account for both specific and general aspects of the field (including transitory events as well as the general "atmosphere"). In short, he described behavior as being a function of both the person and the environment. The Lewinian approach does not, however, appear to have engendered much research relating to person-environment interaction, possibly because it did not involve specific predictions of interactions between identified pairs of person and environmental variables.

The theory developed by Murray (1938) has a number of features in common with that of Lewin but, in addition, proposed an explicit set of individual and environmental constructs, with implicit or explicit expectations about how they should interact. Perhaps for this reason some interactional research has emerged using the constructs of this theory. (As indicated earlier, however, some of the constructs and instruments have become so popular in themselves that the interactional aspects of the theory have been relatively neglected.) Murray developed a set of "need" constructs to describe the individual (including needs for abasement, achievement, affiliation, aggression, autonomy, dominance, exhibition, recognition, succorance), and a parallel set of "press" constructs to describe the degree to which the environment was likely to satisfy or frustrate the various needs. For each need, in other words, there was a related press. A specific need-press combination was called a "thema." Murray distinguished between the objective environmental situation (or "alpha press") and the subjective situation (or "beta press"). Stern (1970) conducted a large-scale investigation in which the Murray framework was applied to assessments of the "matches" between college students and the college environments. Thistlethwaite (1960) investigated "college press" on various student outcomes, but did not investigate interactions with student needs.

Social learning theories (e.g., Rotter 1954, Mischel 1973) can also be seen as interactional. The person side of the equation in these approaches is represented by cognitive factors (for example, expectancy, reinforcement values) which help the individual to identify relevant situational characteristics and select his behavioral responses in those situations. Rotter (1955) describes the situation as containing cues which arouse the individual's expectations for reinforcement, with the meanings of the cues dependent on the individual's prior learning history. Mischel used the term "discriminative facility" to describe individuals' selection of situations in which to perform certain behaviors. Mischel's approach

> emphasizes the crucial role of situations (conditions) but views them as informational inputs whose behavioral impact depends on how they are processed by the person. It focuses on how such information processing hinges, in turn, on the prior conditions which the individual has experienced. And it recognizes that the person's behavior changes the situations of his life as well as being changed by them (1973: 279).

Solomon (1977), in a related approach, has suggested considering motivation as a set of individual preferences for being in situations characterized by particular combinations of relevant dimensions, these dimensions being constructed by the individual as a result of prior experience.

Approaches to interactionism which emphasize person-environment "fit" or "match" have been proposed by French et al. (1974) and by Pervin (1968). French et al. consider personal adjustment to reflect the goodness-of-fit between person characteristics and environmental characteristics. They distinguish between subjective and objective fit, and between "opportunity-need" fit (in which the person's needs and values constitute "demands" which are to be met by environmental "supplies") and "ability-demand" fit (in which the environmental role presents demands or requirements which are to be met by the person's skills or abilities). They predict that poor fit on these various dimensions will produce poor adjustment, personal strain, and coping or defensive behaviors. Some research has been generated by this approach, with generally confirmatory results. For example, Kulka (1974) administered questionnaires to high school students to assess subjective person-environment fit in high school. "Ability-demand" discrepancies related to self-esteem and social competence measures (with the smaller discrepancies associated with the higher levels of self-esteem and competence), while the "opportunity-need" discrepancy related to school attitude measures (with smaller discrepancies relating to more positive attitudes). Ability-demand fit was also related to absences from school; the best fit produced the least absences.

Levinson (1959) discussed person-environment fit in organizations. He suggested that the problem of poor fit between organizational role requirements and individual personality is most severe in rigid organizational structures because less diversity is tolerated and a narrower range of role definitions is imposed than in looser organizational structures. Four types of responses were listed as available to "incongruent" members of organizations with rigid structures: they may attempt to change themselves, they may leave the organization, they may remain in "apathetic conformity," or they may attempt to gain sufficient power to change the organization. Pervin (1968) reviewed a number of studies demonstrating that interactions between personal characteristics and both the "noninterpersonal environment" (for example, task difficulty) and the "interpersonal environment" (for example, leadership style) can influence both performance and satisfaction. He called for an interactional approach which includes both subjective and objective environment and which looks at both person and environment characteristics in terms of the same constructs or dimensions. (French, Lewin, and Rotter have also held this latter view.)

Hunt (1971) has discussed several "matching models" which take a more developmental perspective. For example, Kohlberg (1966) has proposed a series of sequential stages of moral development in individuals, and suggests that the environment can be characterized in terms of its potential for inducing people to operate at one or the other of these developmental levels. Kohlberg predicts that progression from one stage to the next is most facilitated when the content of the child's environment is primarily consistent with the moral level just above the child's current level.

Interactional psychology is described by Endler and Magnusson as "concerned with the scientific investigation of the complex interplay of persons and situations in determining behavior" (1976b: 968). They list four "essential . . . features of modern interactionism:

1. Actual behavior is a function of a continuous process or multidirectional interaction (feedback) between the individual and the situation that he or she encounters.
2. The individual is an intentional active agent in this interaction process.
3. On the person side of the interaction, cognitive factors are the essential determinants of behavior, although emotional factors do play a role.
4. On the situation side, the psychological meaning of the situation for the individual is the important determining factor" (ibid.).

It will be noted that two types of interaction are included in this definition: in one, person and environment act jointly to influence behavior; in the other, person and environment reciprocally influence each other (this latter type of interaction is referred to as "transactionalism" by Pervin 1968). This distinction is also noted by Buss who feels that most of the research evidence available refers to the former, joint-effects type of interaction (1977). He also states that the methodology which has been developed to assess the effects of that type of interaction is inappropriate for the analysis of the reciprocal-effects type. He is critical of much of the interactionist theory which, he feels, has not maintained sufficiently the conceptual distinction between these two types of interactionism. He feels that the two types of interaction represent basically different, and contradictory, paradigms. While this distinction seems a valid one, it does not necessarily follow that the two forms of interaction are incompatible. It seems possible to develop an interactional model which could include reciprocal effects between persons and situations, and joint effects of persons and situations on behavior as well. Statistical methodologies such as path analysis would seem appropriate for empirical investigations of such models. It is only with an extreme form of organismic transactionalism, in which it is considered inadmissable to distinguish conceptually between persons and situations, that this criticism may apply.

CHARACTERIZING THE SITUATION

Numerous systems for describing and categorizing persons have been developed, based on needs, motives, values, cognitive styles, and so forth. Less progress has been made toward the development of relevant categories and typologies of situations. Yet in order to elaborate a system of person-situation interactions, it is necessary to characterize situations in at least as much detail as persons. While a number of the theorists mentioned above have advocated using the same dimensions to assess persons and situations in order to facilitate comparisons and matching, this seems to be not an essential element of the theories but more a methodological recommendation. It seems to be an empirical question as to whether this is the strategy which will ultimately lead to the greatest advances in knowledge. A strategy which begins by developing descriptive systems which attempt to encompass most parsimoniously the natural variation in each separate component (person and situation) before examining interrelationships and interactions would seem to be another viable alternative, particularly in investigations of interactions in natural situations. Systems which have used the same constructs to describe both levels (e.g., Murray 1938) have generally begun from a conceptualization of person needs and then constructed parallel situational dimensions. While this is not an unreasonable approach, it does not seem likely to produce as accurate a characterization of situations as of persons.

Some work has been done toward identifying significant dimensions of specific environmental settings, including organizational climates, small-group structures, typologies of correctional institutions. Detailed descriptions of situational events, behavioral "episodes," and "settings" have been provided by ecological psychologists but have not led to the development of general categorizations or typologies of situations (and are not intended to).

Frederickson (1972) emphasized the importance of developing taxonomies of natural situations. He recommended conducting factor analytic studies to identify empirically important situational dimensions, and suggested that cluster analysis could then be applied to these situational factors to produce situational clusters or "types." Members of each type would be characterized by similar profiles on the various situational dimensions. This procedure was followed in the present study which is described in subsequent chapters.

As Ekehammar (1974) suggests, the social-scientific climate seems in recent years to be shifting more and more toward interactionism. Discussions and research in the area have been increasing. Confirmed, or even highly probable, knowledge about the nature, range, and necessary conditions for producing interactions is, however, as yet relatively primitive. It can probably be said with a fair degree of certainty that person-situation interactions exist, but more elaborated explanations of why, where, and how must await further research and further theoretical development.

2 *STUDENTS AND CLASSROOMS*

Just as with social science in general, research on the determinants of academic achievement and other educational outcomes has also been, with occasional exceptions, predominantly noninteractional. One stream of research has attempted to identify instructional programs and procedures which would prove effective for students of all types and has tended to ignore individual differences in reactions to the programs. Another stream has concentrated on identifying individual aptitudes, motives, and other characteristics which best predict educational outcomes, independent of variations in instructional treatments; the emphasis here has been on identifying students most likely to succeed, and has often been used for selection purposes.

Yet, parallel with the social science developments discussed in Chapter 1, there has been a minor but continuing interest in student-treatment interactions which has, in the last decade or so, become a substantial field of inquiry, pursued by large numbers of educational researchers. It is interesting, however, that although there seems to be a strong contemporary current that is hospitable to the notion of interactions between persons and settings, this state has been reached largely independently in the field of education and in the more general areas of social science. Major compilations have recently appeared in each of these areas: a massive review and critique of research on interactions between students and educational treatments by Cronbach and Snow (1977); and two edited collections of papers by Endler and Magnusson, one a collection of previously published theory and research in the area (Endler and Magnusson 1976a), the other a collection of papers prepared for an international symposium on person-environment interaction (Magnusson and Endler 1977). Examination of these volumes shows that each area is referring to an entirely different body of research for its evidence, with almost no overlap between them, in spite of the close formal convergence of their aims and assumptions. Studies in each tradition commonly refer to Cronbach's (1957) paper as the source of the modern-day interest in interactions, but from there the two areas diverge. Apart from a hesitancy at straying beyond the boundaries of one's own discipline (which, of course, may also account for some of the resistance to interactionism which is inherently interdisciplinary), this lack of apparent mutual knowledge and communication between fields, in spite of the convergence in trends, may also perhaps be attributed to the fact that they focus on different sets of variables. Educational research concentrates on predictions of achievement, on situational variations between educational treatments, and on student measures which are considered relevant to academic work—largely cognitive ability measures, but including some personality variables as well. The more general social science research relevant to interactionism has largely related to personality theory and measurement, and has focused on "traits," on behaviors which can be considered to represent those traits, and on situations which may elicit them. Educational research has also been more concerned with practical application—with identifying individuals most likely to benefit from different specific treatments or programs—while social science (and psychological) research has focused on more abstract theoretical principles—deciding whether person-environment interactions "exist" and, if so, how potent they are.

The research which will be described in subsequent chapters was concerned with children's experiences in elementary schools. It is therefore the prior educational research which is most explicitly relevant, and the remainder of this chapter is devoted to the discussion of this prior research. It appears useful, however, to consider the results of that research, and the present research as well, in the light of other attempts to explore person-environment interactions. Before discussing the interactional research which has been done in education, we will consider that research which has been generally more prevalent (at least until recently), which is aimed at identifying important "main effects" on educational outcomes.

NONINTERACTIONAL RESEARCH
IN EDUCATION

Measures of cognitive ability (for example, IQ) and prior achievement are commonly found to be very strong predictors of academic outcomes. These also, of course, represented the only class of "trait" variables which were found in Mischel's (1968) review to be relatively stable and cross-situationally consistent. Possibly because of the overwhelming importance of these factors, educational researchers have had difficulty in identifying other factors which consistently and independently relate to academic achievement.

Some personality factors which have fairly consistently been found to correlate with achievement (such as locus of control) also show moderate correlations with IQ, and thus may not represent entirely independent relationships.

The dominance of cognitive ability factors has not led to the abandonment of the search for other important factors, however, nor should it. If the ultimate aim of educational research is to improve educational practices and outcomes, it must focus on those aspects of education which are potentially manipulable. Thus there have been, and continue to be, large quantities of research concerned with exploring educational environments—in particular, the classroom. Some classroom studies have focused on the teacher while others have examined the classroom "climate"; some have been "naturalistic" and correlational (identifying variables occurring in natural classroom settings and examining their relationships with student outcomes) while others have been "experimental" (predefining and developing distinct treatments, and examining their effects on comparable groups of students). Some of the research of each of these types is considered below.

STUDIES OF TEACHING

Early research on teachers (as discussed by Gage 1972, Dunkin and Biddle 1974, and others) was directed toward identifying determinants and correlates of teacher effectiveness. The primary predictors investigated in these studies were personal characteristics of teachers, including intelligence, knowledge of subject matter, personality characteristics, and interests. These factors were typically correlated with supervisor or principal ratings of teacher effectiveness, and, occasionally, with test scores of students. Some of this research also looked at gross aspects of the classroom setting (class size, curriculum, and so forth) in relation to outcomes. There were relatively few attempts, however, to look at what actually transpired in the day-to-day life of the classroom. The most extensive series of early studies on teacher effectiveness was directed by A. S. Barr, at the University of Wisconsin. Much of this work, summarized in Barr (1961), related teachers' personality traits to ratings of teacher effectiveness. But a small amount of this body of research also involved observations of teachers and students in classrooms, including one study published in 1929.

During the 1940s and 1950s, a number of observational studies of teaching were conducted which investigated a small number of behavioral-style dimensions related to (and in some cases influenced by) the "autocratic," "democratic," and "laissez faire" leadership styles which were experimentally manipulated by Lewin, Lippitt, and White (1939) in their classic studies of leadership styles and group social climates. The concept labels and some of the specific components varied from study to study, but the basic dimensions seemed similar in such style or atmosphere descriptions as "teacher-centered versus student-centered," "integrative versus dominative," and "pre-clusive" versus "conjunctive" versus "inclusive." Flanders' approach to classroom "interaction analysis" concentrated on identifying "direct" and "indirect" styles, and was also derived, in part, from this tradition (1970). These concepts generally defined, on the one hand, teachers who controlled events in the classroom, gave students relatively little leeway to participate, did most of the talking, and tended to be strict, and, on the other, teachers who gave students more opportunity to participate in and to direct classroom events, to interact with each other, and to determine goals.

Other studies, done at about the same time, manipulated these dimensions experimentally in classroom situations. Although much of the research on these dimensions has been characterized by inconsistent findings between studies, there is at least an indication that the more "indirect," student-centered approaches are more likely to influence students' complex cognitive skills and "insight." The use of these dimensions has been criticized by Dunkin and Biddle (1974) on the grounds that they confound teacher "directiveness" (etc.) with teacher "warmth." This seems a valid criticism, in at least some of the studies. Teacher-centeredness often seems to involve sternness and coldness, student-centeredness to involve permissiveness and warmth. Thus, any findings obtained for this dimension could result more from warmth than from teacher-centeredness (or from the combination of the two).

Other studies of teacher and student behavior in classrooms have taken a more strictly empirical approach, with fewer initial expectations about the kinds of teacher behaviors likely to be most effective. These have typically collected information on a broad range of specific variables, which in some instances are related one by one to various outcome measures, and in others are first grouped into empirical dimensions (through the use of factor analysis or related techniques) or into conceptual dimensions (based on theoretical expectations or logical connections within and among subsets of variables) before being related to outcomes. A great many observation systems have been developed for use in such studies. Some involve the use of relatively small sets of mutually exclusive categories, scored either for every distinct unit of behavior as it occurs, or at pre-selected time intervals (every three seconds). The Flanders (1970) system is the best known example of this type. Other systems (called "sign" systems) involve larger numbers of categories which are tallied if they occur within specified time periods of greater duration. A system of this latter type may have more than 100 variables; the observer watches the class for a given length of time (perhaps five minutes), then checks or tallies each behavior which occurred during the period. A system of this type has been developed and used by Soar et al. (1971). The mutually-exclusive category systems have the advantage of allowing the researcher to explore specific sequences of action and reaction, and responses to prior contingencies in the classroom; "sign" systems are capable of obtaining measures on a very large number of variables, some of which may occur relatively rarely.

Perhaps the most widely used type of observation instrument, historically, has been the rating form. Although early studies used ratings to assess "effectiveness," later forms have involved global ratings of general aspects and dimensions of teaching and the classroom environment. For example, Ryans (1960) had observers rate teachers on 18 seven-point global scales (including "partial-fair," "autocratic-democratic," "aloof-responsive," and "harsh-kindly") and students on four scales (including "apathetic-alert" and "obstructive-responsible"). Scales such as these have been repeatedly criticized for the high degree of inference which they require on the part of the observer. While this is undoubtedly a valid criticism, it is also true that there may be general aspects of behavior and group "climate" which may be unmeasurable through less inferential procedures. The authors' practice in observational studies (in classrooms and elsewhere) has been to combine global ratings with less inferential types of observations; relationships between the two sources of data often turn out to be very instructive. It has also been pointed out that the distinction between categorical systems and rating systems has tended to decrease in more recent applications, with some categorical systems including some relatively inferential items, and some rating systems containing references to highly discrete and specific behaviors and events (Rosenshine and Furst 1973).

Students and teachers themselves have also functioned as sources of information about teacher behavior and classroom climate. Questionnaires in which students are asked to describe specific teacher behaviors and styles have been developed and used in several studies (Ryans 1960, Solomon 1966a). Typically, class means on each item are taken to represent "objective" descriptions of the teacher behavior in question. Another possible use for instruments of this type would be to investigate the perceptions of teacher behavior and classroom atmosphere held by various individual students or subgroups of students within the class, and to relate differences in these perceptions to differences in antecedent factors and outcomes. Although this has not been done to any great extent, a few studies have employed methodologies of this type (e.g., Dowaliby and Schumer 1973). Teacher questionnaires have been used to obtain information about teachers' goals and objectives and the general organization and conduct of activities in their classrooms. In recent years, a number of scales have been developed in which teachers are asked to respond to specific questions which, when combined, provide evidence about the "openness" or "traditionalness" of the teacher's classroom (Walberg and Thomas 1971, Traub et al. 1972).

Some studies of teaching have focused on one or another of these methodologies; others, attempting to capitalize on the advantages of the different approaches, have combined them. For example, Solomon et al. (1963) obtained factors representing dimensions of teacher behavior which combined data obtained from a categorical observation system (based on tape recordings of verbal interactions in classrooms), a set of observer's global ratings, class means on various items from a student questionnaire, and items from a teacher questionnaire asking teachers for their goals and motivations for teaching.

Several reviews of the research on observational studies of teaching were published in the early 1970s, each of these providing a description of the current status of the field. It may be worth noting, parenthetically, that the research to be described here in later chapters was initiated during the same period as that in which these reviews appeared. They can therefore also be considered as descriptions of the field as it was at the start of the present study.

In a useful discussion, Soar (1972) suggested that a number of teacher behavior research findings were consistent with an "inverted-U hypothesis." This hypothesis states that there are optimal levels of various teacher behaviors associated with different outcomes. He applied this hypothesis to teacher indirectness (as well as some other teacher variables), presenting evidence that the optimal point for complex-abstract outcomes (creativity) is higher than that for moderately abstract outcomes (vocabulary), which is higher than that for the least abstract outcomes (reading). Although Soar believed that this hypothesis could account for contradictory results between studies concerning the same outcome (they might have sampled behavior ranges on different sides of the optimal point for that outcome) or for the failure of some experiments using extreme-groups designs to show effects (they might have eliminated the optimal point through the use of this design), he did not feel that enough studies had explored curvilinear trends to clearly substantiate the hypothesis.

Rosenshine and Furst (1973) identified nine variables for which they found evidence of consistent relationships with measures of academic growth in children: (1) teacher clarity of communication, (2) variability (flexibility), (3) enthusiasm, (4) task-oriented or businesslike behavior, (5) use of criticism (negatively related), (6)

teacher indirectness (this was found usually to have shown positive
relationships with learning, although often not statistically significant), (7) provision of the student with opportunities to learn criterion
material (including such components as topics covered and amount
of emphasis devoted to different topics), (8) use of structuring comments, and (9) use of multiple levels of questions or cognitive dis-
course.

Dunkin and Biddle (1974) considered much of the same research,
but drew somewhat more limited conclusions. Although they suggest
that positive findings can serve as valuable clues and guides for further
research and for educational practices, they did not believe that the
findings accumulated as of that date should be considered as anything
more than tentative. They discussed a broad range of methodological
flaws which they believed made it unwarranted to draw definitive conclusions from this body of research. Among these flaws were small
and nonrandom samples, instrument inadequacies, design problems,
too little replication, too little interplay between experiments and
field studies, too few attempts to vary study contexts, and too few
studies with multivariate designs.

Since these reviews were published, several large-scale
observational studies have been conducted which seem to represent
significant improvements over most prior research and which meet
the standards implied by several of the Dunkin and Biddle criticisms:
they included large samples, well-designed and sophisticated instru-
mentation, multivariate designs, and in some cases, replication
across years and across variations of some contexts (such as social
class of student body and grade level). There is also a certain amount
of consistency between them in results. Findings from a number of
these are incorporated in a valuable recent review by Medley (1977).

Stallings and Kaskowitz (1974) described a study involving
extensive observations of classes participating in the evaluation of
the "Follow Through" program. This program is intended to continue
where Head Start leaves off—to give special assistance to disadvantaged children during the early years of elementary school. The
overall program was designed as a "planned variation" quasi experiment, whereby a number of "sponsors" developed distinct educational
plans or "models," each based on a coherent theoretical or philosophi-
cal approach. Each sponsor's model was implemented in a number
of projects, divided among several different geographical sites. For
the purpose of the overall evaluation, "control" classrooms, as similar to the project classrooms as possible, were selected at each
project site. Seven models were selected (from about 20 which were
involved in the Follow Through program altogether) for the Stallings-
Kaskowitz observational study. These represented a broad range of
approaches, including some which involved the use of manipulated

reinforcement contingencies, some which emphasized cognitive development (with a Piagetian orientation), and some which developed "open" classrooms with much student autonomy and decision making. The study included first grade and third grade classrooms from a variety of sites (including a non-Follow Through control classroom at each grade level at each site). After eliminating classrooms without baseline data, their final sample included 105 first grade classrooms and 58 third grade classrooms. Although the overall Follow Through program was set up with a quasi-experimental design, the Stallings-Kaskowitz analyses merged data from the different sponsors (and the control settings) so that they could relate outcomes to actual variations in classroom process rather than to differences in the intended programs of the different sponsors. (Other reports on Follow Through, which describe the outcomes achieved by the different sponsors, have also been produced, and will be described below.)

Observers spent three days (five hours each day) in each classroom, and used three different observational instruments to record information about the physical arrangements of the class, materials in use, the activities and groupings in the classroom, and various specific interactions between children and adults. Baseline achievement was assessed with the Wide-Range Achievement Test, reading and mathematics achievement by the Metropolitan Achievement Test, problem-solving skills among third graders by Raven's Progressive Matrices, and Locus of Control by the Intellectual Achievement Responsibility scale.

The effects of individual variables on outcomes were examined with partial correlations which controlled for the baseline prior-achievement scores. Numerous sizable and significant correlations were obtained. Reading achievement was found to be positively correlated with the length of the school day, the amount of time students spent actually engaged in reading activities, the use of systematic instructional patterns (involving the use of positive reinforcement), the use of textbooks and programmed materials, students' task persistence, the use of small groups for first grade students, and groups of nine or more for third grade students. A similar set of variables was found to be positively related to achievement in mathematics: length of the school day; time spent in mathematics activities and in discussions of mathematics concepts and problems; the use of systematic procedures, texts, and programmed instructional materials; student persistence; and the use of small groups for first graders and large groups for third graders. The researchers also reported evidence of an interaction with the ability level of students. Classes composed primarily of low-ability students showed the best performance in mathematics if much class time was spent on math and if the teacher gave students a great deal of praise. The influence of these variables was less pronounced in classes of high-ability students.

The study also provided evidence that the less traditional academic outcomes were promoted by different sets of teacher and classroom variables. Nonverbal problem solving was highest in classrooms which were flexible, involved varied materials, many activities, much student choice, one-to-one interactions between students and teachers, and much open-ended questioning. Children's acceptance of responsibility for their own successes was related to flexibility of classroom procedures, while acceptance of responsibility for failures was highest in the more structured classrooms. Student absences were highest in the structured classrooms, lowest in those characterized by child independence, much questioning and self-initiation of activities by children, and extensive open-ended questioning.

Thus, to summarize these results, gains on achievement tests related most clearly to the amount of time spent in structured activities, while more abstract cognitive performance related to classroom flexibility and "open-endedness." Students' enjoyment of school (as indirectly indexed by the rate of absences) also was apparently greater in the more flexible settings. This distinction between the classroom correlates of the more concrete and the more abstract types of outcomes is reminiscent of the results of the author's prior research in adult classrooms (Solomon et al. 1963), which showed that the clarity of teacher communication and teacher lecturing related to "factual gain"; while teacher energy, aggressiveness, flamboyance, and a moderate position on a permissiveness-control dimension related to "comprehension gain." These results are also consistent with the discussion by Soar concerning the distinction between, and the differences in the antecedents of "simple, concrete" and "complex, abstract" learning outcomes (1972).

Another set of analyses of data from Follow Through classrooms was reported by Soar and Soar (1972). Their sample consisted of eight kindergarten and first grade classrooms from each of seven sponsors, plus two comparison classrooms for each sponsor. Two observers, using different observation instruments, each spent a day in each classroom relating to verbal and nonverbal behaviors of teachers and students. Audio tapes of the classes were also made and later scored with two additional instruments. Rather than analyze observation items individually, Soar and Soar first reduced the data through separate factor analyses of the items from each observation instrument and of student regressed gain scores. Two gain-score factors were obtained, which were consistent with Soar's distinction between simple-concrete and complex-abstract growth. Analysis of the relationships between these two factors and the various factors obtained from the observation instruments indicated that, consistent with the Stallings and Kaskowitz findings, simple-concrete growth was promoted by "highly focused learning tasks," while complex-abstract growth was promoted in settings in which students were allowed more freedom and autonomy. Soar and Soar also investigated both linear and nonlinear trends, which seemed to indicate that teacher direction was positively and linearly related to simple-concrete growth, while moderate levels of teacher direction were optimal for promoting complex-abstract growth. Similar trends were also found for the use of drills by the teacher.

For another large-scale investigation of teaching, Brophy and Evertson (1976) selected second and third grade teachers who had produced stable outcomes, as indicated by the achievement performance of their students over a three-year period. They also replicated their study in two successive years, and investigated about 30 classrooms each year. Several different instruments were used in this research, including a low-inference categorical observation system, high-inference global ratings, checklists, and questionnaires. Achievement was measured with the Metropolitan Achievement Test (using adjusted gain scores). Many of the classrooms in this study were composed largely of students of lower socioeconomic backgrounds; in others, students of high socioeconomic status (SES) predominated. Many of the analyses reported by Brophy and Evertson indicate that the teaching approaches which were successful in classrooms with mostly low-SES students were different from those which were successful when high-SES students predominated.

The following teaching practices were found to be positively related to achievement gains in the low-SES classrooms: a relatively slow pace, encouragement of student-initiated comments, teacher acceptance of "callouts," teacher praise for good efforts (even if unsuccessful), general teacher supportiveness, clarity of teacher presentations, opportunity for immediate practice of demonstrated skills (with immediate feedback), provision of cues, seeking of improved responses with repeated questioning, use of positive encouragement and praise, use of symbolic rewards, and teacher "showmanship." Effective teachers of low-SES students also maintained fairly restricted and structured settings. In contrast, high-SES classrooms showed the best levels of academic achievement with teachers who used a fast pace, gave many response opportunities, suppressed "call-outs," were challenging and demanding, used symbolic rewards, provided students with academic criticism, and did some "scolding," but also allowed students some independence.

Brophy and Evertson considered the SES distinctions to represent motivational differences in the students (this was suggested by observations of the students' behavior in these classrooms). The low-SES students appeared to be uncertain of their academic skills, to fear failure, and to be anxious in the school situation. The task undertaken by the effective teacher therefore involved allaying these fears through a slow pace, involving clear presentation of information in a noncompetitive setting and accompanied by much praise for students' efforts. The high-SES students, on the other hand, tended to be self-confident, motivated, and competitive. The effective teachers therefore had to counter the students' competitive tendencies (which could get in the way of the learning tasks) but at the same time to provide activities which would maintain the motivation and interest of these students.

The Brophy and Evertson findings for the low-SES classrooms seem quite similar to those reported for the two Follow Through studies described above (Soar and Soar, Stallings and Kaskowitz). The Follow Through populations were, of course, composed primarily of disadvantaged students; this, therefore, indicates some convergence across the studies. It is also interesting that both the Stallings-Kaskowitz and the Brophy-Evertson studies investigated, and found, interactions with student characteristics: ability level in the former, SES in the latter. Neither of these studies was essentially interactional in its basic conception. They were designed primarily to identify potent main effects of teaching, and did not obtain enough information about various student characteristics to do thoroughgoing investigations of interactions. Yet, these studies are among the first large-scale investigations of teaching behaviors to investigate and demonstrate interactions with student background characteristics at all. While the interpretations and theoretical meaning of the interactions would be more complete and convincing if additional measures of child personality and motivational characteristics had also been included (particularly in the Brophy-Evertson study where SES was assumed to represent certain clusters of such variables), the interpretations offered do seem plausible and the existence of the interactions undeniable. It remains for further research to elucidate the dynamics behind these interactions.

Evidence of interactions with another student variable, age, was provided in another large-scale naturalistic investigation conducted by McDonald and Elias (1976). This study involved about 2,500 pupils, in the classrooms of 41 second grade and 54 fifth grade teachers, in eight California school districts. Tests assessing achievement in reading and mathematics (including standardized tests and new tests developed to measure more specific objectives) were given to all participating students in the fall and spring of a single school year, as were measures of students' attitudes towards reading and mathematics. Information on children's expectations, cognitive styles, and other characteristics was also obtained, some of it from instruments administered to children, some from teachers and parents. Data on teacher behavior and classroom activities were obtained from direct observations and from coded videotapes. A large number of observational items were reduced to 22 scores per teacher, representing seven areas: instructional time, instructional content, instructional material, instructional organization, instructional activity, social-control interactions, and pupil behavior. Separate observations were conducted during reading and during mathematics instruction.

Relationships between the observational variables and students' achievement gains were investigated separately for each of the four settings: second grade reading, fifth grade reading, second grade math, and fifth grade math. The patterns of relationships obtained were different in the different settings. Effective teachers of second grade reading had students do much monitored independent work, coupled with brief and frequent teacher contacts involving specific questioning, explanation, and feedback. They also used a variety of materials (related to a limited range of content), kept the children on task, and spent relatively little time on getting things organized, or teaching the children in groups. Classes which did well on reading at the fifth grade, however, were characterized by greater amounts of teacher discussion and sustained interaction with students involving explanation and questioning. They also devoted much time to reading instruction overall and to direct individual instruction in reading. McDonald suggests that the differences between the practices found effective in reading instruction at these two grade levels reflect differences in instructional objectives—with second grade instruction focusing on the acquisition of basic skills and fifth grade instruction on more complex comprehension skills.

A somewhat parallel set of differences was found between effective math instruction variables at the second and fifth grades. The most effective second grade classrooms were characterized by directed seat work, with teachers moving around the class a good deal, teaching a variety of math skills. Group teaching was more effective at the fifth grade, as were whole-class instruction and varied organizational arrangements.

Although the specific effective behaviors varied, McDonald suggested that a common principle could account for the findings in the different settings—that of "direct instruction." Teachers have a common immediate behavioral objective of maintaining student attention and on-task behavior. The means of achieving this vary according to the developmental level of the child and the content of the learning task. For second graders, acquiring basic skills can be achieved best with a large amount of individual work and individual instruction; for fifth graders, particularly in math instruction, larger group settings may be more effective. In whatever setting and whatever the learning objective, however, it seemed important for the instruction to be carried out in a <u>direct</u> manner, with a clear explanation (or elicitation from students) of what is to be learned, with provision of suitable conditions for attempting what is to be learned, and with frequent feedback to the child about performance." Most of McDonald's findings referred to patterns of teacher behaviors rather than single variables. Relatively few single teaching variables were found related to learning. But when they were combined into naturally occurring groupings, meaningful sets of outcomes emerged: "This study suggests that it is different patterns and structures of teaching acts that influence changes in learning rather than single omni-effective teaching performances (McDonald 1976: 20).

Rosenshine (1976a, 1976b) has also discussed the concept of "direct instruction," and has suggested that convergences in the findings of a number of these recent studies, particularly those involving low-SES student populations, may be seen as indicating the effectiveness of this general mode of instruction. He includes as components of direct instruction (1) the amount of time spent on academic activities, (2) seat work with structured materials, (3) the use of narrow, direct, and focused questions, (4) immediate feedback to students, (5) closely monitored group work, (6) teacher control, dominance, and businesslike behavior, (7) systematically organized sequences involving small steps, and (8) clear goals—all combined with teacher warmth, conviviality, and use of praise. Although the concepts of direct instruction described by McDonald and Rosenshine are not identical—Rosenshine focusing somewhat more on specific activities, McDonald on the objectives of the activities—they are generally quite consistent. Rosenshine's inclusion of teacher warmth as a component of direct instruction is interesting, particularly in light of Dunkin and Biddle's criticism of that research in the "democratic-autocratic-laissez faire" tradition which typically confounded teacher "warmth" with "democratic" behavior and "coldness" with "autocratic" behavior. Thus, when these patterns were created experimentally, teachers who were "benevolent autocrats" tended not to be represented. Yet such a pattern would have come closest to the concept of "direct instruction," as defined by Rosenshine. Perhaps this body of research, which contrasted democratic and autocratic (or parallel) styles, showed relatively inconsistent findings because the most effective patterning of teacher behavior was not represented.

More recent data consistent with the above conclusions concerning the effectiveness of "direct instruction" have been reported by Wellisch et al. (1977) and Kirschner Associates (1977). The former study, part of a national evaluation of the Emergency School Aid Act (ESAA), involved intensive observations in 26 schools, focusing on classroom organizational climates, reading and math instructional practices, resources used, and general school practices. Its findings indicated, in general, that academic growth was enhanced by teachers who strongly and clearly structured many aspects of the classroom environment. There was also evidence that student task attending played a mediating role—that students were more task-oriented and, therefore, achieved more in more structured settings. The Kirschner Associates study evaluated compensatory education in 14 school districts distributed throughout the country. Reading and mathematics instructional units in first and third grades were investigated. The findings generally indicated that an "opportunity" dimension (composed of elements referring to the amount of instructional time available and the degree of overlap between skills taught in the class and items on the achievement tests) related to achievement in the first grade settings, while elements of an "individualization" dimension (in particular, matching student tasks with mastery and/or pretest levels) were more important at the third grade level.

STUDIES OF CLASSROOM "CLIMATES" AND INSTRUCTIONAL PROGRAMS

Several writers have argued for increasing the "ecological validity" of educational research in general, and research on classrooms in particular (Snow 1974, Shulman 1970, Doyle and Ponder 1975, Doyle 1978). While such comments have most frequently been made with regard to educational experiments—where the suggestion is that the variables manipulated should represent elements which actually exist and operate in natural situations—they have been applied to "naturalistic" research as well (by Doyle, in particular). Naturalistic studies which isolate or abstract individual variables and consider their effects separately—without examining their patterns of combinations with other variables, their functioning within situational contexts, or their contributions to an overall situational "atmosphere"— are not accurately representing the total set of elements which may be important in producing various outcomes. Studies of educational "climates" are one way of approaching the problem of ecological validity. Rather than looking at separate, isolated facets of teacher or student behavior, they attempt to define dimensions of general atmosphere which represent patterned combinations of teacher behaviors, student behaviors, and general class activities. Although a number of approaches to the assessment of total classroom climates rely on the use of student questionnaires (Anderson and Walberg 1974, Moos 1978), objective observations can be used for the purpose as well.

Studies which attempt to contrast different educational programs can be considered, in part, to be looking at different "climates," particularly if the programs are not limited to purely cognitive components. Studies of this type, however, frequently fail to investigate the degree to which the intended programs have actually been implemented; if outcome differences are then found, it is difficult to know to what they should be attributed.

Comparison Of "Follow Through" Models

The Project Follow Through "Planned Variations" evaluation involved one of the largest studies of this type to be undertaken. Naturalistic studies of teacher behavior by Soar and Soar (1972) and by Stallings and Kaskowitz (1974)—each of which was based on subsets of the Follow Through data—have been considered above. The overall evaluation, however, examined the outcomes achieved by each of the models for the total set of sponsors. The major report of this evaluation was completed in 1977 (Abt Associates 1977). Although they did not have direct information about adequacy of implementation of the different models, Stallings and Kaskowitz reported data that indicated that implementation was somewhat better for the more "structured" models (1974). The evaluators classified the models—according to sponsors' major goals—as "basic skills," "cognitive-conceptual," or "affective-cognitive." Student outcomes were assessed with achievement tests, and with measures of nonverbal problem solving (Raven's matrices), self-esteem, and locus of control. The major findings indicated, first, that there was great variation in student performance across project sites within models and, second, that the more structured "basic-skills" approaches most consistently produced gains in measures of basic skills and, to some degree, in self-concept. A reanalysis of the data reported by Kennedy (1978), used the project rather than the individual student as the unit of analysis. Results were presented as average project effects. With this analysis, the two basic-skills models ("direct instruction" and "behavior analysis") produced gains in language and math computations, but not in reading comprehension, math problem solving, or nonverbal problem-solving. Their gains were thus at the "simple-concrete" pole of the dimension identified by Soar (1972). Outcomes produced by other sponsors' projects tended to be null or negative on all measures. While these results seem to be in at least superficial agreement with the notion of the effectiveness of "direct instruction" discussed earlier, and in at least partial agreement with Soar's discussion of the relationships of different teaching behaviors with different types of outcomes, some additional comments made by Kennedy concerning the meaning of these results are worth noting. Aside from apparent differences in implementation effectiveness, noted above, she points out that the measures and the testing situations were differentially relevant to the different programs. Programs with unique sets of nontraditional goals would not be adequately assessed through the use of standardized instruments and testing procedures. She felt that this applied not only to the achievement tests, but to the other assessment instruments as well. As evidence for this point, she cites data presented by one sponsor (High/Scope Foundation) showing that a language production test—which was developed to represent their specific objectives and which used testing procedures which paralleled their typical classroom activities— demonstrated strong positive effects for that sponsor's model. Although it would be impossible to develop a battery of instruments which accurately reflected the intended outcomes of this many programs, these findings do suggest that one should be extremely cautious in generalizing from results such as these.

Comparison of "Open" and "Traditional"
Approaches

A number of studies reported in recent years have contrasted the effects of "open" and "traditional" educational climates. These followed a number of years during which open education was the subject of much discussion and controversy (Plowden 1967, Blackie 1971, Kohl 1969, Silberman 1970, Featherstone 1971, Hassett and Weisberg 1972), but relatively little research.

Several attempts have been made to analyze the characteristics of open education in terms of basic dimensions (Bussis and Chittenden 1970, Walberg and Thomas 1971), and some classroom inventories and observation forms were developed in order to determine objectively the degree to which various classes met the several criteria of "openness" (Walberg and Thomas 1971, Traub et al. 1972). A number of the areas and dimensions covered in these instruments are also important in other instruments used to assess classroom climate and teaching characteristics (including student autonomy and independence, self-initiation of tasks, teacher performance of a consultative role, and variety of simultaneous activities).

Haddon and Lytton (1968) compared creativity measures of British eleven and twelve-year-old children in "formal" and "informal" schools just prior to completing their "primary" school careers. The formal and informal schools were different mainly in that the latter emphasized self-initiated learning to a much greater degree. Children from the informal schools scored significantly higher on the measures of divergent thinking (creativity) and also showed higher correlations between creativity and intelligence. A follow-up study with the same children after a four-year lapse (Haddon and Lytton

1971) found that the between-group difference in creativity was maintained. Similar results were obtained by Oberlander and Solomon (1973), showing that students in "multi-grade, multi-age" classrooms scored significantly higher on verbal and nonverbal measures of fluency, flexibility, and originality (components of creativity) than did students in "self-contained" classrooms. Scores on one creativity index, "alternative uses," were found to be higher for children in open classes by Owen et al. (1974), while Wilson et al. (1972) found "productive thinking" greater in "open plan" schools. Ramey and Piper (1974), however, reported reversed differences for different types of creativity; children in an open school scored higher on "figural creativity" while those in a traditional school scored higher on "verbal creativity." No differences in creativity between open and traditional schools were found by Wright (1975) or by Forman and McKinney (1978).

Children in open, rather than traditional, classrooms show more positive attitudes toward school, according to studies by Wilson et al. (1972), Traub et al. (1974), Tuckman et al. (1974), Epstein and McPartland (1975), Franks and Dillon (1975), and Groobman (1976). However, Klaff and Docherty (1975) and Marshall (1976) found no systematic open-traditional differences in attitudes toward school. Some of these studies also found that students in the open classes had more positive self-concepts, while Groobman (1976), Klaff and Docherty (1975), Ruedi and West (1973), and Inman (1977) did not find significant differences in self-concept between the two types of class. Traub et al. (1974) and Franks and Dillon (1975) also reported evidence of greater independence, initiative, and autonomy in open schools, while Epstein and McPartland (1975) found greater self-reliance in open classrooms, and Reiss and Dyhdalo (1975) reported that children in open-space classrooms showed greater persistence at difficult tasks. Wilson et al. (1972) found no differences in "curiosity"; Owen et al. (1974) found none in "locus of control"; and Wright (1975) found none with measures of personality and cognition between the two types of class. Academic expectations and aspirations were found not to be significantly differentiated between class types in studies by Groobman (1976) and Epstein and McPartland (1975). Bennett (1976) found that increases in both motivation and anxiety were greatest in "informal" classrooms.

Varying results have been reported concerning academic achievement in open and traditional schools. Harckham and Erger (1972) found greater reading achievement in British inner-city "informal" than "formal" schools, but found no differences between the two types of schools in suburban areas. Schnee (1975) found school openness to relate positively to reading scores, while Marshall (1976) found teacher flexibility and student choice related to reading

growth in grades one through three. No significant overall differences in academic achievement were found by Tuckman et al. (1974),
Owen et al. (1974), McPartland and Epstein (1978), or Groobman
(1976). Traub et al. (1974), however, found higher achievement test
scores in traditional, than in open, inner-city schools, and Ruedi
and West (1973) found "academic adequacy" (self-rated) to be greater
in traditional, than in open, sixth grade classes. Better achievement
in traditional than open classes has also been found by Rentfrow and
Larson (1975), Wright (1975), Bennett (1976), Franks and Dillon
(1975), Inman (1977), and Forman and McKinney (1978).

In summary, the above studies generally show (1) some evidence
of superiority in creativity, liking for school, self-reliance, and
initiative for the "informal" or "open" classrooms; (2) a clear recent
trend toward better academic achievement (as measured by standardized tests) in "traditional" ones; and (3) little evidence concerning
various psychological characteristics—values, social behavior, and
the like. It is interesting that many of these latter characteristics
are precisely those which developers of "open" programs have stated
as primary goals.

If it can be assumed that the "traditional" classes in these
studies contained more of the elements of "direct teaching" than did
the "open" classes, the above results for academic achievement seem
consistent with the earlier results described for the recent large-
scale observational studies of teaching. However, as with the Follow
Through evaluation, it should be borne in mind that the achievement
tests used may have been particularly appropriate to the objectives
of the traditional classes, but less so to those of the open ones.

STUDIES OF INTERACTIONS BETWEEN STUDENT
AND TREATMENT CHARACTERISTICS

Studies Involving Open Education

The view has often been expressed that "open" types of education might be more suitable for some children than for others. Indeed,
some of the differences in results obtained by Brophy and Evertson
(1976) for children of different SES levels suggest this. The expectation that such differences exist was one of the notions originally
impelling the research which we will be describing in later chapters.

A few studies on open education have explored this possibility.
White and Howard (1970) found that underachieving seventh grade
boys who believed that the outcomes of their efforts were externally
controlled did better in a self-directed than a teacher-directed class,
while those boys who believed that they themselves were responsible

for the outcomes of their efforts did equally well in either type of class. The same independent variable, "locus of control," was used in a study by Judd (1974) with somewhat different results: He found that those believing in internal responsibility for outcomes tended to have more positive concepts of themselves as learners and more positive attitudes toward school when in "open-space" schools, while those believing in external responsibility for outcomes had more positive self-concepts and school attitudes in traditional schools.

Arlin (1975) also found that "internals" were more satisfied in open than in traditional classrooms, while Parent et al. (1975) found that they performed better in a "low-discipline" minicourse (with "externals" performing better in a "high-discipline" one).

Klein (1975) found that children low in anxiety scored higher on creativity in open than in traditional classes; Papay et al. (1975), on the other hand, found that low-anxiety second graders performed better in mathematics in traditional classes while high-anxiety second graders performed better in "individualized multiage" classrooms. Ward and Barcher (1975) reported that high-IQ children obtained higher reading and creativity scores in traditional than in open classrooms.

A few of the previously cited studies which compared overall effects between open and traditional classrooms also included some consideration of interactions with child characteristics. Thus, Epstein and McPartland (1975) reported evidence at several grade levels of a more positive relationship between school "openness" and achievement for high-SES children than for low-SES children; they also examined interactions with other measures of family environment (such as authority structure), but found no consistent significant effects. Rentfrow and Larson (1975) found that black girls showed better reading and mathematics achievement in open classes, while black boys and white children in general did better in traditional classes. Reiss and Dyhdalo (1975) reported that "persistent" boys learned more in open classrooms, "nonpersistent" boys, in traditional ones.

The study by Bennett (1976) also explored the interaction of student and classroom characteristics in the context of "formal" and "informal" education. Although, as noted, he found generally superior academic performance in the more "formal" settings, there were some variations for particular subgroups of students. Low-achieving boys deviated from the general trend and achieved best in reading in classrooms that were informal or "mixed"; this same group of boys also achieved best in mathematics in the informal classrooms.

Bennett also cluster analyzed children on the basis of personality profiles, producing eight "types." The performance of each of the types of children was compared across the three general class settings—formal, informal, and mixed. Reading achievement was distinctly highest in formal classrooms for "saints" (stable extrovert motivated conformists) and for "unmotivated introverts," while reading achievement was highest in the mixed classrooms for "unmotivated stable extroverts" and "motivated neurotic" students. In mathematics, seven of the eight types performed best in formal classrooms. The exception, "sinners" (contentious nonconformers), did best in the informal classrooms. With respect to achievement in English, all types did well in the formal classrooms, although one (the "anxious conformists") did slightly better in the mixed.

Other Research on Student-Treatment
Interactions

The investigation of interactions between student characteristics and educational treatments has been a relatively minor part of the research on open education. In other areas of educational research, the search for student-treatment interactions has become fairly extensive in the last decade or so. In addition to the comprehensive methodological and substantive review and critique of the entire area recently published by Cronbach and Snow (1977), reviews and discussions have also been produced by Berliner and Cahen (1973), Bracht (1970), Hunt (1971, 1975) and Tobias (1976). The label most commonly applied to this area of investigation is "aptitude-treatment interaction" (ATI), although the phrases "trait-treatment interaction" and "attribute-treatment interaction" have also been used. All of these terms seem too limiting. Cronbach and Snow (1977), however, who use the former, consider "aptitude" to be a general term referring to any individual characteristic which may help predict an outcome and "treatment" to be any aspect of an educational program provided to students. Hunt (1975) prefers the term "person-environment interaction"; it is more inclusive, and allows for the consideration of interactive effects for total persons (rather than, or in addition to, abstracted attributes of persons), and of total environments or situations. Thus, an investigation could include the school atmosphere, in addition to the classroom, as part of the impinging "environment."

Most of the research which has been reported has involved short-term experiments, usually manipulating one or two treatment characteristics and examining interactions with one or two person attributes (for example, anxiety and intelligence). A smaller body of research has involved field experiments in which experimental treatments are distributed among two or more teachers or classrooms, students (in some cases) are assigned randomly to the different treatments, and interactions between the treatments and measured student characteristics are examined for their effects on measured outcomes. A large-scale investigation by Goldberg (1969) is a good example of this approach. Another research approach which has been applied to this problem is a completely natural-state approach. In this approach, which has been the least frequently used, characteristics of existing educational settings are determined (through observations, student questionnaires, and teacher questionnaires), measures of student characteristics are obtained, and the effects of interactions (and main effects) on educational outcomes are determined.

Several studies of the latter type have been conducted by McKeachie and his associates. In one study, McKeachie (1961) found that students with strong needs for affiliation did best in classes of "warm" teachers; intelligent students and those with strong needs for power did best in classes which provided them with opportunities for assertion; students with strong needs for achievement did best with teachers who provided many "achievement cues"; and anxious students did best in classes which were clearly organized and structured. In a later study (McKeachie et al. 1966) it was found that students scoring high in need for affiliation received the best grades from teachers who gave many affiliative cues (as determined from student ratings), while the reverse was true for students low in need for affiliation; however, a subsequent study (McKeachie et al. 1968), which investigated the relationship of the combination of need for achievement and perceived achievement cues to grades in several courses, produced negative results.

Grimes and Allinsmith (1961) reported an interaction involving student anxiety; highly anxious (and compulsive) children progressed better in reading with a structured (phonic) treatment than with an unstructured (whole word) treatment. Dowaliby and Schumer (1973) found that anxious students learned best in "teacher-centered" (rather than "student-centered") classes while Tallmadge and Shearer (1971) found that anxious subjects did better with an "inductive discovery" treatment and that low-anxiety subjects did better with an "expository deductive" treatment. Peterson (1977) obtained a complex four-way interaction involving student ability, student anxiety, structuredness of instruction, and amount of class participation. Calvin et al. (1957) found that less intelligent students did better when problem-solving sessions were conducted in an authoritarian rather than a permissive manner, while more intelligent students did equally well with either approach. Daniels and Stevens (1976) found that college students with extremely "external" locus-of-control scores clearly did better in a "traditional" (teacher-controlled) eight-week psychology course, while those with extremely "internal" scores did better in a "self-directed" (contract) course.

Beach (1960) demonstrated that "sociable" college students learned more in a small-group section, while less sociable students learned more in a lecture section of a college course. In a study by Domino (1971), students scoring high on the personality measure, "achievement via conformance," learned most and were most satisfied in a class taught in a "conforming" way (lectures, high structure), while those scoring high on "achievement via independence," did so in one taught in an "independent" way (active student participation, unstructured). Haigh and Schmidt (1956) gave students the choice of being in directive or nondirective classes and found, as they predicted, no differences in outcome between the groups, all students being in their preferred settings. The study is flawed, however, by the lack of control groups. McKeachie (1963) has summarized some of the studies in this area as showing "that a certain type of student, characterized as independent, flexible, or in high need for achievement, likes and does well in classroom situations which give students opportunity for self-direction" (: 1158).

In spite of the fact that large numbers of ATI studies have been done, relatively few solidly established and validated generalizations can as yet be made. Cronbach and Snow (1977) have conducted the most extensive survey of this literature, including a careful examination of the methods and data-analytic procedures, and, in some cases, reanalysis of the data. They have summarized the trends which they feel are well established in this body of research (as of about 1975).

Among the individual characteristics included in ATI research have been general abilities, specialized abilities, and personality traits or styles. Some of the clearest findings have occurred with general abilities. Generally, high-ability students appear to benefit from the opportunity to organize and process information themselves, while low-ability students do better if much of the organizing is presented to them. Among other studies, strong support for this generalization has been provided by a program of research conducted by Hunt (1971, 1975). It has been found consistently, in the Hunt research, that students with a high "conceptual level" (referring both to cognitive complexity and interpersonal maturity) perform best with low structure, or are unaffected by variations in structure, while those with a low "conceptual level" are benefited by greater degrees of structure (operationalized, in different studies, through lecturing, presenting rules before examples, and so forth). Apparently, high-ability students benefit from settings which require their own intellectual performance, low-ability students from those in which there are no such requirements or the intellectual content is provided to the students directly.

Among the specialized abilities which have been investigated in ATI research are spatial and mathematical abilities, memory, and prior learning experience. Of these, prior learning experience has shown the clearest interactions with instructional variables. Students who have had prior experience with a particular treatment (usually a specialized procedure of some sort) are most likely to perform well under that treatment. Quite a few studies have looked at interactions with various personality characteristics. The general variable which has shown the greatest evidence of interactive effects is called "constructive motivation" by Cronbach and Snow. These interactions have indicated, in general, that constructively motivated students perform best in classroom situations which are less directive, more spontaneous, and require students to take more active roles. (This generalization is consistent with McKeachie's conclusion, noted above.)

RATIONALE FOR THIS RESEARCH

The research project which is the subject of this book combined many elements of the various streams of research that have been described. The intention was to investigate person-environment interaction in the context of the elementary classroom. "Environment" was conceived of as a combination of teacher behaviors, classroom atmosphere, and general student behaviors; "person" characteristics included aspects of personality, cognitive variables, and prior achievement; and "outcomes" were conceived broadly to include academic achievement, cognitive skill, attitudes, and values.

The research was begun with an interest in the distinction between "open" and "traditional" education, but it was soon discovered that this was neither a clear nor a simple distinction. "Open" seemed to mean many different things to different people (as did "traditional," for that matter), in spite of some efforts that had been made to define and operationalize open education. Moreover, the differences between actual classroom manifestations of "openness" were even greater than those between the different conceptual discussions and prescriptions. It became quickly evident, therefore, that it would be necessary to observe the actual happenings in classrooms and not to depend on arbitrary a priori classifications. It was also noted that many of the various suggested elements and components of "openness" were identical or similar to variables which had been measured in studies of teacher behavior or classroom atmosphere; thus, it seemed feasible to adapt or develop instruments which could determine the degree to which these various elements (in addition to other elements) were found in a broad range of classrooms, not just those designated clearly "open" or "traditional." Once this decision had been made, the focus of the research had, in essence, been shifted from a primary concern with "openness" to a concern with the effects, more generally, of different classroom atmospheres (some of which might contain elements of "openness").

The research evidence which had been produced up to the time of the initiation of the planning of the study gave little clear evidence as to the effects of open education. (The subsequent five or so years has not changed this picture greatly—except for a greater accumulation of evidence indicating that students score higher on standardized achievement tests in traditional than in open classes.) Two possible reasons for the inconsistencies between studies were considered: first, classrooms (or schools) categorized as "open" or as "traditional" might not be really comparable across studies; second, each type of classroom might be effective only for certain subgroups of students. Although this latter possibility had been discussed, no research which explored it directly had been reported when the investigations began (a few have been done since then, as noted above). Thus, it was decided both to look at classroom characteristics objectively and to examine the possibility of interactions between these classroom characteristics and various relevant student characteristics.

Because the researchers were interested in trying to represent a number of distinct classroom environments, and also in examining empirical groupings of classroom variables and of classrooms, it was decided that the study should be "naturalistic" rather than "experimental." Although some ideas had been derived from prior research (and other sources) about what were probably the most important classroom behavior characteristics to investigate as components of the classroom environment, few preconceived notions were held about the various distinct combinations of these components which might turn out to be important. Therefore, it was considered less appropriate to create and manipulate environments or climates than to examine their natural groupings empirically. While experiments are, of course, better suited for the attribution of causal relationships, they are necessarily artificial, and are unable to deal with complex relationships among large numbers of variables. The classical experimental paradigm, whereby one or two independent variables are manipulated in a given study, does not seem well suited for the examination of the kinds of varied groupings and interactions which occur in natural settings. It seems a serious distortion of the facts of the situation to investigate small numbers of variables in isolation when, in fact, they combine with many other variables to comprise a unified total, a "field." This is not to say that experiments have no value. It would seem a reasonable strategy to identify important variables or groupings in naturalistic studies; then to investigate them further in series of experiments in which the various elements comprising an empirical grouping can be varied systematically to determine the relative potency of each. (For an application of a similar strategy, see Gage et al. 1978.)

A number of decisions grew out of the desire to represent empirically the natural complexity of the classroom situation. One was that the study should be multivariate and that the classroom should be reflected through measures which referred to numerous aspects of classroom life, including physical arrangements, teacher behavior, student behavior, general activities, and so on. It also seemed to follow that the statistical handling of these measures should utilize the natural groupings of variables. Too many studies have used multivariate observation instruments, and then analyzed the data as a series of separate items. This procedure seems to ignore the multivariate complexity of the classroom situation—the classroom "ecology"—as much as any univariate controlled experiment. In fact, by treating the variables separately, this procedure implicitly assumes that a set of correlations is simply an analog for a series of one-variable controlled experiments, but without the control such experiments afford. Therefore, multivariate procedures such as factor analysis were chosen to identify natural groupings and dimensions in the data.

For somewhat related reasons, both categorical tallies and global ratings were also included in the observation instrument. Although global ratings are prone to "halo" problems, they can reflect aspects of classroom atmosphere which cannot be represented well by specific behavioral categories. They also tend to be highly reliable and to have good predictive validity (Dunkin and Biddle 1974, Brophy and Everston 1976).

The use of global observer ratings and of factor analysis has been criticized, however, on the grounds that they are difficult to use in training teachers. It has been suggested that tallies of specific behaviors which can provide information about minimal or optimal frequencies are potentially more useful to teachers than information about effective "dimensions" or ratings which cannot be tied down to concrete recommendations. It seems, though, that this argument makes possibly unwarranted assumptions about the nature of the correlational data and about the process by which prescriptions for teaching are learned and incorporated into teaching practices. In the first place, it assumes that individual variables which show significant relationships with measures of learning are independent contributors to that outcome. But if such variables combine with others in empirical groupings, then no single one can be considered as a separate entity, and providing training on that variable alone will not accurately represent the total behavioral pattern for which it may be serving as proxy. Secondly, it seems likely that prescrip-

tions for teaching, even if stated in terms of specific frequencies of
specific behaviors, are probably translated by teachers into more
global cognitive constructs which can then be used to develop meaningful and consistent patterns and approaches to teaching. If this is so
(and it is yet an unanswered research question as to whether it is),
then the use of factors or global ratings, or both, for instructional
purposes may be as effective, or even more effective, than the use
of specific categories of behavior for they would provide teachers
with these cognitive constructs directly.

The crux of this study is the application of an attribute-treatment
interaction approach to naturalistic observations of classrooms. Two
major purposes were to identify (1) those aspects of teacher behavior
and classroom climate which are powerful enough to produce effects
for all types of students and (2) those aspects which showed different
effects for different subgroups of students. As pointed out earlier,
few, if any, of the previous large-scale naturalistic studies of teaching or classroom climate have investigated the possibility of interactions with student characteristics in a thoroughgoing, systematic
way. The intent was to obtain a broad sampling of classroom characteristics and a broad sampling of those student characteristics which
were expected to be relevant to important dimensions of classroom
life, and then to examine their various joint and direct effects on a
large set of outcomes. Cognitive measures, motives, dispositions,
and situational preferences were included as student characteristics.
A few of these measures reflected certain of the approaches to interactionism described in Chapter 1. For example, based on the notion
that motivation can be conceptualized as a series of preferences for
being in situations with particular sets of requirements and demands
(Solomon 1969, 1977), a series of questionnaire items was developed
which asked students to state their preferences among alternate sets
of hypothetical classroom characteristics. It was expected that students would do best in classrooms which most closely matched their
stated preferences. From previous research on "generalizers" and
"specifiers" (Solomon 1977), a measure of "generality of strong
achievement-task preferences" was derived. It was assumed that
students with more general preferences would show few interactions
with situational characteristics, while those with more specific
preferences would show many such interactions. The other student
characteristics measured were also selected for their potential interaction with classroom characteristics. They included intrinsic motivation, achievement motivation, fear of failure, need for approval,
structured role orientation versus personal expression orientation,
locus of control, and locus of instigation (referring to the degree to
which one feels responsible for initiating one's own activities).

Because a broad range of types of classrooms were to be included in the study (at least some of which were to represent aspects
of "openness") it was considered necessary to include measures of
various educational outcomes, not just traditional academic ones.
Proponents of different educational programs and philosophies have
argued that schools should try to promote the development of general
cognitive skills and abilities, interpersonal skills, social attitudes
and values, and positive self-concepts in addition to (and, in some
schemes, apparently in preference to) basic academic skills. Measures relating to all these areas were adapted or developed, with the
expectation that classes would generally produce positive effects in
those areas which they most strongly emphasized. While these measures were relatively brief and relatively experimental, and therefore
could not be expected to match the well-established reliability of
standardized achievement tests, it seemed essential to include a
varied and broadly representative set of such outcomes. Therefore,
in addition to standardized achievement tests, measures of the following outcomes were also obtained: inquiry skill; creativity; writing
skill; attitudes toward self, school, and other children; orientation
toward educational tasks; and the children's own evaluations of their
learning and their classes.

Finally, the study included some methodological explorations.
These were not part of the original plan, but developed in the course
of the research. They involved finding ways of characterizing classrooms and students and of investigating the interactions between the
two sets of characteristics. As stated earlier, social scientists with
interactionist orientations have stressed the need for broader sampling
of situations and for the development of taxonomies of natural situations. The same point has also been made with respect to educational
situations and settings (e.g., Shulman 1970, Hunt and Sullivan 1974).
The possible utility of developing taxonomies of student types (each
of which might benefit from a distinct type of teaching approach) has
also been discussed, among others, by Good and Power (1976). A
combination of multivariate techniques, including factor analysis and
cluster analysis, was employed to obtain a set of classroom "types"
and a set of student "types"; their interactions were then examined
using analyses of variance. Other procedures for examining interactions and main effects were also explored and will be described in
subsequent chapters.

3 THE PILOT STUDY

Because the research plan required the adaptation or development of several instruments and analytical procedures, a fairly large pilot study was initially conducted. Although the primary purpose of this pilot study was to develop and refine instruments, measurement techniques, and analysis procedures, it was also expected that it would provide preliminary data relevant to hypotheses about which student characteristics "fit" best in different kinds of classrooms. The pilot study was conducted in six classrooms, three "open" and three "traditional." The later, "main" study was to involve a much larger number, so that measures of specific descriptive dimensions of classrooms could be obtained and investigated for direct effects on educational outcomes, as well as for interactions with the individual child characteristics. This chapter presents a brief description of the methods and results of this pilot study. A full description of the pilot study was presented in a previous report (Solomon and Kendall 1974), and supplementary analyses from the pilot study have been reported in three additional papers (Solomon and Kendall 1975, 1976, 1977).

At the outset, numerous measures of individual preferences, motives, and orientations were obtained from fourth grade children in two sets of classes, three "open" and three "traditional." Some of these measures were developed for this research, some were adapted from the authors' prior research, and some were adapted, or taken directly, from the research of others. Among these measures were achievement motivation, fear of failure, personal expression versus structured role orientation, locus of control, intrinsic motivation, social desirability, "bureaucratic" orientation, and preferences for various sets of hypothetical class characteristics. Detailed structured observations of the activities and organization of each class subsequently were made by four teams of two observers, each team making one visit to each class. Near the end of the school year, questionnaires measuring inquiry skill, creativity, several school-related attitudes, and class and self-evaluations, as well as the California Achievement Test, were administered to the children. At the same time, teachers filled out questionnaires describing their class activities, organization, and objectives, and also made a set of 30 ratings of the behaviors, orientations, skills, and abilities of the children in their classes. The children were also asked to indicate their parents' occupations on one of the questionnaires; a crude index of socioeconomic status was later derived from this. Measures of the children's academic ability and performance, taken a year previously at the end of the third grade, were obtained from school records. Complete data were available on 92 children: 56 boys and 36 girls. All data were collected in the spring of 1973.

Comparison of the two types of class, in terms of the observation and teacher description categories, showed that students in the open classes had more opportunity to make choices and influence decisions about class activities, were more likely to be involved in group activities, and were more likely to cooperate with one another. There were more varied activities, more different activities going on simultaneously, and more stimuli of various sorts in the open classes. Teachers in open classes spent more time consulting with students and leading discussions, while those in traditional classes spent more time lecturing, making formal presentations, and disciplining students.

The various sets of measures obtained on the individual children were factor analyzed. The following names were assigned to the factors which emerged in each set:

1. The third grade ability and achievement measures were included in a single factor analysis and produced a single factor, called prior achievement.

2. The measures of preferences, orientations, and motives were analyzed together, resulting in four factors, compliant-comforming orientation, personal-control orientation, autonomous-achievement orientation, and preference for open situations.

3. The various measures of cognitive skills and knowledge obtained at the end of the fourth grade were included in a factor analysis, and produced three factors: achievement test performance, inquiry skill, and creativity.

4. Five factors were derived from the various measures of school-related attitudes: self-confidence, democratic attitudes, concern for others, decision-making autonomy, and value on self-direction.

5. The class and self-evaluation items produced three factors: enjoyment of class, social involvement (friends), and perceived disruptiveness in class.

6. Five factors emerged from the analysis of the teachers' ratings of the students: <u>autonomous intellectual orientation</u>, <u>democratic, cooperative behavior</u>, <u>perseverant achievement behavior</u>, <u>involvement in class activities</u>, and <u>undisciplined activity</u>.

The prior achievement and preference-orientation factors, plus the index of "socioeconomic status," a derived measure of "impulsiveness-activity level," and a dichotomous categorical representation of "type of class" (open or traditional) were used as independent variables in a series of stepwise multiple regression analyses (done separately for boys, girls, and the total sample) with each of the remaining factors, plus a measure of "writing quality" as dependent variables. Prior achievement and socioeconomic status were entered first in each analysis, so that all other effects were those which occurred after these had been accounted for. Interactions were incorporated into these analyses by entering the products of the type-of-class measure (scored 1 for open, -1 for traditional) and each of the other independent variables. These product terms were the last set of variables entered into each equation, following the entry of all the independent variables. Although there were numerous significant direct relationships between the personal orientations and the outcome measures, the primary concerns of this research were with the interactions between individual characteristics and type of class, and with any overall effects of type of class on outcomes; only these latter two types of effects are discussed in this summary.

The patterns of relationships with the various outcome measures were generally different for boys and girls. The measures of autonomous achievement orientation, preference for open situations, and socioeconomic status produced the largest numbers of significant interactions with type of class for boys, while the measures of prior achievement, compliant-conforming orientation, and personal-control orientation produced the most for girls. Three significant type-of-class main effects were found for boys; those in open classes were more involved in class activities than those in traditional classes, but persevered with achievement tasks less and did less well on the fourth grade achievement tests (when performance on the third grade test was accounted for). Girls in open classes scored higher on decision-making autonomy, self-direction, democratic, cooperative behavior, and involvement in class activities than did those in traditional classes. Only two of these outcome measures were not additionally influenced by interactions: involvement in class activities for boys and democratic, cooperative behavior for girls.

The obtained interactions were generally interpreted as showing ways in which individual child characteristics fit in with the orientations and activities typical of the different types of class.

The autonomous-achievement orientation was considered more consistent with the typical activities of open classes (involving greater
exploration and self-direction). The higher boys scored on this
orientation, the more likely they were to be creative and concerned
for others in open classes and the less likely they were to persevere,
perform well on achievement tests, or show undisciplined activity in
open classes. The finding for perseverant behavior also occurred
for the total sample.

The personal-control orientation was judged to be more appropriate to an open class situation, which allowed children greater
opportunity to exert effective influence on the selection, initiation,
and outcomes of their own activities. Children of both sexes who
scored high on this orientation showed greater decision-making
autonomy and less undisciplined behavior in open classes. Girls
scoring high also showed stronger autonomous intellectual orientations in open than in traditional classes.

Children who stated preferences for open situations were expected to be more comfortable and to find more acceptable outlets
for the expression of their needs in open, rather than traditional,
classes. Boys who stated such preferences scored higher on autonomous intellectual orientation, decision-making autonomy, and writing
quality in open classes. Children in the total sample who scored
high on preference for open situations persevered more and showed
better writing skills in open classes.

The interactions obtained with socioeconomic status were also
interpreted in terms of children's comfort with the different types
of class. It was thought that higher-status children might feel more
familiar and comfortable with the kinds of activities prevalent in
open classes and that lower-status children might feel more comfortable in traditional classes. It was found that boys of high socioeconomic status were more self-directing in open classes and those
of low socioeconomic status were more socially involved and performed better on the achievement test in traditional classes. No
interactions with SES were found for girls or for the total sample.

The compliant, conforming orientation was considered more
consistent with the norms and expectations of traditional classes;
girls scoring high on this measure were more socially involved in
traditional classes.

An interaction showing that impulsive/active girls were more
self-directing in open classes was attributed to a greater opportunity
for girls with this orientation to express and satisfy needs in the
open class situation.

A high level of prior achievement was considered to represent
a potential for skill development. Boys with high levels of prior
achievement showed more creativity in open classes, where there

were presumably more activity options relevant to the development of such skills. Prior achievement was also considered an attribute more likely to be highly valued in the traditional classes; girls with high levels of prior achievement were more socially involved and less undisciplined in traditional than in open classes.

For both boys and girls, there were many more instances in which there were significant interactions but no significant type-of-class main effects than there were instances of significant type-of-class main effects but no significant interactions. This was considered to verify the potential fruitfulness of an approach which investigates the joint effects of individual characteristics and class-room characteristics over that of an approach which is limited to investigating the overall effects of classroom characteristics alone.

After the above analyses had been completed, it was decided to reanalyze the data with a different approach. The initial procedure had involved factor analyzing various individual student characteristics, and then examining interactions between type of class and each of the resulting factors. Even though each of the various regression analyses contained all of the interaction terms, the approach essentially tried to assess the separate contributions of each of the student dimensions to the outcomes, when combined with the type-of-class variable. This approach seemed insufficient, because it did not allow one to judge what the effects were for individuals as complete entities; it broke them up into separate components. It seemed desirable to try to represent students in terms of total profiles rather than separate abstracted dimensions, and then to examine the interactions of these total profiles with the classroom designations. Therefore, another set of data analyses was attempted. First, a cluster-analysis procedure (Lorr and Radhakrishnan, 1967) was applied to the student factors representing prior achievement and four "preference-orientation" dimensions. Each resulting "cluster" comprised an average profile of scores on these five factors. Students identified as members of each cluster could be considered to represent an empirical "type."

Six clusters were obtained, with "memberships" (N's) ranging from 11 to 19. Cluster 1 contained children who were high prior achievers and showed an "independent and internally motivated approach to achievement" (Solomon and Kendall 1976). Members of cluster 2 were low in prior achievement and seemed to feel little control over their environments. Cluster 3 members appeared to be personally motivated and directed, but not academically oriented. Those in cluster 4 showed moderately high prior achievement, preferred structured settings, felt in control of their environments, and scored low in "autonomous-achievement orientation." Cluster 5 members expressed a strong preference for open situations, were moderately high prior achievers, tended to be noncompliant, and were not achievement-oriented. Students in cluster 6 scored quite high on "compliant, conforming orientation," and in the moderate range on all other factors.

Interactions between type of class and cluster membership were examined with analyses of variance. Because the within-cluster N's were small, it was not possible to include the sex of student as a variable in these analyses. Significant interactions were obtained with five of the outcome variables. Children in the two clusters characterized by high levels of prior achievement (clusters 1 and 5) showed better achievement test performance in traditional than in open classes. The cluster containing the lowest prior achievers (cluster 2) showed no differentiation between class types on any of the dependent variables. Children in cluster 3, who seemed to be internally directed, but not achievement-oriented, were more self-directing and autonomous in open classes, but performed better academically in traditional ones. The results obtained for children in clusters 4 and 6 were the most difficult to interpret. Children in cluster 4, with relatively high levels of prior achievement, a preference for structured situations and a strong personal-control orientation, showed more decision-making autonomy in open classes, but more self-direction in traditional ones. It was judged that their personal-control orientation led them to appreciate the decision-making opportunities in open classes (similar to the students in cluster 3 who also scored high on personal-control orientation, and showed more decision-making autonomy in the open classes), while their preference for structure may have led them to be more self-directing within the clearer limits imposed by traditional settings. Finally, cluster 6 children, whose most salient characteristic was compliance, scored significantly higher on creativity in open than in traditional classes, a finding which was approximately the reverse of the initial expectations, but could perhaps be interpreted as indicating compliance to the norms of the open classroom setting. These analyses are described in more detail in Solomon and Kendall (1976).

Although there are suggestions of consistency between the two sets of analyses at a few points, they are, of course, not really comparable. One looked at single dimensions, the other at total profiles; one found many interactions within sex groups, while the other looked only at total sample effects. The cluster-based approach seems more attractive conceptually, but far more work appears needed before its virtues and limitations are completely understood.

The N's in this pilot study were, of course, small, the instruments for the most part, unvalidated, and the analysis techniques exploratory. Therefore, the results obtained by either approach were not considered to be more than tentative and suggestive. At the least,

however, the results indicated the potential utility of an analytic
approach which investigates effects for learner "types" rather than,
or in addition to, isolated dimensions or characteristics of learners.
In the subsequent larger study, to be described in the following pages,
a similar cluster analysis approach was applied to the identification
of classroom types as well as student types, and the interactions
between the two were examined. This was not the sole approach,
however; the main effects of, and interactions between, various
individual dimensions of students and of classrooms were also examined.

4 THE MAIN STUDY: GENERAL PLAN AND DATA COLLECTION PROCEDURES

GENERAL PLAN

Design

The aims of this research were (1) to identify natural groupings of classroom variables (with components representing the contributions of teachers, students, physical arrangements, and general activities); (2) to identify empirical "types" of classrooms; (3) to identify important dimensions of student motivational, attitudinal, and cognitive characteristics; (4) to identify empirical "types" of students (based on natural groupings of these characteristics); (5) to investigate direct effects of the classroom variables and types on various indexes of student progress (academic, cognitive, affective); and (6) to investigate the possibility of joint or interactive effects of various combinations of classroom and student dimensions and types on the same indexes of school progress. These aims necessitated a large variety of instruments and a large sample of classrooms.

Because various aspects of the data collection and data analysis promised to be quite complex, it was decided at an early stage to limit the sample to a single grade level. Fourth grade was selected for two reasons: (1) a desirable precondition was the maximization of the variability between the different classrooms in the study, and several school system administrators suggested the variability was likely to be greater at the lower grades. (2) At the same time, it was planned to administer a number of questionnaires to the students, and therefore a grade level high enough that the reading requirements of these instruments would not present problems to large numbers of the students was required. Fourth grade seem a suitable compromise for meeting both of these requirements.

Students and teachers in 50 fourth grade classrooms in a single county school system participated in the study. The students were all given portions of an achievement test during the spring of the

1973-74 academic year. Data from a different achievement test,
taken in the spring of the previous year (when the students were
finishing the third grade) as part of the school system's regular testing program, were also available for use as premeasures or covari-
ates. Other instruments measuring educational "outcomes"—including
cognitive skills, self-esteem, and various social attitudes and values—
were administered at both the beginning and end of the 1973-74
academic year. Measures of several school-related motives, preferences, and orientations of the children were also obtained near the
beginning of the school year. The 50 classrooms were broadly
sampled so as to be likely to represent various classroom types.
Each classroom was visited by trained observers on eight different
occasions during the school year. These observers made tallies
and ratings of a great many categories of teacher behavior, student
behavior, classroom activities, and classroom "atmosphere."

Data Analyses

The data analyses were primarily aimed at investigating the
joint (as well as separate) effects of classroom characteristics and
child characteristics (preferences, motives, and so on) on the various indexes of outcomes. Two major data analytic procedures were
used throughout this study: factor analysis and analysis of variance.
Factor analysis was used to reduce large numbers of items or scores
in particular sets of data to smaller numbers of basic characteristics
or dimensions. Analysis of variance was used to investigate joint
effects of child characteristics and classroom characteristics on
each outcome measure.

Factor analysis is a statistical procedure for reducing redundancy in a set of data by grouping items or scale scores based on
their interrelationships (or intercorrelations). It is used to form
composite indicators which represent a maximal amount of information with a minimal number of constructs (or "dimensions"). Each
factor's meaning is inferred from an examination of the pattern and
relative weights (or "loadings") of the items. (A "loading" is essentially the correlation of the item with the overall factor.) The items
with the highest loadings are the most important in determining the
meaning of the factor. The factors in most of the analyses were
"rotated" to "orthogonal simple structure"; the rotated factors
resulting from this procedure tend to be uncorrelated with each
other and to be maximally simple and meaningful.

A combination of methods was used to determine the number
of factors to retain and rotate in the various analyses to be described
in later chapters. Generally, the number of factors with eigenvalues

of one or greater was considered an upper bound, while the number indicated by the "scree" test (Cattell 1966) was considered a lower bound. Different rotations within this range were examined, and the one which produced the most meaningful groupings of items was retained in each case. Each of the factor analysis tables which appear in this report present the item loadings, communalities (h^2, the combined contribution of an item to all the factors within one factor analysis), eigenvalues (the variance accounted for by a given factor), the total variance in the set of items, and the percentage of the total variance accounted for by each factor.

Analysis of variance is used to determine the impact or effect of one or more "independent" variables upon a "dependent" variable. When the analysis includes two or more independent variables, it partitions the overall effect on the dependent variable into several sources: those indicating the direct (or "main") effect of each independent variable by itself, and those indicating joint (or "interaction") effects of various combinations of the independent variables. A result showing that highly motivated children learned best in "self-directed" classes and that poorly motivated children learned best in "teacher-directed" classes would be an example of an interaction; the effect is a joint product of the two independent variables, child motivation and class-type.

The analyses of variance in this study were done with the data so organized that the individual class was the unit of analysis. This was deemed appropriate because the children were grouped in classes and the different children within a single class could not be considered to be independent. The specific procedures used for these analyses are described later. Class-level analyses were not done in the pilot study because there were an insufficient number of classrooms to make the procedure feasible.

Some other specialized data analysis procedures were also used in the study, including cluster analysis and multiple regression analysis. These were not used as pervasively as the two just mentioned, and will be described briefly when they are introduced.

RECRUITMENT OF CLASSROOMS
AND CHILDREN

While the pilot study had involved a small number of classrooms, designated beforehand as either "open" or "traditional," the intent with the main study was to avoid preselection according to class type, but rather to try to have a broad range of classrooms represented. The initial plan was to attempt to recruit 50 classrooms; this seemed about the maximum number that could be handled given the research design and the resources available.

The research plan and objectives were presented to several area principals' meetings (the county in which the study was done is divided into six administrative areas). Those principals who expressed interest were given written descriptions of the plan and forms to return after consultation with their fourth grade teachers. In some cases, visits to the schools were also made and the plan discussed with the teachers. Because the research plan required obtaining descriptions of classroom characteristics which would be equally representative of the environment experienced by all students in any particular class, it was necessary to eliminate classrooms which were very "departmentalized"; therefore, classrooms which did not contain a minimum of 12 children who spent at least half of their time together were not included in the sample.

The 50 classrooms in the study were in 26 schools which were spread throughout the county but concentrated in the more urbanized areas. Early in autumn of 1973 letters describing the project were sent to parents of all fourth grade children in the selected classrooms, asking their permission for their children's participation. Children whose parents refused (about ten in all) were not given any of the tests and questionnaires, and were not rated by teachers. The final sample of children (after eliminating a few with very incomplete data, or with evidence of consistent "patterned" response on several of the administered questionnaires and tests) comprised 1,292 fourth graders: 645 boys and 647 girls. Other grade levels were represented in some of the classrooms, but were not included in the study.

All schools were in Montgomery County, Maryland, a relatively affluent county immediately north and northwest of Washington, D.C. On a coding of family "bread winner's occupation" obtained from school records, the following distribution was obtained:

unskilled or semi-skilled workers	67	(5.2%)
skilled workers	136	(10.5%)
clerical and sales, technicians	171	(13.2%)
managers, proprietors, owners of small businesses, semi-professionals	492	(38.1%)
executives, owners of large businesses, top administrators, professionals	426	(33.0%)

The average achievement level of the children was relatively high (as it tends to be for the county as a whole). Mean national percentile scores on the Iowa Test of Basic Skills which most of the children in the sample had taken at the end of the third grade ranged from 60.36 (reference materials) to 68.19 (spelling), with the mean for the total battery composite score at 67.52. The Cognitive Abilities Test, also administered at the end of the third grade, showed national percentile means, for the children in this sample, of 65.85 for verbal, 70.94 for quantitative, and 66.03 for nonverbal ability.

CLASSROOM OBSERVATIONS

The classroom observation system used in the present research was a revision of the system used in the pilot study. It includes sections for making observations of general classroom activities, classroom atmosphere, teacher activities, and student activities. It is, in part, a "sign" system (Medley and Mitzel 1963) and in part a series of global rating scales. The sign system section includes some items which were adapted from a system developed by Soar et al. (1971). The observer using this section of the observation system watches the class for a period of five minutes, then goes through a long list of activity categories ("teacher starts or shifts individual task or activity," "teacher gives requested help," "student-student academic discussion," "student starts or shifts activity on own," "simultaneous individual and group activities"), checking each category that occurred during the period. When the tallying for one period has been completed, another five-minute observation period is begun. Six observation periods are tallied in this way, in each observation session.

The global ratings were developed in part from the authors' previous research (Solomon et al. 1963, Solomon et al. 1969), and in part from the general literature comparing different types and styles of education. These atmosphere ratings use six-point scales and are made after the conclusion of the observation session. Among the items included are: "S's (students) talked very freely/S's talked only at T (teacher) direction," "S's mostly uninvolved in class activities/S's highly involved in class activities," "classroom is relatively devoid of stimuli/full of stimuli," "classroom is calm/excited," "T encouraged exploration/discouraged exploration," "T frequently gave individual attention/never gave individual attention." The observation form also contains a cover sheet on which the observers note characteristics of the classroom arrangement (number of adults present, desk arrangements, amount of student work displayed, accessibility of equipment and materials).

The instrument used in the pilot study contained a total of 277 items, 24 on the cover sheet, 182 in the sign system, and 71 global rating items. In revising this instrument for the main study, items with low reliabilities or low frequencies of occurrence (in the sign section) were eliminated. Some low-frequency items which were similar in content were combined into single items. Many of the retained items were rewritten, particularly rating items which had produced skewed distributions. The format of the instrument was also changed somewhat, and a few new items were added. After the final selection of items for the revised scale had been made, an observer's manual, giving item definitions and general instructions for use of the instrument, was written.* The revised form contains 249 items, including 17 on the cover sheet, 162 in the sign section, and 70 global rating items.

The observers were trained with videotapes made of five class sessions. These tapes were viewed and scored repeatedly in daily training sessions held during a two-week period. After each scoring period, the tallies and ratings of all observers were compared and discussed; sometimes a section of the tape was replayed to aid this process. By the end of the training period, good interobserver agreement appeared generally to have been reached (this was not formally assessed, however). There were eight observers, each of whom, following this training, made one visit to each of the 50 classrooms in the study. There were two major reasons for using this design for the observations: it allowed the use of an analysis of variance approach to assess reliability (to be described later) and, through combining observations across observers, it minimized the possible effects of observer biases or differential perceptions. One additional observer was trained as an alternate and made three class-observation visits (to avoid having regular observers visit classrooms which included their own children). These visits were spread out through the school year, ranging between the end of October and the end of April, with approximately three weeks between successive visits to each class. The visits were balanced, as much as possible, between mornings and afternoons and between different days of the week.

TEACHER DESCRIPTIONS OF
CLASSROOM ACTIVITIES

In order to get the teachers' views of the characteristics, organization, and typical activities of their classrooms, they were asked, near the end of the school year, to respond to a 64-item questionnaire, "Teacher Description of Classroom Activities." An earlier version of this questionnaire containing 49 items had been used in the pilot study, and was derived in part from a questionnaire

---

*The manual, the observation form, and all instruments used in this research can be obtained from the authors.

developed by Traub et al. (1972). With the revised questionnaire, teachers made ratings on six-point scales which described the positions of their classes with respect to a number of characteristics: the amount of free time available to students; participation of children in making rules, defining goals, selecting activities, initiating their own tasks, evaluating their own work, determining their own learning objectives; the amount of time the teacher spends presenting planned lessons, acting as "resource person," acting as discussion leader; the amount of plan changing, number of classroom rules, individuality of learning objectives, amount of structuring and sequencing of tasks. Part of the purpose of this questionnaire was to obtain information about some aspects of the classes which might not be easily accessible to observers (for example, student participation in goal setting, planning, and evaluation).

MEASURES OF ATTITUDES, VALUES, AND SELF-ASSESSMENTS

In late September and early October of the 1973-74 academic year, two questionnaires were given to the children participating in the study; each questionnaire was administered on a different day, with about a week between administrations. A parallel pair of questionnaires was administered to the children in late April and early May. In order to have the questionnaires administered in the various classes at about the same period in the school year, it was necessary to employ a large number of questionnaire administrators. A total of 14 people performed this role in the fall administration, 11 in the spring. Some of them were graduate students at local universities, some were mothers of children in the school system, and some were both. Nine of them also served as the classroom observers (and alternate).

The administrators read the questionnaire instructions and each item aloud while the children read to themselves. Although this was not necessary for most of the children, it made it possible to avoid making special administration arrangements for children with low reading skill. These two sets of questionnaires contained measures of certain values, attitudes, and self-assessments which are among the educational-outcome indexes in this research. They were administered at both times to give an indication of the child's initial and final status with regard to each measure. A list of these indexes, with sample items, follows.

1. Assertion responsibility (four items): This is one of four "democratic attitude" subscores adapted from previous research

(Solomon et al. 1972). It refers to the responsibility to state one's own position, even if it seems unpopular or unlikely to prevail. The child was asked to indicate degree of agreement (on four-point scales) with items including:

> "Four kids are making up some rules for a new game. Three of them agree on a rule; the fourth one doesn't like it. Since the others agree, he should not say anything about it."

> "Your family is planning an outing. You already know that everyone else except you wants to go to a museum. You should not say what you want to do."

2. Willingness to compromise (four items): This is another of the "democratic attitude" subscores, which also asks for the child's agreement or disagreement.

> "Two friends are trying to decide what to do on a Saturday afternoon. One thinks they should go to a movie; the other thinks they should go to the park. Each should just do what he wants to by himself." (If children disagreed, they were asked to "write in what you think they should do," and this response was scored for degree of compromise.)

> "When two people argue about something, one of them is right and one is wrong."

3. Equality of representation (four items): Another "democratic attitude" subscore.

> "When the kids in a class at school are voting on something, the kids who are always making noise should not be allowed to vote."

> "New members should be in a club for a while before they get to vote on things."

4. Equality of participation (four items): The last of the "democratic attitude" subscores.

> "When kids are playing games, the ones who don't know how to play should get to play as much as anyone else."

"Kids who get in trouble on one trip should not get to
go on the next trip."

5. Cooperation versus competition (nine items, expanded from
four in the pilot study): This measure was developed for this research.
The children were asked to state agreement or disagreement on four-
point scales.

"Classes are best when everyone tries to do better
work than everyone else."

"It is better for a bunch of kids to work together paint-
ing one big picture than for each kid to try to paint the
best picture."

6. Value on group activities (twelve items): This measure was
adapted from one used in prior research (Oberlander and Solomon
1973); it asked for statements of agreement or disagreement (four-
point scales).

"People in group projects have a very good time working together."

"You learn more by working on math problems by
yourself than with a group of kids."

7. Value on task self-direction (six items): This measure was
developed for this research and asked for statements of agreement
or disagreement.

"When you want to find out more about something, you
should just go to the library and see what you can dig
up, without getting help."

"If you want to fix a broken toy, you should ask for help
right away so you won't waste a lot of time on it."

8. Value on decision-making autonomy (ten items): This measure was adapted from previous research (Oberlander and Solomon
1972) and also asked for agreement or disagreement on four-point
scales.

"Teachers should be the ones to decide what kids should
work on in school."

"Kids should be the ones to decide if they need to do homework."

9. Tolerance for differences (value on heterogeneity) (four items): This measure was adapted from prior research (Oberlander and Solomon 1972).

"The best kind of neighborhood to live in is one with people who are the same in their hobbies, jobs, and interests."

"If a new kid came to school who talked and dressed differently from the others, it would be best for him to try to be more like everyone else."

10. Concern for others (nine items): This measure was developed for this research.

"A kid has enough schoolwork of his own to look after without worrying about other kids'."

"It is important for you to take extra time to help kids who don't understand something."

11. Self-esteem (twelve items): This measure was adapted from one developed by Davidson and Greenberg (1967). Children were asked to state the frequency (on a five-point scale ranging from "always" to "never") with which each of a series of phrases accurately described them.

"I think I am:
. . . a good worker in school."
. . . not the way I would like to be."

12. Class and self-evaluations (eight items): This was a set of items, developed for this research, asking children to evaluate the class and their own learning and enjoyment during the school year. Since it referred to what had happened during the year, it was given only in the spring.

"How much do you think you have learned in school this year?" (Answered with a five-point scale ranging from "not much" to "more than ever before.")

"How much fun have you had in school this year?" (Answered with a similar five-point scale.)

MEASURES OF INQUIRY SKILL, WRITING
QUALITY, AND CREATIVITY

The questionnaires measuring attitudes and values also included some items intended to measure children's inquiry skill, writing skill, and creativity. Each of these items required written responses; different sets of items were developed or selected for the pre- and postmeasures.

1. Inquiry skill: The inquiry skill items, following the research approach of Allender (1968), posed problem situations and asked the child to state a strategy for solving the problems. The emphasis was on the child's ability to develop a potentially effective approach to reaching a solution. There was one inquiry item at the beginning of each of the four questionnaires. The items used in the first two (for the pretest measures) were:

A Problem

Pretend you are an engineer trying to decide on the best place to build a bridge across a river. What would you do to help you decide? Write down the things you would do to help you decide.

A Mystery

You are hiking with some friends and come across a "ghost town." How could you find out why no one lives there any more? Write down the things you could do to find out.

The items used in the posttest questionnaires were:

A Problem

Pretend that you are the mayor of a small city and you are trying to find a good spot to put a new playground. How would you figure out what was the best spot? Write down the things you could do to help you figure it out.

A Mystery

You come home and find your room messed up, although it was neat when you left. You wonder whether it got messed up by the wind, a burglar, or someone just fooling around. How would you figure out which it was? Write down the things you could do to find out.

The last two of these items had also been included in the pilot study. The coding system was simplified somewhat from that used in the pilot study to eliminate some apparent between-category redundancy in the initial system. Each of the item answers was scored, in the present study, for the number of "informative responses" (number of suggested steps which would produce information useful to the solution of the problem), number of "site-extended responses" (those which involved ranging beyond the geographical site of the problem), and for the overall completeness of the response to the problem (a rating, made on a four-point scale). To eliminate overlap between the first two of the above categories, the "site-extended" total was converted to a percentage by dividing it by the total number of appropriate responses.

2. Writing quality: The same items used to measure inquiry skill were also rated for the clarity, expressiveness, and coherence of the written communication shown in the responses to these items. Although the same coders who scored the items for inquiry also did the writing-quality rating, they were instructed to make this judgment independent of the adequacy of the inquiry response; if the response was written clearly and well, it was to receive a high rating even if it constituted a poor approach to the inquiry problem. This rating was also made on a four-point scale.

3. Creativity. The creativity items, taken from Wallach and Kogan (1965), were placed at the ends of the same questionnaires. The four "uses" items and the four "patterns" items which in the original Wallach and Kogan research had shown the highest item-total correlations with their respective subtest totals were selected for the present investigation. Two of each type of item were used in the pretest questionnaires and two in the posttest questionnaires, with two items per questionnaire. The pretest "uses" items were "chair" and "button"; the children were asked to write down as many different uses of each as they could think of. The posttest uses items were "cork" and "shoe" and were presented with the same instructions. The "patterns" items consisted of geometric line drawings, to which the children were to respond with as many different perceptions as possible ("Write down all the things you think this could be."). The two pretest patterns items consisted of a small circle above (or next to) a large half circle, and three straight, horizontal, parallel lines, two long and one (between them) short. The posttest patterns were four circles next to three sides of a rectangle and five short, parallel, staggered lines. There were no time limits for these items, which were described in the questionnaires (and by the administrators) as "games." The creativity items had been placed at the beginnings of questionnaires in the pilot study; this placement made it difficult to avoid time limits completely. In the present study, therefore,

the creativity items were placed at the end of the questionnaires, and the inquiry items (with nine-minute time limits) at the beginning.

As was the case in the pilot study, each of the creativity items was scored for "fluency" (the number of appropriate responses) and "uncommonness" (the number of responses below a specified frequency of appearance). For the items used in the pilot study ("button," "cork," and the last two "patterns" items described above), the frequencies were determined by making a list of all responses used by the total pilot study sample and counting the number of people giving each. After an examination of the distributions with different percentage cut-off points, it was decided, in the pilot study analysis, to define an "uncommon" response as one given by 10 percent of the sample or less for the uses items, and one given by 1.5 percent of the sample or less for the patterns items. These gave similar, and statistically workable, distributions for the different types of items. In the main study analysis, the same lists and cut-off points were used for the repeated items (if an appropriate response in the new study did not appear in the old list for the same item, it was considered to be uncommon). For the items which were new to the main study, it was necessary to make up new lists of items and frequencies. This was done with a random selection of seven of the classrooms, in which about 180 children had responded to these questionnaires (about 14 percent of the total sample). The same percentage cut-off points for the uses and patterns items were used for these new items as for those repeated from the pilot study. When the total sample was coded for these items, the designation of each response as common or uncommon was derived from the list which had been developed from the subsample; appropriate responses which did not appear in the subsample list were considered uncommon. A similar procedure to that used for the "site-extended" inquiry category was used to remove overlap between fluency and uncommonness; the number of uncommon responses was converted to a percentage by dividing it by the total number of appropriate responses for the same item. These two coding categories were similar, but not identical, to those used by Wallach and Kogan.

Because the above two coding categories seemed insufficient to reflect the variety and richness of some of the children's responses, two additional coding items were devised. Each was a rating which referred to the total set of responses to a single stimulus, and each used a four-point scale. The first of these was "elaboration," defined in the coding instructions as "the degree to which . . . responses are detailed and spelled out, specifically described, embellished." The second was a rating of "imaginativeness," defined as "the degree to which . . . responses evidence the play of imagination; uses responses which deviate from ordinary uses of and settings for (object), and patterns responses which involve shifts of perspective or scale, viewing object rotated, upside-down, from above or underneath, would be among indices of this quality."

MEASURES OF SCHOOL ACHIEVEMENT
AND SOCIOECONOMIC STATUS

After the last questionnaire had been administered, three more visits were made to each class (usually by the same administrator) to give sections of the California Achievement Test. These visits were about a week apart, and ranged between the middle and end of May (with the exception of three classes which had to be rescheduled, and had their last session during the first week of June). In order to reduce the testing time, a few of the CAT subtests were eliminated from this testing, including mathematics problems, fractions, and punctuation. The tests which were given were first visit: reading (vocabulary, comprehension); second visit: mathematics (computation and concepts); third visit: language (capitalization, usage and structure, spelling). To obtain indicators of prior achievement, national percentile scores of the achievement tests which most of the children in the sample had been administered by the school system a year earlier (Iowa Test of Basic Skills and the Cognitive Abilities Test) were obtained from school records.

To determine socioeconomic status, information about the occupational status of the children's parents was obtained from the schools. The occupation of the family breadwinner was coded on a five-point scale, on which 1 represented "unskilled or semiskilled workers," and 5 represented "executives, . . . professionals, owners of large businesses."

TEACHERS' RATINGS OF STUDENTS'
CLASSROOM BEHAVIOR

Near the end of the school year, the teachers were asked to make ratings of the individual children in their classes with an 11-item rating form called "Teacher Views of Students." In the pilot study, a 30-item scale had been used, with five-point scales, and the teachers were asked to divide their classes into relatively equal fifths with respect to each rated attribute. Because the teachers in that study felt the rating procedure to be both difficult and time consuming, several changes were made. The number of items was reduced (with items selected to represent the qualities found to cohere into factors in the pilot study), the scale was changed to a four-point scale, and the directions were changed. Among the attributes rated were "highly active, energetic," "self-controlled," "works well with other children," "highly involved in class activities," "cooperative, does what is asked," and "perseveres with tasks." With regard to each attribute, teachers were asked to give a rating of 1 if the attribute was "not at all, or only slightly characteristic of the child (compared with others in the class)" and a rating of 4 if the attribute was "highly or extremely characteristic of the child." These ratings were also considered to represent measures of outcomes in this research.

MEASURES OF PREFERENCES, ORIENTATIONS, AND MOTIVES

Two questionnaires, containing measures of personal dispositions which were expected to interact with differences in classroom characteristics to influence various outcomes, were administered to the children in the study from early to mid-October. All of these measures had been included in the pilot study; most were revised to some degree before being used in the main study. All scales contained multiple-choice or paired-alternatives types of items. Following is a list of these measures, the number of items in each, and two examples of the items included in each scale.

1. Personal expression versus structured role orientation (12 items): This measures children's relative preference for situations in which they are free to express themselves and impose their own objectives versus those which are highly structured, with various role obligations clearly spelled out. It was developed for this research. Items include:

"I would rather (a) be in a place where I know exactly what I am supposed to do (b) be in a place where I pick what I want to do."

"I would rather (a) follow a time plan, so I know what I'll be doing at different times (b) do things as they come, with no time plan."

2. Fear of failure (ten items): This measure was also developed for this research.

"I would rather (a) keep working on a math problem I haven't been able to solve (b) stop working on a math problem that is too hard, and find an easier one."

"I would rather (a) work a puzzle I know I can do
(b) work a hard puzzle I've never done before."

3. Intrinsic-extrinsic motivation (12 items): This measures
one's tendency to strive for the sake of the pleasure of engaging in
the activity per se rather than for obtaining rewards from external
sources; the measure was adapted from an instrument developed for
a previous study (Oberlander and Solomon 1972).

"Peter is reading a book. Why? (a) He wants to find
out more about something. (b) His teacher will give
him 'extra credit'."

"Sally is writing a story. Why? (a) She likes writing
stories. (b) She wants to please her parents (or
friends)."

4. Class characteristics preferences (26 items): This series
of items was developed for this research. It asks children to state
preferences for different sets of classroom characteristics, many
of which describe attributes believed typical of either "open" or
"traditional" classes.

"I would most like a class where (a) the kids choose
what they want to do (b) the teacher and kids together
plan what to do (c) the teacher plans what the kids will
do."

"I would most like a class where (a) kids talk to each
other or the teacher whenever they want to (b) kids
can talk only when the teacher calls on them (c) kids
can talk to each other a little, if it's needed for what
they're doing."

5. Locus of control (intellectual achievement responsibility)
(20 items): This measure, developed by Crandall et al. (1965b),
refers to the children's acceptance of responsibility for their own
successes and failures (as opposed to attributing them to external
sources). It produces subscores referring to internal attribution of
successes (I+) and internal attribution of failures (I-), as well as a
total score. For the present investigation, the scale was shortened
from 34 to 20 items by taking the ten I+ items and the ten I- items
which had obtained the highest item-total correlations in the pilot
study. The retained items include:

"When you do well on a test at school, is it more likely
to be (a) because you studied for it, or (b) because the
test was especially easy?"

"When you forget something you heard in class, is it
(a) because the teacher didn't explain it very well, or
(b) because you didn't try very hard to remember?"

6. Locus of instigation (15 items; expanded from 12 in the
pilot study): This measure was developed for this research and is
based on some theoretical notions discussed by Solomon and Oberlander
(1974). It measures the child's belief that he or she is generally
responsible for initiating his or her own activities. It is differentiated
from locus of control in that it refers to the instigation rather than
the outcomes of behavior.

"When I practice an instrument, it is usually because (a)
I just started without thinking (b) I was told to, or had
to (c) I was asked to, and agreed (d) I decided to."

"When I join a club, it is usually because (a) I was
asked to, and agreed (b) I was told to, or had to (c)
I decided to (d) I just came across it by accident."

In scoring this scale, the "I decided to" responses were given a value
of 3; "I was told to" responses a value of 1; and the other responses
(referring to chance and to agreeing after being asked), a value of 2.

7. Achievement motivation (20 items): The version of this
measure used in the pilot study was developed by Wiener and Kukla
(1970). It was slightly revised for use in the present study.

"I prefer jobs (a) that I might not be able to do (b)
which I'm sure I can do."

"After I lose at a game (a) I want to play again right
away (b) I want to do something else for a while."

8. Generality-specificity of strong task preferences (12 items):
This measure was adapted from prior research (Solomon 1977). The
child is asked to state his degree of liking for each of a set of 12
varied tasks, using a six-point rating scale, ranging from "I would
like doing this very much" and "I would like doing this fairly well"
to "I would dislike doing this pretty much" and "I would hate doing
this." Among the rated tasks were "following complicated directions
to put together a model," "making a big snowman with some friends,"

and "practicing dart throwing to become a better shot." The measure
of "generality" is derived by counting the number of strong preferences stated ("very much"). It was thought that the performance of
children with more specific and narrow preferences would be more
differentiated across classrooms than those with broader and more
general preferences.

9. Social desirability (24 items): This measure was developed
by Crandall et al. (1965a), and refers to the child's tendency to endorse
statements that are socially acceptable or socially valued, even when
they are not likely to be accurate. This tendency has been thought
to relate to a need for approval. The measure was shortened for
this study (it contains 48 items); the 24 items with highest item-total
correlations in the pilot study were retained. In responding to the
scale, the child is asked to state whether each of a series of statements is true or false.

"When I make a mistake, I always admit I am wrong."

"I never forget to say 'please' and 'thank you.'"

10. Bureaucratic orientation (school environment preference
schedule - SEPS) (24 items). This measure comprised a separate
instrument, which was administered during the same session as one
of the other questionnaires. It was developed by Gordon (1968), and
is based on Weber's theory of bureaucracy. It measures a preference
for being guided by established authorities, institutions, and rules,
and a general conforming orientation. The child is asked to state his
degree of agreement (on a 5-point scale) with each of a series of
items, including:

"A student should always do what his teacher wants
him to."

"Older people are in the best position to make important decisions for young people."

5 DERIVING DIMENSIONS OF CLASSROOM ENVIRONMENT

INSTRUMENT RELIABILITY
AND REFINEMENT

The reliability of each item in the observation form was assessed with an analysis of variance approach, with classrooms and observers treated as independent variables. "Intraclass correlations" were derived from these analyses for each observation category (Guilford 1956, Williams 1973). The classroom-by-observer interaction constituted the error variance term in the intraclass correlation computation, so that the coefficient represents the degree to which an item differentiates between classrooms, and does so in the same way for different observers:

$$r_{kk} = \frac{MS_{classrooms} \quad (MS_{classrooms \times observers \quad interaction})}{MS_{classrooms}}$$

Items with reliabilities of less than .30 or mean frequencies of less than 1 per session were eliminated from further analyses, with the exception of a few which seemed of sufficient theoretical importance to include in spite of low reliability. Eight groups of items which were related but insufficiently reliable or frequent by themselves were combined: For example, "games (entertainment)" and "games (educational)" were combined into a single "games" category, and "two or more different simultaneous group activities" and "two or more different simultaneous individual activities" were combined into "two or more different simultaneous activities."

A single score was derived for each individual sign system item in a given classroom by summing the tallies within sessions (across the six observation periods), and then summing these totals across the eight observers. The global ratings were also summed over the eight observers who visited each classroom. After elimina-

71

tions and combinations, a total of 205 items remained: 17 on the cover sheet, 119 in the sign section, and 69 global rating items. The reliabilities of the final set (including the new item combinations) are shown in the columns at the far right of Tables 5.1 through 5.7. The reliability of the teacher class descriptions could not be assessed because there was only one set of judgments for each class, and no a priori scales for which to determine the degree of internal consistency.

FACTOR ANALYSES OF CLASSROOM OBSERVATIONS AND DESCRIPTIONS

One important purpose of this project was to identify dimensions of classroom environments. A series of factor analyses (see Chapter 4) was used to accomplish this, using programs contained in the Statistical Package for the Social Sciences (SPSS) (Nie et al. 1975). Because there were too many items in the observation form and the teacher-description questionnaire to be handled in a single analysis even after the elimination of the least reliable items, the teacher questionnaire and each section of the observation form was analyzed separately to begin with, and the resulting factors were rotated obliquely. Factor scores derived from each of these "first-order" factors were then factor analyzed themselves. The first-order factors were rotated obliquely in order to maximize their intercorrelations for the "second-order" analysis. Factors resulting from the second-order analysis were rotated orthogonally.

Observation Form Cover Sheet

Analysis of these items produced five factors, accounting for 72.7 percent of the total variance. Factor loadings, item reliabilities, item communalities (h^2), and related information are presented in Table 5.1. Items are presented in order of their contributions to the successive factors, not their original order in the instrument.

The first factor is the strongest, and has the largest number of high-loading items. The first item in the factor refers to the physical openness of the space; another set of items represents physical aspects of the classroom environment which are apparently associated with such openness: "number of interest centers," "carpeted floor," "teacher-made wall displays" and "signs and pictures on walls." Another pair of high-loading items refers to the accessibility of equipment and materials to the children. This factor was labeled, "physical openness, accessibility of material and equipment to stu-

TABLE 5.1

Factor Analysis of Observation Form Cover Sheet Data

| Items | Loadings on Factors | | | | | h^2 | r_{kk} |
	1	2	3	4	5		
Openness of space	-.83	-.29	.11	.55	.49	.90	.98
Number of interest centers	-.83	-.02	.36	.55	.33	.84	.89
Carpeted floor	-.82	-.27	.17	.50	.33	.77	.99
Background noise	-.80	.01	.02	.22	.30	.69	.70
Percent teacher-made wall displays	-.80	-.14	.00	.14	-.21	.81	.80
Accessibility of materials	-.74	.01	.55	.39	.30	.77	.79
Accessibility of equipment	-.67	-.17	.33	.37	.36	.56	.75
Signs and pictures on walls	-.64	-.15	.53	.33	.20	.62	.82
Percent commercial wall displays	.28	.91	-.11	-.27	-.03	.88	.83
Percent student-made wall displays	.44	-.74	.08	.14	.23	.90	.82

(continued)

Table 5.1 (continued)

Items	Loadings on Factors					h^2	r_{kk}
	1	2	3	4	5		
Inanimate things from environment (rocks, sand)	-.05	-.03	.80	.12	.16	.66	.83
Plants in room	-.05	-.07	.72	-.17	.00	.59	.92
Animals, etc. in room	-.29	.01	.56	.32	.54	.58	.89
Judged crowdedness	.27	.10	-.02	-.83	-.18	.70	.80
Number of grade levels*	-.45	-.18	.18	.71	.37	.61	*
Tables/desks not in rows	-.19	-.35	-.03	.63	-.25	.61	.87
Number of adults in space	-.48	-.36	.25	.43	.77	.80	.90
Number of children in space	-.35	-.48	.07	.02	.76	.81	.91
Percent of variance	38.3	11.5	10.1	6.8	6.1		
Eigenvalue	6.89	2.07	1.81	1.22	1.10		

*Not an observation-system item; values were assigned according to general information regarding the classes. No reliability was assessed.

Source: Compiled by the authors.

dents." The high loading of one additional item, "background noise," indicates that classes characterized by such openness also have a relatively high level of noise. It will be noticed that all of these high loadings are negative. Physically open classes with accessible materials and equipment would thus show low scores on this factor.

The second factor is defined by two items, "percent of commercial wall displays" (with a high positive loading) and "percent of student-made wall displays" (with a high negative loading). The factor is called, therefore, "commercial versus student-made wall decorations."

The third factor has the highest loadings for three similar items: "inanimate things from environment," "plants in room," and "animals, etc. in room." This factor is summarized as representing "extracurricular stimuli."

The fourth factor seems to represent a combination of gradedness and crowdedness. Classes scoring high on this factor would tend to include two or more grade levels and to be relatively uncrowded. This factor is termed "multigraded, uncrowded versus single-graded, crowded."

The last factor also contains only two high-loading items, "number of adults in space" and "number of children in space." Thus, this factor is termed, "number of children and adults in class area."

General Organization and Activities Section
of Observation Form

Three factors were produced by the analysis of the items in this section, accounting for 49.1 percent of the variance. The results of this analysis are shown in Table 5.2.

The first factor has a single high positive loading for "all same group activity" (plus a moderate positive loading for "all same individual activity") contrasted with high negative loadings for "simultaneous individual and group activities," "reading," "number of different subjects or topics during observation period," "two or more different simultaneous activities," and for a few other items which refer to different topics or activities. An accurate general designation of this factor would seem to be "common versus varied simultaneous activities."

Three items with moderate negative loadings form the most consistent combination contributing to the second factor: "audio-visual equipment in use," "games," and "student-made materials in use." These are considered to be the nucleus of the factor which is called "unusual 'fun' activities." Posed against these is a single

TABLE 5.2

Factor Analysis of Observation Form General
Organization and Activities Items

Items	Loadings on Factors			h^2	r_{kk}
	1	2	3		
Simultaneous individual and group activities	-.80	-.34	-.18	.76	.55
All same group activity	.74	-.15	.02	.59	.29
Reading	-.73	.16	.11	.58	.43
Number different subjects or topics during observation period	-.70	-.34	-.21	.62	.63
Structured writing	-.65	-.08	.15	.44	.31
Textbooks in use	-.63	-.03	.04	.40	.59
Two or more different simultaneous activities	-.58	-.44	.18	.54	.44
Teacher-made materials in use	-.43	-.40	.09	.34	.34
Commercial materials in use	-.33	.05	-.11	.13	.53
Creative writing	-.29	.00	.04	.09	.51
All engaged in same individual activity	.49	.70	-.10	.71	.51
Audio-visual equipment in use	.30	-.48	-.10	.35	.45
Games	-.01	-.43	.06	.19	.27
Student-made materials in use	-.10	-.42	-.25	.24	.09
Problem solving/logic	.24	-.31	.22	.21	.30
Disruptive activity shift	.05	-.06	.80	.64	.58
Smooth activity shift	.10	.09	-.45	.22	.30
Projects/experiments	.01	-.23	-.36	.18	.35
Percent of variance	26.6	12.3	10.2		
Eigenvalue	4.80	2.22	1.83		

Source: Compiled by the authors.

76

high positive loading for "all same individual activity" suggesting that these activities tend not to occur as single class-wide activities, and that there is a degree of overlap between the first and second factors.

The third factor contains a high positive loading for "disruptive activity shift" and a moderate negative one for "smooth activity shift." The factor is therefore called "disruptive versus smooth shifting of activities."

Teacher Activities Section of Observation Form

The factor analysis of the items recording observations of teacher activities (shown in Table 5.3) produced five factors, accounting for 54 percent of the total variance. The first factor, called "teacher hostility, annoyance, criticism," contains high loadings for such items as "shows annoyance, anger," "orders," "scolds, shouts, or punishes," "criticizes behavior," "uses sharp tone," "warns," and "uses sarcasm." The pattern seems clear and unambiguous.

The second factor includes several items which refer to teachers' interactions with students. Most of these describe ways in which teachers promote student verbal participation: "asks for clarification," "asks convergent question," "calls on student," "encourages student expression," "listens attentively," "verbally prods," "asks individual a question," "disagrees with S (Student) idea (with explanation)," and "amplifies student comment." The factor is called "encouragement of active (verbal) student participation."

The third teacher-activities factor poses high positive loadings for several items which refer to teacher involvement with individuals or small groups within the class ("gives requested help," "talks about one or more students' work," "interacts with one student," "interacts with subgroup," "gives unrequested help," "touches/hugs student," "asks group a question") against high or moderate negative loadings for items which refer to teacher interaction with the class as a whole ("asks class a question," "interacts with total class," and "talks to total class"). The factor was labeled "teacher interaction with individuals or subgroups versus total class."

The fourth factor contains elements of teacher warmth (with high or moderate loadings for "smiles," "praises student work or comments," "socializes with students," and "praises/approves behavior") and teacher expressiveness ("tells personal opinion, experiences, likes," "ranges from topic or encourages same," "tells implications or consequences," "gives speculative, hypothetical material"). Moderate loadings for "plans with students" and

TABLE 5.3

Factor Analysis of Observation Form Teacher Activities Items

Items	Loadings on Factors					h^2	r_{kk}
	1	2	3	4	5		
Shows annoyance, anger	.90	.03	-.03	-.14	-.41	.87	.56
Orders, commands	.86	.02	.03	-.17	-.32	.77	.54
Scolds, shouts, or punishes	.85	-.12	.04	-.03	-.01	.77	.61
Criticizes behavior	.82	.00	-.06	.06	-.33	.72	.67
Uses sharp tone	.80	-.08	.01	-.04	-.06	.66	.54
Uses firm tone	.80	-.02	-.07	.00	-.32	.68	.46
Warns	.77	.05	.12	-.19	-.41	.69	.49
Criticizes student work or comments	.75	.32	.15	-.03	-.27	.70	.61
Uses sarcasm	.64	.11	-.08	-.09	.00	.45	.56
Ignores, rejects S idea (no explanation)	.55	-.09	-.20	-.12	-.22	.36	.25
Invokes/announces classroom/discipline rule	.50	-.16	-.08	.25	-.24	.40	.27
Talking to one student, no interaction	.38	.13	.19	-.20	.10	.26	.18
Asks for clarification	.09	.79	.00	.08	.15	.66	.26
Amplifies or explains student comment	-.01	.77	-.07	.32	.03	.68	.24
Asks convergent (1 answer) question	.03	.71	.21	-.24	-.23	.68	.36
Gives answer, complete or incomplete	.14	.71	.26	.15	-.13	.60	.20
Calls on student (after no offer)	.22	.71	.03	-.11	-.08	.57	.36
Elicits implications or consequences	-.22	.66	.05	.19	.43	.63	.27

Calls on student (after offer)	-.06	.64	-.50	.15	-.07	.75	.53
Gives factual material	-.14	.63	.07	.19	-.26	.55	.45
Encourages student expression	-.22	.59	.10	.41	.54	.71	.20
Listens attentively to student	-.16	.56	.46	.33	.38	.66	.48
Verbally prods	.33	.53	.20	.00	.27	.51	.30
Asks individual a question	.28	.52	.52	-.23	.09	.56	.22
Disagrees with S idea (with explanation)	.38	.47	.19	.00	.06	.39	.38
Gives requested help	.02	-.13	.73	-.09	.02	.58	.43
Talks about one or more students' work	-.05	.13	.73	.22	.02	.60	.30
Asks class a question	.05	.26	-.73	.38	-.04	.76	.55
Interacts with one student	.00	.03	.67	.18	.28	.55	.36
Interacts with subgroup	-.31	.32	.61	-.07	.05	.55	.44
Interacts with total class	-.02	.36	-.59	.51	.05	.73	.54
Gives unrequested help	.19	.28	.57	-.16	-.17	.46	.33
Touches/hugs student	.00	-.09	.54	.33	-.12	.48	.48
Asks group a question	-.17	.47	.54	-.21	.09	.56	.34
Talks to total class (no interaction)	.36	-.25	-.49	.36	-.05	.56	.58
Works alone at desk or table	.03	-.24	-.41	-.14	-.04	.23	.60
Distracts S(s) from disruptive activity	.25	.14	.32	.11	.01	.20	.37
Tells personal opinion, experiences, likes	.02	.36	-.01	.70	.29	.62	.62
Smiles	-.49	.24	.29	.60	.35	.71	.73
Praises student work or comments	-.32	.42	.31	.60	.03	.67	.37
Socializes with students	-.41	-.12	.18	.53	.21	.50	.28
Ranges from topic or encourages same	-.31	.45	-.15	.53	.16	.56	.26

(continued)

Table 5.3 (continued)

Items	Loadings on Factors					h^2	r_{kk}
	1	2	3	4	5		
Plans with students	-.12	-.06	.07	.51	.49	.47	.24
Participates in student activity	-.19	-.01	-.21	.50	.11	.31	.38
Tells implications or consequences	.31	.34	-.07	.48	-.14	.47	.46
Gives speculative, hypothetical material	-.22	.31	-.14	.40	.31	.36	.32
Praises/approves behavior	-.06	.15	.09	.37	.15	.17	.26
Talks with adult	.07	-.15	.02	.33	.04	.15	.32
Suggests, guides	-.23	.18	.25	.22	.76	.67	.32
Asks divergent question (many answers)	-.07	.26	-.20	.28	.73	.69	.28
Drills students (rote, repetitive work)	.07	.35	.14	-.14	-.61	.55	.61
Encourages elaboration of idea or activity	-.24	.43	.19	.41	.60	.65	.29
Talks to subgroup (no interaction)	.13	.10	.38	-.10	-.52	.44	.37
Gives directions	.27	-.08	.91	.21	-.44	.32	.23
Starts, shifts, or ends activity	.21	.09	-.16	-.07	-.36	.19	.21
Reads aloud	.14	.06	-.05	.02	-.26	.08	.37
Percent of variance	17.7	14.1	10.4	6.9	4.9		
Eigenvalue	9.91	7.88	5.84	3.86	2.72		

Source: Compiled by the authors.

"participates in student activity," in conjunction with these other high loading items, convey an impression of friendly and nondominating interaction with students. The factor is called "personal expression, warmth, friendliness."

The fifth factor was called "encouragement of student expressiveness, exploration versus drilling," primarily because of high positive loadings for "asks divergent question" and "encourages elaboration of idea or activity," a moderate one for "encourages student expression," and a high negative loading for "drills students (rote, repetitive work)." There is also a high positive loading for "suggests, guides," indicating that teachers who encourage student expressiveness, do so in a rather indirect way.

Student Activities Section of Observation Form

Items from this part of the form also produced five factors, which accounted for 63.6 percent of the total variance. This factor analysis is shown in Table 5.4.

Items defining the first factor refer to students smiling, cooperating with, helping, and responding to one another, raising (and answering) questions, speculating and experimenting. The factor is called "interstudent cooperation, friendly interaction while working," which seems to represent the most salient cluster of characteristics represented.

The second factor is called "general student disruptiveness, hostility" because of the set of consistent high loadings for such items as "student ignores or rejects teacher request or demand," "student teases student—unfriendly," "students horseplay," "students shout," "students fidget," "students argue," "student expresses annoyance," and "student frowns, cries." (These are negative loadings, so the quality we have identified would be represented by low scores on the factor.)

Two qualities are evident in the items with high loadings on the third student-activities factor: active, largely verbal student participation in academic classroom activities and teacher direction of this participation. The items manifesting one or both of these qualities include "five or more students attending to teacher," "student gives solicited question or comment," "student offers response," "student answers teacher question," "student gives factual material," and "student listens, watches." The label assigned to the factor is "attentive, responsive verbal class participation (academic) under teacher direction."

Three items with high positive loadings form the nucleus of the fourth factor. Each of them indicates a request for help or atten-

TABLE 5.4

Factor Analysis of Observation Form Student Activities Items

Items	Loadings on Factors					h²	rkk
	1	2	3	4	5		
Five or more students smile	.76	-.09	-.20	.09	-.33	.63	.67
Student answers student question	.69	-.18	-.13	.57	-.31	.70	.44
Student builds on teacher or student comment	.69	-.13	.06	-.04	-.03	.52	.06
Students work together	.66	-.16	-.12	.58	-.65	.83	.62
Students share, cooperate	.65	-.02	-.23	.41	-.49	.62	.35
Student raises question or makes comment	.65	-.21	.17	.11	-.08	.48	.29
Student gives opinions, experiences, likes	.64	-.16	.04	-.06	-.29	.49	.48
Student helps (teaches) student	.63	.09	-.11	.42	-.46	.59	.38
Student gives feedback, evaluation	.61	-.05	.05	.23	-.34	.43	.15
Inter-student academic discussion	.60	-.14	-.11	.56	-.27	.59	.45
Student teases student(s) (friendly)	.53	-.43	-.32	.09	-.40	.58	.45
Student experiments with material, equipment	.50	.13	-.46	.23	-.14	.50	.31
Student gives speculative, hypothetical material	.41	.16	.23	.07	.29	.41	.23

Student ignores or rejects T request, demand	.10	−.86	.06	.11	.00	.75	.71
Student teases student(s) (unfriendly)	−.03	−.78	−.03	.27	−.07	.66	.60
Students horseplay	.40	−.77	−.33	.11	−.42	.88	.78
Students shout	.34	−.76	−.28	.04	−.16	.74	.72
Five or more students fidget	−.03	−.75	.16	−.27	.16	.70	.61
Students argue	.36	−.74	−.19	.32	−.18	.69	.64
Student expresses annoyance	.23	−.68	−.19	.49	−.07	.68	.45
Student(s) talk about nonclass topic	.16	−.67	−.13	.40	−.46	.70	.74
Two or more Ss not attending to T (when expected)	.00	−.67	.41	−.06	.44	.76	.58
Three or more Ss move around aimlessly	.33	−.64	−.14	.40	−.59	.80	.71
Student criticizes (disapproves) student	.34	−.63	−.06	.43	.02	.62	.48
Student frowns, cries	−.07	−.60	.14	.14	−.07	.41	.27
S tries to stop other's disruptive behavior	.52	−.57	−.09	.09	−.37	.62	.44
Two or more Ss apparently daydreaming	−.24	−.55	.38	−.05	.23	.53	.50
Student waits	−.32	−.46	.09	.11	.35	.46	.22
Five or more Ss attending to teacher	−.01	−.09	.85	−.18	.40	.80	.39
S gives solicited question or comment	.09	−.15	.82	−.19	.06	.74	.22
S offers response (raises hand)	−.16	.17	.78	−.34	.56	.84	.61
Student answers teacher question	−.09	.03	.68	.35	.00	.67	.39

(continued)

Table 5.4 (continued)

Items	Loadings on Factors					h²	rkk
	1	2	3	4	5		
Student gives factual material	.13	.19	.57	.16	-.15	.48	.09
Student listens, watches	.08	-.17	.55	-.43	.36	.55	.44
Student-teacher discussion of work	.08	-.15	.03	.73	-.29	.57	.31
Student seeks attention of teacher	.22	-.20	.24	.70	.02	.64	.32
Student seeks feedback, evaluation	.15	-.26	-.18	.70	-.19	.53	.30
Student asks for directions or help	.02	-.18	-.48	.70	-.30	.69	.29
Five or more Ss move purposefully	.28	-.01	-.31	.66	-.58	.66	.56
Student starts or shifts activity on own	.35	.01	-.09	.44	-.86	.83	.54
One-half class or more working intently, with teacher attention	-.20	-.05	.30	-.04	.73	.58	.37
S gets or replaces materials, equipment on own	.30	-.15	-.33	.63	-.70	.75	.48
One-half class or more working intently, without teacher attention	.13	.35	-.38	.39	-.67	.71	.49
Students form own work group	.43	-.26	.05	.56	-.65	.72	.47
Student(s) work on floor	.30	-.17	.18	.16	-.59	.48	.81
Percent of variance	27.2	15.3	9.3	7.2	4.7		
Eigenvalue	12.22	6.88	4.19	3.22	2.11		

Source: Compiled by the authors.

tion from the teacher ("student seeks attention of teacher," "student seeks feedback, evaluation," and "student asks for directions or help"). Another item, "student-teacher discussion of work" also refers to student-teacher interaction, the activity possibly resulting from the student's request. A final high-loading item refers to students moving "purposefully"; this item seems less closely tied in with the others (but could in many cases reflect movement toward the teacher to get the desired help or attention). The factor is accordingly labeled "student-initiated interaction with teacher."

The last student-activities factor contains a set of high negative loading items which refer to various self-initiated (or self-sustained) activities ("student starts or shifts activity on own," "student gets or replaces materials, equipment on own," "one-half of class or more working intently, without teacher attention," and "students form own work group") contrasted with a high positive loading for an item reflecting a non-self-sustained activity ("one-half of class or more working intently, with teacher attention"). The factor is called "student independent, autonomous activity" (another negatively scored factor).

Student Ratings Section of Observation Form

Results of the factor analysis of the global ratings of student classroom behavior are shown in Table 5.5. This analysis produced three factors, accounting for 81.9 percent of the total variance. The ratings were each made with six-point scales, with the two extremes labeled. The item names, at the left of the table, present both poles, with the one given the score of six presented first in each case. Thus, an item with a positive loading can also be considered to have a negative loading when considered from the perspective of the opposite pole.

The first factor is by far the strongest of the three in this analysis. Its high-loading items contrast classes in which the students followed prescribed plans, had no alternatives, worked at a common pace, moved little, were compliant and teacher-dependent, had no voice in planning, and participated in common activities with those in which they followed their own interests, made choices, worked at their own pace, moved much, were independent and self-sustaining, were responsible for planning class activities, and participated in varied simultaneous activities. This factor is called "students controlled, structured, common-paced versus independent, autonomous, varied."

The second factor, called "eager involvement, interest versus uninvolvement, boredom," shows high loadings for items representing

TABLE 5.5

Factor Analysis of Observation Form Student Ratings

Items	Loadings on Factors			h^2	r_{kk}
	1	2	3		
Followed prescribed plan vs. followed own interests	.93	-.37	-.42	.88	.71
Constantly making choices vs. had no alternatives	-.92	.48	.35	.88	.74
Common pace aimed at vs. worked at own pace	.90	-.27	-.20	.83	.64
Moved very little vs. moved very much	.89	-.17	-.39	.82	.78
Students were independent vs. were compliant	-.89	.19	.51	.85	.70
Work teacher-dependent vs. self-sustaining	.88	-.48	-.55	.87	.59
Totally responsible for class activity planning vs. had no voice in planning	-.87	.46	.43	.81	.74
Varied simultaneous activities vs. single common activities	-.79	.31	-.05	.74	.62

	I	II	III	IV	V
Talked only at T direction vs. talked freely	.76	-.07	-.48	.68	.86
Were passive (receiving) vs. active (productive)	.63	-.62	-.30	.59	.58
Seemed extremely interested vs. seemed bored	-.20	.96	.25	.95	.63
Highly involved vs. uninvolved in class activities	-.24	.95	.20	.90	.64
Appeared happy vs. unhappy	-.42	.89	.26	.82	.66
Showed no initiative vs. much initiative	.60	-.74	-.32	.70	.63
Worked on convergent tasks most of time (vs. never)	.41	-.32	-.96	.93	.44
Worked on divergent tasks most of time (vs. never)	-.46	.37	.91	.87	.48
Percent of variance	56.8	16.3	8.8		
Eigenvalue	9.09	2.61	1.42		

Source: Compiled by the authors.

extreme interest, involvement, happiness, and initiative at one set of poles, and boredom, uninvolvement, unhappiness, and lack of initiative at the other.

The third factor contains two items with very high loadings: one negative, "worked on convergent tasks most of the time (versus never)"; and one positive, "worked on divergent tasks most of the time (versus never)." Convergent tasks have one or a limited set of definite correct answers or outcomes (for example, mathematical problems, puzzles); divergent tasks are "open-ended" and can have a large or unlimited number of appropriate outcomes (art, creative writing, hypothetical speculations). This factor is called "divergent tasks versus convergent tasks."

Classroom Ratings Section of Observation Form

The factor analysis of the global ratings of the general class-room atmosphere is presented in Table 5.6. Three factors were retained and rotated, accounting for 79 percent of the total variance.

The first factor was labeled "relaxed, friendly, accepting versus tense, hostile, rejecting." This dimension contrasts classes which were rated, at one extreme, as friendly, accepting, relaxed, person-oriented, cooperative, and creative with those rated, at the other, as hostile, rejecting, tense, not person-oriented, not cooperative, and uncreative.

The positive extreme of the second factor is defined by item poles defined as "businesslike," "quiet," "orderly," "not at all spontaneous," "calm," "rigid regarding procedures," "task-oriented," "tidy," "not at all carefree," with "many rules," and an "orderly sequence of activities"; the negative pole by such qualities as "noisy," "unruly," "spontaneous," "excited," "flexible," "untidy," and "jovial." The factor is named "calm, orderly task orientation versus excited, unruly spontaneity."

The third factor is defined primarily by three items with very high loadings: "extremely varied versus repetitive," "diverse versus common materials and books in use at same time," and "full versus relatively devoid of stimuli." The factor is called "diversity, variety of stimuli versus repetitiveness, commonality, sparseness."

Teacher Ratings Section of Observation Form

Results of the factor analysis of the observers' ratings of the teachers' classroom behavior are presented in Table 5.7. Five factors resulted from this analysis, accounting for 78.9 percent of the variance.

TABLE 5.6

Factor Analysis of Observation Form Class Ratings

Items	Loadings on Factors			h^2	r_{kk}
	1	2	3		
Hostile vs. friendly	-.93	.03	-.40	.88	.61
Rejecting vs. accepting	-.91	.04	-.43	.86	.66
Relaxed vs. tense	.90	-.41	.54	.87	.72
Extremely vs. minimally person-oriented	.89	-.25	.53	.80	.62
Frequently vs. never cooperative	.83	-.07	.54	.72	.56
Uncreative vs. creative	-.79	.21	-.74	.76	.64
Not oriented vs. oriented to novel, unusual	-.73	.40	-.70	.71	.64
Leisurely vs. rushed	.63	-.42	.62	.57	.66
Extremely vs. not at all business-like	-.17	.94	-.28	.89	.76
Extremely noisy vs. quiet	.03	-.93	.14	.89	.85
Unruly vs. orderly	-.13	-.91	.00	.93	.83
Behavior extremely vs. not at all spontaneous	.44	-.88	.35	.85	.79

(continued)

Table 5.6 (continued)

Items	Loadings on Factors			h^2	r_{kk}
	1	2	3		
Excited vs. calm	-.01	-.81	.08	.69	.57
Flexible vs. rigid regarding procedures	.63	-.79	.63	.91	.74
Extremely vs. minimally task-oriented	-.37	.79	-.46	.70	.60
Many vs. no rules in evidence	-.64	.79	-.55	.89	.75
Orderly vs. random sequence of activities	-.25	.78	-.53	.72	.75
Very tidy vs. untidy	-.09	.78	-.21	.61	.83
Extremely vs. not at all carefree, jovial	.65	-.77	.50	.86	.75
Extremely varied vs. repetitive	.64	-.27	.90	.84	.65
Diverse vs. common materials and books in use at same time	.31	-.24	.86	.76	.55
Full vs. relatively devoid of stimuli	.52	-.18	.80	.65	.75
Percent of variance	50.3	22.8	5.9		
Eigenvalue	11.07	5.02	1.30		

<u>Source</u>: Compiled by the authors.

Items defining the positive pole of the first factor represent teachers who were critical, impatient, punitive, insensitive, unprotective, sometimes sarcastic, cold, and somewhat uncomfortable appearing. These are contrasted with, at the other pole, praising, patient, nonpunitive, sensitive, protective, nonsarcastic, very warm, and comfortable teachers. The dimension represented seems quite clear, and is called "coldness, criticism versus warmth, praise."

The second factor seems to represent teacher dynamism and activation. Its high-loading items contrast, at the negative poles, flamboyance, dramatics, energy, vocal expressiveness, gesturing, enthusiasm, humor and laughter, clarity and rapidity of speech, and immediacy of feedback with, at the positive poles, dryness, lack of energy, vocal monotonousness, paucity of gesturing, lack of enthusiasm, little humor or laughter, incoherence and slowness of speech, and little or nonimmediate feedback. The factor is called "lethargy, dryness versus energy, flamboyance."

The degree of control manifested by the teacher appears to be the major element represented by the third factor. The positive pole is defined by nonpermissiveness, a narrowly defined range of acceptable behavior, direct control, discouragement of student autonomy, and nonacceptance of student procedural suggestions or expressiveness; the negative pole by permissiveness, a broad range of acceptable behavior, little direct control, promotion of student autonomy, and acceptance of student procedural suggestions and expressiveness. The label for this factor is "teacher control, dominance versus permissiveness, encouragement of student autonomy."

The fourth factor is defined primarily by two high-loading items: "never versus frequently gave individual attention," and "never versus frequently consulted with individuals or small groups." The factor is called "individual attention, consultative role" (with the named pole of the factor corresponding to the negative item loadings). A third item, "direct and immediate feedback," also has a moderate loading and seems consistent with individual attention and consultation.

Three items form the nucleus of the fifth teacher-rating factor: "emphasized comprehension, analysis versus memory, rote," "discouraged versus encouraged exploration" (a negative loading), and "often versus seldom controlled indirectly." The first two were given greater weight in defining the factor as "emphasis on student comprehension, exploration versus memory, rote" (although indirect control does not seem inconsistent with this characteristic).

Teacher Questionnaire

The factor analysis of the items in the teacher questionnaire describing classroom organization and activities is presented in

TABLE 5.7

Factor Analysis of Observation Form Teacher Ratings

Items	Loadings on Factors					h²	r_kk
	1	2	3	4	5		
Mostly praising vs. mostly critical	-.90	-.37	-.29	-.24	.52	.89	.76
Very patient vs. impatient	-.87	-.12	-.59	-.12	.45	.91	.70
Punitive vs. not at all punitive	.86	.19	.45	.09	-.62	.87	.72
Insensitive vs. sensitive to students	.85	.53	.38	.16	-.44	.88	.68
Not protective vs. protective, sheltering	.82	.28	-.02	.09	-.26	.74	.49
Never vs. frequently used ridicule, sarcasm	-.80	.10	-.37	-.19	.37	.78	.74
Very warm vs. not at all warm	-.77	-.64	-.39	-.07	.43	.89	.67
Extremely comfortable, confident vs. uncomfortable	-.52	-.51	-.25	.32	.48	.68	.39
More attention to girls vs. to boys	-.41	-.26	.03	-.37	.41	.42	.58
Flamboyant, dramatic vs. dry	-.13	-.94	-.09	-.10	.20	.90	.73
Unenergetic vs. very energetic	.25	.93	-.05	.16	-.20	.89	.73
Monotone vs. varied, expressive voice	.14	.92	-.11	.11	-.06	.88	.68
Gestured constantly vs. very little	-.11	-.92	-.12	.03	.21	.88	.69
Highly enthusiastic vs. unenthusiastic	-.45	-.90	-.10	-.09	.28	.89	.72
Never vs. often used humor	.37	.79	.27	-.11	-.27	.74	.71
Often vs. seldom laughed	-.55	-.78	-.24	.06	.43	.82	.68
Vague, unclear, incoherent vs. extremely clear, coherent	.39	.61	-.34	.01	-.27	.67	.33

Seldom vs. often gave direct and immediate feedback	.19	.60	.04	.58	.16	.77	.25
Spoke very slowly vs. very rapidly	-.38	.57	-.04	.23	.06	.64	.74
Highly vs. not at all permissive	-.30	-.12	-.93	-.24	.33	.89	.79
Accepted narrow vs. broad range of behavior	.30	.11	.92	.28	-.33	.89	.80
Always vs. seldom exercised direct control	.46	-.08	.76	.19	-.70	.86	.72
Discouraged vs. promoted S independence, autonomy	.46	.25	.73	.27	-.65	.78	.64
Neither sought nor accepted procedural suggestions (vs. did both)	.35	.31	.71	-.09	-.55	.71	.64
Encouraged vs. discouraged open student expressiveness	-.60	-.37	-.62	-.05	.45	.68	.48
Never lectured vs. mostly lectured	-.13	.14	-.53	-.38	.52	.57	.54
Never vs. frequently gave individual attention	.16	.09	.23	.91	-.16	.85	.56
Never vs. frequently consulted with individuals or small groups	.19	.01	.30	.88	-.32	.86	.43
Emphasized comprehension, analysis vs. memory, rote	-.30	-.38	-.22	-.11	.84	.77	.39
Discouraged vs. encouraged exploration	.66	.36	.56	.24	-.73	.83	.56
Often vs. seldom controlled indirectly	-.49	.05	-.45	-.15	.69	.62	.25
Percent of Variance	40.5	19.0	8.6	7.0	3.8		
Eigenvalue	12.66	5.90	2.67	2.16	1.17		

Source: Compiled by the authors.

Table 5.8. These factors are somewhat less clear and more difficult
to interpret than those produced by the different sections of the observation protocol. While the eigenvalues and percent of variance
accounted for by the four factors shown in this table (36.7 percent)
may seem to suggest that a larger number of factors would have been
appropriate, rotations of several different numbers of factors were
examined in this analysis, as in most of the other factor analyses in
this study, and the result presented here is the rotation which produced the most meaningful and most interpretable factors. One item
included in this analysis ("S's 'flow' back and forth between different
sections of open class area") was not included in the original questionnaire; the information was added before data analyses as a result of
comments made by some teachers when responding to the questionnaire. In cases where the teachers had not made such comments,
information for this item was reconstructed by one or more of the
observers who had visited the class.

The items which load most highly on the first factor generally
refer to the degree to which the teacher alone controls, directs, and
makes decisions about student and class activities, and the degree
to which the students participate in such functions. Teachers at the
positive pole of this factor take sole charge of planning evaluation
procedures, evaluating students' work, forming subgroups, planning
the sequence of activities, deciding on needed tasks and activities,
making rules, and so on, while, in classes at the negative pole, the
students either participate in or by themselves perform these activities. The factor was accordingly named "teacher control, decision
making versus student autonomy, participation in decisions and class
direction."

Two basic elements appear to be encompassed by the second
factor from the teacher questionnaire. Most of the items with highest
loadings refer to the teacher's interacting with individuals or subgroups, and attending to the varied needs of the different students,
as opposed to interacting with the total class, and treating the class
in a relatively undifferentiated way. These items represent the
individualization of evaluation procedures and learning objectives,
and the predominant setting or focus of student activity and teacher
attention—total class versus individual or small group. Another set
of consistent items, with somewhat lower factor loadings, refers to
the degree to which class plans and activities are subject to change.
This is indicated directly in one item with a moderate loading ("plans
changed very frequently versus seldom"), but is also evident in related
items which refer to freedom to experiment and manipulate materials
and to carry discussions into unexpected directions. The factor was
named "individualization, flexibility versus nondifferentiation, rigidity."

TABLE 5.8

Factor Analysis of Teacher Questionnaire

Items	Loadings on Factors				h²
	1	2	3	4	
Ss participate in (vs. T alone plans) all evaluation procedures	-.75	.28	.06	-.03	.60
No joint planning sessions (T and Ss) vs. several sessions a week	.69	-.21	-.01	.09	.49
Ss participate in (vs. T alone) evaluation of S work	-.68	.06	.22	-.01	.52
T places Ss (vs. Ss place themselves) in subgroups	.67	-.07	.39	.19	.63
T (vs. Ss) plans sequence of activities	.63	.06	.13	.31	.50
Ss (vs. T) provide main directing force in class	-.61	.15	.07	-.25	.39
Ss (vs. T) decide what tasks need work at any given time	-.60	.36	-.04	-.39	.50
Ss (vs. T) determine most classroom procedures	-.58	.25	.43	-.22	.54
T almost never (vs. most of time) acts as discussion leader on S-initiated topics	.56	.04	.26	.00	.42
T almost never (vs. most of time) acts as "resource person"	.56	-.18	.05	.36	.39
T (vs. Ss) determines Ss' activities	.55	-.32	.32	.18	.48
T attention directed to subgroups almost never (vs. most of time)	.54	-.05	-.01	-.17	.36

(continued)

Table 5.8 (continued)

Items	Loadings on Factors				h²
	1	2	3	4	
At least one hour per day (vs. almost no) independent study time available	-.52	.20	.09	.02	.30
Classroom rules made by Ss vs. by T	-.51	.23	.36	-.13	.39
Ss usually all engaged in same activity vs. engaged in many different activities simultaneously	.51	-.46	-.28	.36	.53
Ss evaluate each others' work frequently vs. not at all	-.47	.17	.22	-.02	.28
Most Ss work at own pace vs. common pace aimed at	-.47	.29	-.15	-.14	.30
Ss spend little (vs. much) time talking about personal experiences, beliefs and opinions	.42	-.27	-.13	.27	.26
Little (vs. almost all) time free for Ss to pursue own interests	.35	.10	-.13	.22	.20
Nothing prescheduled vs. all activities occur according to prearranged time schedule	-.31	.30	.25	-.10	.22
Ss "flow" back and forth at will between different sections of open class area	-.24	.12	-.01	-.15	.07
T almost never (vs. most of time) gives prepared oral presentations	-.30	.72	-.05	-.12	.55
Evaluation procedures different for each vs. same for all Ss	-.13	.69	-.11	-.08	.49
Subgroups change very often vs. seldom	-.24	.65	-.03	-.10	.44

T attention directed to class as whole almost never vs. most of time	-.18	.62	.26	-.25	.48
Learning objectives set separately for each child vs. same for all	-.23	.60	-.04	.06	.41
Ss expected to resolve own conflicts or arguments vs. conflicts, etc. stopped quickly by T	-.40	.56	-.24	-.22	.49
Ss do most of work in small groups vs. as individuals or total class	-.09	.55	.00	.03	.32
T almost never acts as discussion leader on topics of own choice vs. does so most of time	-.16	.54	-.08	-.28	.35
Ss do not (vs. frequently) help one another	.47	-.50	-.05	.17	.40
Ss work at many "centers" vs. at own desk or table	-.27	.49	.13	-.27	.33
Plans changed very frequently vs. seldom	-.16	.49	-.14	.02	.28
Ss free to experiment and manipulate materials vs. expected to use as instructed	.11	.48	-.03	-.07	.27
Discussions kept closely topic–relevant vs. allowed to wander	-.25	-.43	.10	.34	.41
Ss spend little (vs. most of) time trying to dis-cover and apply basic principles	.24	-.40	.08	-.17	.27
Few (vs. many) rules for acceptable behavior	-.36	.39	-.10	-.23	.27
Ss (vs. T) decide on arrangement of furniture and equipment	-.19	.38	.14	-.36	.26
Ss expected to participate in all vs. may choose not to participate in any class activity	.08	-.33	.00	.13	.12
Little (vs. very strong) emphasis on having pleasant, happy time in class	.01	-.27	-.18	-.21	.17

(continued)

Table 5.8 (continued)

Items	Loadings on Factors				h²
	1	2	3	4	
Ss expected to solve most problems themselves vs. get immediate help	-.16	-.22	-.03	.02	.09
Average number of hours per day with children in own class (or "homeroom" or "core")	-.16	.04	.70	.10	.53
Typical number of room changes per day for Ss	-.14	.13	-.64	.02	.46
Number teachers instructing Ss during typical day	-.19	.25	-.64	-.14	.51
Number of "departmentalized" subjects	.28	.24	-.60	.05	.51
Class is never (vs. daily) informed which Ss did best work	.03	-.04	-.49	-.40	.42
T attention directed to individual Ss almost never vs. most of time	.44	-.01	.44	.13	.41
Most vs. none of the class work involves memorizing	-.13	-.28	.43	.03	.30
Most instructional materials commercial or developed by T vs. developed by Ss	.36	.08	-.37	.27	.33
Ss leave classroom freely without permission vs. with permission	-.06	.18	.28	-.65	.52
Ss grouped according to ability or achievement level for all (vs. for no) subjects	.01	.18	-.08	.63	.47

T (or school guidelines) determine what Ss should learn vs. Ss decide what they want to learn	.05	.01	.13	.57	.34
T describes or demonstrates methods of learning and problem solving vs. Ss develop and use own methods	.26	.18	.26	.56	.50
Little (vs. much) effort to keep Ss within sight of T	-.05	.01	.00	-.55	.31
Ss start themselves (vs. T starts Ss) on tasks	-.26	.18	-.03	-.51	.30
Ss may talk only when called on vs. at any time	.17	-.33	-.35	.50	.45
Ss leave seats with permission vs. at will	.13	-.38	-.38	.50	.49
Frequent vs. no testing	-.05	-.19	.24	.49	.33
Little (vs. much) overt emphasis on getting work done and done well	-.20	.11	-.09	-.48	.25
Much (vs. no) homework	.27	-.20	.31	.47	.37
Most learning tasks "open-ended" vs. clearly organized and sequenced	-.38	.11	-.11	-.46	.32
Arrangement of furniture and equipment changed rarely vs. frequently	.01	-.29	-.17	.39	.25
Parents or volunteers participate little (vs. much) in classroom activities	.27	.05	.00	.38	.21
Classroom rules enforced by Ss vs. by T	-.28	.29	.26	-.35	.28
Help initiated by T perception of need vs. S request	.04	-.07	-.04	.33	.11
Ss get material or equipment only with permission vs. at any time	.03	-.22	.04	.27	.11
Percent of variance	16.6	7.1	6.5	6.5	6.5
Eigenvalue	10.80	4.59	4.25	4.25	4.20

Source: Compiled by the authors.

99

The third factor is defined primarily by four highly loaded items: "average number of hours per day with children in own class," "typical number of room changes per day for students," "number of teachers instructing students during typical day," and "number of 'departmentalized' subjects." The first of these has a positive loading, the rest, negative. The fourth item, referring to "departmentalization" seems to be central to this factor. Since children in departmentalized situations spend less time with "homeroom" or "core" teachers, change rooms more often, and are taught by more teachers than those in "self-contained" situations, the first three items would seem to be logical concomitants of the fourth. The factor was called "self-containedness versus departmentalization."

The most consistent set of items with high or moderate loadings on the fourth factor seems to reflect a dimension of "restrictiveness versus freedom" (which is the name assigned to the factor). These items refer to freedom to leave the classroom, be out of the teacher's sight, talk, leave seats, and get equipment and material. A few other items (for example, "students develop and use own methods," "much versus no homework") are not inconsistent with this designation of the total factor.

Second-Order Analysis of Classroom Factors

A total of 33 factors was produced by the eight factor analyses of classroom activities just described. Factor scores were derived for each of these factors with the "complete estimation method" (Harman 1960). These factor scores represent the position of each classroom on each factor. The scores then served as the input for a second-order factor analysis of classroom dimensions. This procedure can be considered analogous to factoring empirically derived scales, as is frequently done in personality research. This factor analysis produced six factors, shown in Table 5.9, accounting for 68.7 percent of the variance.

The first of these factors shows particularly high loadings for four of the first-order factors: "relaxed, friendly versus tense, rejecting," "involvement, interest versus boredom," "teacher hostility, annoyance, criticism," and "coldness, criticism versus warmth, praise" (the last two with negative loadings). The factor was named "warmth, friendliness, involvement, interest, versus coldness, hostility, boredom." Two of these high-loading first-order factors refer to teacher behavior, and one refers to child behavior, and one to general classroom atmosphere. The new factor should thus be considered to reflect all these elements. Some of the moderate loadings suggest that "friendly" classes tend also to include many stimuli

TABLE 5.9.

Second-Order Factor Analysis of Classroom Measures

First-Order Factors (items)	Loadings on Factors						
	1	2	3	4	5	6	h²
Relaxed, friendly vs. tense, rejecting[f]	.91	-.16	-.02	-.04	.08	.24	.92
Involvement, interest vs. boredom[c]	.89	.11	-.07	-.06	.09	.23	.88
Teacher hostility, annoyance, criticism[c]	-.87	-.04	.04	-.06	.09	.02	.77
Coldness, criticism vs. warmth, praise[g]	-.84	.05	-.11	.02	-.09	.05	.73
Emphasis on S comprehension, exploration vs. memory, rote[g]	.69	-.08	-.28	.00	-.14	.48	.80
Extra-curricular stimuli[a]	.57	-.12	.05	-.35	-.04	-.07	.47
Unusual "fun" activities (neg)[b]	-.48	.38	.33	-.06	-.22	.01	.54
Calm, orderly task orientation vs. excited, unruly spontaneity[f]	.06	.92	.06	.08	.05	-.17	.88
Teacher control, dominance vs. permissiveness, encouragement of S autonomy[g]	-.23	.80	.22	.01	.10	-.24	.81
General student disruptiveness, hostility (neg)[d]	.53	.75	-.06	.01	-.03	.06	.86
Ss controlled, compliant, orderly vs. independent, autonomous, varied[e]	-.31	.65	.54	.31	.02	-.20	.95

(continued)

Table 5.9 (continued)

First-Order Factors (items)	Loadings on Factors						h²
	1	2	3	4	5	6	
Inter-student cooperation, friendly interaction while working[d]	.51	-.57	.01	.04	.16	.43	.80
Disruptive (vs. smooth) shifting of activities[b]	-.44	-.57	-.03	.13	-.20	-.16	.61
Physical openness, accessibility of material and equipment to Ss (neg)[a]	-.28	.52	.37	.17	-.14	.10	.54
Restrictiveness vs. freedom[h]	-.10	.50	-.01	.29	.32	-.04	.45
Individualization, flexibility vs. nondifferentiation, rigidity[h]	.08	-.44	.09	-.05	.02	.18	.24
Ungraded, roomy vs. graded, crowded[a]	.01	-.39	-.33	-.34	-.03	.39	.52
Common vs. varied simultaneous activities[b]	.08	-.05	.83	.43	.03	-.06	.89
Student independent, autonomous activity (neg)[d]	-.27	.33	.74	.21	.21	-.04	.82
Diversity, variety vs. repetitiveness, commonality[f]	.48	-.31	-.61	-.30	.03	.22	.84
Self-containedness vs. departmentalization[h]	-.10	.05	-.53	-.14	.26	-.05	.38
T individual attention, consultative role (neg)[g]	-.11	.10	.20	.83	.18	.20	.82
S-initiated interaction with T[d]	-.02	-.14	-.18	-.82	.00	.05	.73
T interaction with individuals or subgroups vs. total class[c]	.09	-.23	-.41	-.73	.10	-.07	.78
Commercial vs. S-made wall decorations[a]	-.02	-.10	.05	.52	-.02	-.21	.32

Attentive, responsive verbal class participation under T direction[d]	-.15	.13	-.14	.16	.86	-.06	.83
Encouragement of active verbal (academic) student participation[c]	-.01	.22	-.23	.10	.82	-.03	.78
T lethargy, dryness vs. energy, flamboyance[g]	-.29	.08	-.22	.15	-.71	-.12	.68
T personal expression, warmth, friendliness[c]	.27	-.27	.49	-.03	.51	.29	.73
No. of children and adults in class[a]	.28	-.27	.24	-.14	.36	-.17	.39
Divergent tasks vs. convergent[e]	.09	-.40	.19	-.06	-.28	.71	.79
T encouragement of S expressiveness and exploration vs. drilling[c]	.27	-.09	-.15	.14	-.03	.71	.63
T sole control, decision making vs. S participation in decisions, autonomy[h]	.02	.10	-.05	.19	-.33	-.58	.49
Percent of variance	25.5	14.3	10.5	8.3	5.3	4.8	
Eigenvalue	8.40	4.72	3.46	2.75	1.74	1.60	

[a]First-order factors from Observation Form Cover Sheet.
[b]First-order factors from Observation Form Organization section.
[c]First-order factors from Observation Form Teacher Activities section.
[d]First-order factors from Observation Form Student Activities section.
[e]First-order factors from Observation Form Student Ratings section.
[f]First-order factors from Observation Form Class Ratings section.
[g]First-order factors from Observation Form Teacher Ratings section.
[h]First-order factors from Teacher Description of Classroom Activities Questionnaire.

Source: Compiled by the authors.

and unusual and varied activities, to emphasize student comprehension, and to show much student cooperativeness and little student disruptiveness.

The next two second-order factors each include elements of student autonomy, but placed in somewhat different contexts. The first of these shows the highest loading for the first-order factor, "calm, orderly task orientation versus excited, unruly spontaneity." Other first-order factors with high or moderate loadings contrast, at their poles, classes in which teachers control and dominate activities, students are compliant and orderly, activity shifting is smooth, and students' behavior is relatively restricted, with those in which students are autonomous, disruptive and hostile (but also cooperative), have access to materials and relative freedom. The general impression produced by the first-order factors at the low end of this dimension is of a type of student autonomy which constitutes not so much a replacement of teacher control by student control, as an absence of control altogether. This factor is termed "teacher control, structure, orderly task orientation versus permissiveness, spontaneity, lack of control."

The student autonomy represented in the next factor relates more specifically to self-directed tasks. Thus the components of the first-order factor, "student independent, autonomous activity" which loads highly on this one refer to students starting or shifting their own activities, working intently on their own, and forming their own work groups. Here the autonomy does seem to represent the replacing of external with internal control. The other high-loading first-order factors are "common versus varied simultaneous activities" and "diversity, variety of stimuli versus repetitiveness, commonality, sparseness." Classes in which the students determine and shift their own activities are likely to display a wide variety of different activities at any given time. The factor is called "imposed, common, repetitive activities versus student-initiated (and -maintained), varied, simultaneous activities."

The fourth of these second-order factors contains three high loadings and one moderate one. The high-loading first-order factors each refer to teacher interaction with individuals or subgroups: "teacher individual attention, consultative role," "student-initiated interaction with teacher," and "teacher interaction with individuals or subgroups versus total class." The factor is named "individualized teacher-student interaction, teacher consultative role" (negatively scored). The first-order factor with the moderate loading, "commercial versus student-made wall decorations," suggests that the individualized class is more likely to make use of student productions in this way.

Classes at the positive extreme of the fifth factor are character-ized by teachers who are energetic, dramatic, personally expressive and warm, and who promote active student academic and verbal participation in class activities, and by students who do participate verbally, actively, and attentively. Classes at the negative extreme have teachers who are relatively lethargic and dry, show little per-sonal expressiveness and warmth, and tend not to actively promote student participation. The factor is called "energetic teacher promo-tion of student verbal (academic) participation."

The last of these second-order factors is named "emphasis on student expressiveness, exploration, and creativity." The highest loadings are obtained for "divergent versus convergent tasks" and "teacher encouragement of student expressiveness and exploration versus drilling." Moderate loadings are also obtained for factors reflecting teacher control versus student autonomy and the teacher's emphasis on student comprehension and exploration.

The six second-order factors are comparable with other attempts to identify basic dimensions of behavioral styles and group atmospheres (including classrooms, families, occupational groups). The first two factors found here are basically the same two which have been found centrally in many of these other investigations: "warmth versus coldness" and "control versus permissiveness." The other factors found here seem more specifically limited to educational settings.

Some other recent attempts to describe basic classroom char-acteristics by factor analyzing observations have been reported by Soar and Soar (1972), Emmer and Peck (1973), and Samph and White (n.d.). Soar and Soar (1972) used four observation systems with a sample of Follow Through classrooms. They factor analyzed each system separately, producing a total of 27 factors, and did not do a second-order factor analysis. Three of these factors seem clearly related to the present "warmth" factor ("warm emotional climate," "teacher negative affect," and "teacher acceptance"), two to the present "control, orderliness" factor ("teacher directed activity" and "teacher evaluation and control") and one, possibly, to "common-ality versus variety of activity" ("free choice versus structured learning in groups"). Their other factors defined different and more specific aspects of the classroom environment than those emerging in the present research. Emmer and Peck reported a second-order factor analysis of five sets of classroom behavior factors, derived from different observation systems. This analysis produced 11 factors, many of which can be related to those in the present study. Thus, the present "warmth" seems represented in their "negative affect" (negatively) and "teacher support for correct response," "control" in "teacher controlling behavior" and "pupil presentation of ideas," "individualized interaction" in "teacher-initiated problem solving," "encouragement of academic participation" in "pupil unresponsiveness" (negatively), and "emphasis on student expressiveness" in "restrictive versus expansive teaching." The Samph and White study constituted a second-order factor analysis of factors derived from six classroom observation systems. This analysis resulted in five factors which seem similar to three of those found in the present study: "warmth" (which compares to the reverse of "negativism" and "teacher nonsupportive behaviors"), "control" (which compares to "teacher directing the communication process" and "teacher monitoring"), and "encouragement of verbal (academic) participation" (which compares to "teacher encouragement of content-oriented interaction").

Other researchers have measured classroom climate through questionnaires in which students describe their classrooms (Walberg and Anderson 1968; Stern and Walker 1971; Trickett and Moos 1973). Each of these instruments contains sets of items describing a priori scales, which are typically not factor analyzed. Some of these scales also seem similar to some of the obtained dimensions in the present study: each of the questionnaires, again, have scales representing aspects of "warmth" and "control". The Trickett and Moos questionnaire relates the most closely to the present results. It contains nine scales representing four "functions": an "affective relationship" function contains three scales—"involvement," "affiliation," and "support"—all of which would seem to be included in the present study's "warmth" factor; a "system maintenance and authority" function contains three scales—"order and organization," "rule clarity," and "teacher control"—which relate to the present "control, orderliness"; a "system change" function contains one scale—"innovation"—which relates to the present "commonality versus variety of activity"; and a "goal orientation" function contains two scales—"task orientation" and "competition"—which seem to relate (not as clearly, however) to the present "encouragement of academic participation."

6 DERIVING DIMENSIONS OF CHILD CHARACTERISTICS AND EDUCATIONAL OUTCOMES

PREFERENCE, ORIENTATION, AND
MOTIVE SCALES

Item Analyses and Reliability

Internal-consistency reliability was assessed for these scales, and for most of the other questionnaire-derived scales in this study, by applying the Spearman-Brown formula to the mean of interitem correlations (Guilford 1956, Nunnally 1967). All of the preference, orientation, and motive scales which had obtained low reliabilities in the pilot study were revised (including both rewriting and adding items) for the present study. In almost all cases, low reliabilities were improved while scales with high reliabilities previously (which were not revised) remained acceptably reliable. The locus-of-control and social-desirability scales, which had been shortened, also maintained acceptable reliabilities. One exception occurred with the achievement-motivation scale. Although five of its 20 items were changed to some degree, the reliability in the present study was actually lower than it had been in the pilot study (.26, as compared with .32). Since many of the achievement motivation items were conceptually similar to those in the fear of failure scale, and since the reliability of that scale was also relatively low (although it had improved as a result of the revision—.46, as compared with .34 in the pilot study), it was decided to factor analyze the combination of items from both scales, and attempt to extract more reliable subgroupings of items. Three factors were derived, and rotated orthogonally. Items which obtained loadings of at least .30 on one factor, and which also clustered together in a meaningful way, were grouped into three new scales. The items in these scales, and their item-total correlations are presented in Table B.1. The first scale is "preference for challenging tasks versus avoidance of risk" and contains ten items, mostly indicating preferences for difficult or risky tasks or games. The second scale is called "preference for inter-personally equal versus dominated situations" and includes five items which reflect liking for games in which "everyone is about the same" or "I am about as good as my playmate" as opposed to those in which "I'm better than anyone else" or "I'm much better than my playmate," and for classroom situations reflecting a similar dimension. The third scale, containing four items, was called "academic motivation," and represents a stated preference for trying to learn and for doing school work over relaxing and playing.

To obtain scales from the 26 questionnaire items which asked children for their preferences among different sets of classroom characteristics, a similar procedure was followed. The items were initially factor analyzed. Although rotations of several numbers of factors were tried, and a three-factor solution produced the most coherent results, none of the rotations was completely satisfying conceptually. Therefore, the three-factor solution was used as a general guideline and nucleus, and items were grouped into scales using the factor information and the researchers' perceptions of meaningfulness of clustering as criteria. Three scales were derived; the item-total correlations are shown in Table B.2. The first, "preference for classes with freedom of activity" (versus restrictive-ness), contained six items reflecting children's preferences for classes in which they would be free to get materials, talk, walk around, etc. at will, as opposed to doing so only at teacher direction. The second class-preferences scale was called "preference for classes which allow children autonomy" (versus classes with teacher control), and also contained six items, mostly referring to preferences for classes in which children rather than teachers make decisions about their activities. The third scale contained four items and was called "preference for classes where students are involved in teach-ing" (versus teacher monopolization). The items in this scale refer to classes in which children (versus the teacher) help each other, check each others' work, teach each other, and talk about each others' work.

The internal consistence reliabilities for these six new scales ranged from .48 to .70. These reliabilities, and those of the other preference, orientation, and motive scales, are presented on the far right of Table 6.1.

Factor Analysis

All of the preference, orientation, and motive scales were included in a factor analysis, the results of which are shown in Table 6.1. Four factors were retained and rotated to orthogonal simple structure.

TABLE 6.1

Factor Analysis of Preference, Orientation, and Motive Scales

Scale	Loadings on Factors				h²	r_kk
	1	2	3	4		
Preference for classes which allow children autonomy (vs. T control)	.73	-.24	-.01	-.20	.63	.70
Preference for classes with freedom of activity (vs. restrictiveness)	.67	-.15	-.06	-.31	.57	.62
I- (responsibility for failures)	-.50	-.07	.28	.06	.33	.70
Preference for classes where students are involved in teaching (vs. T monopolization)	.48	-.08	-.05	.03	.24	.48
Personal expression vs. structured role orientation	.45	-.38	.04	-.04	.35	.54
Social desirability	-.08	.66	.08	.13	.46	.83
Bureaucratic orientation (SEPS)	-.21	.62	-.10	-.12	.45	.84
I+ (responsibility for successes)	-.34	-.10	.52	-.03	.40	.57
Intrinsic motivation	.00	-.26	.52	.14	.36	.66

(continued)

Table 6.1 (continued)

Scale	Loadings on Factors				h^2	r_{kk}
	1	2	3	4		
Locus of instigation	-.01	.12	.51	.00	.28	.53
Preference for interpersonally equal (vs. dominated) situations	-.17	.01	.43	.27	.29	.61
Generality of strong task preferences	.03	.16	.25	.10	.10	.69
Academic motivation	-.17	.35	.10	.44	.36	.48
Preference for challenging tasks (vs. risk-avoidance)	-.16	-.19	.32	.40	.32	.61
Percent of variance	22.9	14.9	9.4	7.2		
Eigenvalue	3.21	2.08	1.32	1.00		

Source: Compiled by the authors.

110

All three of the class characteristics preferences scales, referring to children's preferences for classes with student autonomy, freedom of activity, and participation in teaching activities, show high or moderate loadings on the first factor. There is also a moderate positive loading for "personal expression versus structured role orientation," and a moderate negative one for I- (responsibility for failures). With the exception of I-, these scales all seem to refer to aspects of student freedom and autonomy. The factor is therefore labeled "preference for classes with student autonomy." The negative loading for I- suggests that students who state a preference for autonomy also tend to deny responsibility for their own failures. It is conceivable that an autonomous classroom situation, where teachers exert relatively little direct control over students and classroom activities, is seen as one where success and failure attributions are made less frequently, and may therefore seem attractive to children who want to avoid such attributions. Although some of the components are different, a similar factor was obtained in the pilot study, and called "preference for open situations."

The second factor contains only two high-loading items, "social desirability" and "bureaucratic orientation." Each of these scales describes an orientation toward compliance with adult-prescribed rules, norms and values. The factor is therefore named "compliant, conforming orientation." A very similar factor was obtained in the pilot study, and given the same label.

The highest loading items on the third factor are I+, "locus of instigation," and "intrinsic motivation." The first two refer to the individual's belief that he or she is responsible for the successful outcomes of his or her own activities, and for the initiation of the activities in the first place; both deal with the individual's feeling of personal control. The third item, "intrinsic motivation," refers to participating in activities for self-defined reasons and rewards (rather than externally defined ones). While not identical with personal control, such a quality seems quite consistent with it. In order to maintain both aspects in the designation of this factor, the name, "personal control/intrinsic motivation," was given to it. These two aspects did not fall in the same factor in the pilot study.

Two items with moderate loadings define the fourth factor, "academic motivation" and "preference for challenging tasks" (versus risk avoidance). These are both scales derived from the original achievement-motivation and fear-of-failure scales. The label "achievement motivation" seems an accurate representation of their combination.

FACTOR ANALYSES OF ACHIEVEMENT TESTS

Subscores from the Cognitive Abilities Test and the Iowa Test of Basic Skills which the children had taken at the end of the third grade were included in a single factor analysis, shown in Table 6.2. Similar to a parallel analysis in the pilot study, a single, clear factor emerged, with no low loadings, and no discernable differentiation between measures of "ability" and of "achievement." This factor is called "prior achievement."

A similar result was produced by a factor analysis of the scales of the California Achievement Test administered to the children in the study at the end of the fourth grade (the year of the study). This analysis, presented in Table 6.3, also produced a single factor with high loadings for all subtests. The factor is named "achievement test performance."

TABLE 6.2

Factor Analysis of Third Grade Cognitive Abilities and Achievement Tests

Subtests	Loadings	h^2
Cognitive abilities: verbal	.91	.83
Cognitive abilities: quantitative	.82	.67
Cognitive abilities: nonverbal	.73	.54
ITBS: Vocabulary	.84	.71
ITBS: Reading	.84	.71
ITBS: Spelling	.80	.61
ITBS: Capitalization	.76	.57
ITBS: Punctuation	.78	.60
ITBS: Language usage	.82	.67
ITBS: Map reading	.82	.67
ITBS: Graphs and tables	.81	.65
ITBS: Reference materials	.86	.75
ITBS: Arithmetic concepts	.84	.70
ITBS: Arithmetic problems	.82	.67
Percent of variance	69.0	
Eigenvalue	9.66	

Source: Compiled by the authors.

TABLE 6.3

Factor Analysis of Fourth Grade Achievement Tests

Subtests	Loadings	h^2
CAT: Reading vocabulary	.81	.66
CAT: Reading comprehension	.84	.70
CAT: Math computation	.77	.60
CAT: Math concepts	.84	.70
CAT: Capitalization	.72	.53
CAT: Language usage	.68	.47
CAT: Spelling	.79	.62
Percent of variance	66.5	
Eigenvalue	4.66	

Source: Compiled by the authors.

CREATIVITY AND INQUIRY-SKILL MEASURES

Reliability

Reliabilities of the measures of creativity and inquiry skill (as well as that of writing quality, which was derived from the same responses as inquiry skill) were assessed in two ways. The first involved an assessment of intercoder agreement. Five classrooms were randomly selected from the total set of classrooms in the study. Creativity, inquiry-skill, and writing-quality responses from these five classrooms were each coded independently by two coders. Intercoder correlations for each of the coding categories and ratings from these items are presented in Table 6.4. With a few exceptions, the correlations appear to be generally adequate.

Reliability was also assessed for the total sample by applying the Spearman-Brown formula to the correlations between the scores assigned to the two items of each type at each testing period. For example, the pretest "uses" scores were derived from two items, "chair" and "button." For each coding category (such as "percent uncommon responses") the correlation between the two items was entered in the Spearman-Brown formula. The summed scores, across the two items of each type, were then used in subsequent factor analyses. Results of these factor analyses, with the reliability

TABLE 6.4

Intercoder Correlations for Selected Subsample
of Protocols (N = 98-101): Creativity, Inquiry Skill,
and Writing Quality

| Item | Creativity Categories | | | |
	Number Appropriate Responses	Percent Uncommon Responses	Elaboration Rating	Imagination Rating
Pretest uses				
Chair	.92	.78	.56	.60
Button	.90	.78	.77	.73
Pretest patterns				
Pattern 1	.95	.79	.76	.79
Pattern 2	.97	.83	.69	.84
Posttest uses				
Cork	.95	.75	.75	.78
Shoe	.98	.89	.71	.66
Posttest patterns				
Pattern 3	.97	.71	.71	.61
Pattern 4	.98	.76	.74	.74

| | Inquiry Skill and Writing Quality Categories | | | |
	Number Informative Responses	Percent Site-extended Responses	Completeness Rating	Writing Quality Rating
Pretest				
Bridge location	.79	.36	.71	.41
Ghost town	.50	.52	.64	.65
Posttest				
Playground location	.78	.31	.71	.67
Disordered room	.84	.15	.59	.55

Source: Compiled by the authors.

TABLE 6.5

Factor Analyses of Pre- and Posttest Creativity and Inquiry Scores

Categories	Pretest Analysis				Posttest Analysis				Pre- Vs. Post- Corrs.
	Loadings		h²	r_{kk}	Loadings		h²	r_{kk}	
	1	2			1	2			
Number appropriate responses, uses items	.60	.37	.49	.60	.70	.28	.57	.66	.42
Percent uncommon responses, uses items	.37	.29	.22	.37	.56	.19	.35	.43	.18
Elaboration, uses items	.41	.25	.23	.46	.61	.11	.38	.51	.31
Imagination, uses items	.54	.40	.46	.45	.82	.22	.72	.59	.35
Number appropriate responses, patterns items	.70	.04	.49	.60	.53	.22	.33	.70	.34
Percent uncommon responses, patterns items	.56	.02	.32	.23	.35	.11	.14	.11	.07
Elaboration, patterns items	.70	.14	.51	.48	.52	.19	.31	.57	.32

(continued)

115

Table 6.5 (continued)

Categories	Pretest Analysis				Posttest Analysis				Pre-Vs. Post-Corrs.
	Loadings				Loadings				
	1	2	h^2	r$_{kk}$	1	2	h^2	r$_{kk}$	
Imagination, patterns items	.88	.04	.77	.54	.69	.24	.54	.54	.28
Number of informative responses, inquiry items	.16	.85	.76	.43	.27	.87	.84	.50	.35
Percent site-extended responses, inquiry items	.05	.42	.18	.13	.07	.19	.04	.00	.12
Completeness of response, inquiry items	.09	.93	.86	.41	.23	.94	.93	.50	.38
Percent of variance	38.6	16.7			41.4	11.9			
Eigenvalue	4.25	1.84			4.55	1.30			

Source: Compiled by the authors.

coefficients, are presented in Table 6.5. Because writing quality was a distinct construct, and seemed of sufficient potential interest to maintain as a separate variable, it was not included in the factor analyses; its reliability, which therefore does not appear in Table 6.5, was .51 for the pretest items and .54 for the posttest items. Correlations between the pre- and posttest administrations of the parallel measures are also presented in this table; the pre-post correlation for writing quality was .43.*

Factor Analyses

The creativity and inquiry items were put into two factor analyses, one including the pretest scores, the other, the posttest scores. The pre- and posttest analyses were generally quite similar. Each produced two clear factors, one representing creativity and one representing inquiry. While the relative ordering of the factor loadings for the creativity factor is somewhat different in the two analyses, with more weight for the patterns items in the pretest analysis, and more for the uses items in the posttest analysis, the general set of loadings is strong enough throughout the creativity categories so that "creativity" seems an appropriate designation of the first factor in each analysis. Each of the inquiry items has its highest loading on the second factor in both analyses. The rating of "completeness" and the "number of informative responses" have very high loadings (almost identical between the two analyses), while the loading of "percent site-extended responses" is very much lower in each case. This factor is called "inquiry skill." The creativity and inquiry items also defined separate factors in the pilot study.

----

*Since seven months intervened between the pre- and postquestionnaire administrations, the children in different classrooms were subjected to different environments and experiences which were expected to have differential effects on various outcomes. These pre-post correlations were expected to be positive, but generally only moderately so. On the whole, this is what occurred, with both the creativity and inquiry indexes, shown here, and the attitude and value scales, shown in Table 6.6. Indeed, very high correlations (as are frequently obtained with test-retest reliabilities over shorter time periods) would be inconsistent with the major goals of this research (to find classroom environment main effects, and environment by person interactions), because too much of the outcome variance would be accounted for by initial status, leaving too little to be allocated to these other sources.

ATTITUDE AND VALUE SCALES

Item Analyses and Reliability

Most of the attitude and value scales were revised after the pilot study. All of the internal-consistency reliabilities were improved as a result of this revision (with the exception of the pretest administration of concern for others which remained the same at .47), but some were not improved enough. Examination of interitem correlations for those still unreliable scales revealed some items which seemed incompatible with their scale-fellows. One item each in the self-direction, compromise, and cooperation scales had numerous negative correlations with the other items in the scale, both in the pre- and posttest administrations. Accordingly, these items were removed and the reliability recalculated. Omitting the bad item from the scale measuring value on self-direction—"If you are puzzled about something, it is always better to try to find the answer for yourself than to have someone tell it to you"—increased the reliability coefficient from .32 to .38 for the pretest, and from .36 to .42 for the posttest—slightly better but still far from ideal. The omitted compromise item was "When you have an opinion, you should stick to it even if everyone says you're wrong"; its removal increased the reliability coefficient from .23 to .37 in the pretest, and from .31 to .50 in the posttest. The item dropped from the value on cooperation scale was "School is nice only if everybody shares everything." Its omission raised reliabilities from .33 to .38 for the pretest, and from .42 to .46 for the posttest. For the subsequent factor analyses of these scales, new totals were calculated with these items omitted.

Factor Analyses

The results of the factor analyses of the pre- and posttest administrations of the value and attitude scales are presented in Table 6.6. Although not identical, the patterns of loadings on the four factors which were extracted in each analysis are generally similar.

The first factor in each analysis is primarily defined by three items, "tolerance for differences," "assertion responsibility," and "self-esteem." The same items comprised also a factor in the pilot study (although self-esteem was relatively stronger in that analysis). The combination of thinking well of oneself (self-esteem), feeling sufficiently sure of oneself to believe in stating one's opinions even if unpopular (assertion), and to accept nonconformists (tolerance for differences) led, as in the pilot study, to labeling this factor "self-confidence."

TABLE 6.6

Factor Analyses of Pre- and Posttest Attitude Scales

	Pretest Analysis						Posttest Analysis						Pre-Vs. Post-Corrs.
	Loadings						Loadings						
Scales	1	2	3	4	h²	r_kk	1	2	3	4	h²	r_kk	
Tolerance for differences (value on heterogeneity)	.59	.08	.29	.05	.44	.61	.41	.21	.36	.00	.35	.62	.45
Assertion responsibility	.35	.32	.29	-.07	.32	.61	.44	.31	.31	.09	.39	.66	.47
Self-esteen	.29	.05	-.01	.04	.09	.75	.28	.04	.04	-.02	.08	.79	.44
Equality of representation	.18	.57	.25	-.12	.44	.47	.12	.67	.23	.18	.55	.48	.38
Equality of participation	.17	.49	.20	.12	.32	.43	.18	.44	.27	-.07	.31	.45	.30
Value on cooperation	.16	.12	.49	.11	.29	.38	.11	.20	.47	-.15	.30	.46	.40

(continued)

119

Table 6.6 (continued)

Scales	Pretest Analysis						Posttest Analysis						Pre-Vs-Post Corrs.
	Loadings				h²	r_kk	Loadings				h²	r_kk	
	1	2	3	4			1	2	3	4			
Concern for others	-.04	.11	.43	-.01	.20	.47	.02	.12	.51	-.02	.27	.58	.32
Compromise	.20	.13	.43	-.14	.26	.37	.23	.14	.51	.09	.34	.50	.43
Value on group activities	.02	.10	.10	.56	.33	.68	-.14	.03	.17	-.36	.18	.74	.29
Value on self-direction	-.01	.06	.06	-.24	.06	.38	-.01	.00	.05	.47	.22	.42	.29
Value on decision-making autonomy	-.18	.27	-.02	-.24	.16	.77	-.13	.10	.01	.25	.09	.79	.46
Percent of variance	21.8	11.8	9.8	9.4			24.2	11.9	9.7	8.5			
Eigenvalue	2.40	1.30	1.08	1.03			2.66	1.31	1.07	.93			

Source: Compiled by the authors.

The second factor includes two of the democratic-attitudes subscales, "equality of representation" and "equality of participation." These scales have a concern with equality as a common element; the factor is therefore named "value on interpersonal equality." (These same two scales were also the prime determinants of one of the pilot study factors.)

The third factor shows a cluster of relatively high loadings for "value on cooperation," "concern for others," and "compromise" (the first two of these helped to define a factor in the pilot study). "Concern for others" seems to be the essential element here; both cooperation and compromise would seem to depend on a willingness to take the other party's needs and objectives into account. The factor is named "concern for the welfare of others."

Although the signs of the item loadings on the fourth factor are reversed between the pre- and posttest factor analyses, it can be seen that the two factors are generally similar except for this reversal. In each case, "value on self-direction" and "value on decision-making autonomy" tended to define one pole of the factor, while "value on group activities" defines the other. ("Autonomy" and "self-direction" comprised separate factors in the pilot study; it seems conceptually more reasonable for them to cluster together.) This factor poses a value on self-determined task activity and autonomous decision making against one on participating in group activities. Group participation requires interacting with others and occasionally giving way to others and letting them determine activities. Thus it may reduce the possibilities of purely personal autonomy. The factor is called "value on self-direction versus group participation."

In order to produce clearly comparable scores for use in subsequent analyses, the factor scores for both of these analyses were produced by applying the factor-score coefficients for only one of them—the posttest analysis—to each set of (standardized) original scale scores. In other words, a common set of scale weightings was used to produce both sets of factor scores (pre- and posttest attitudes).

FACTOR ANALYSES OF STUDENT CLASS AND SELF-EVALUATIONS AND OF TEACHERS' RATINGS OF STUDENTS

Student Class and Self-Evaluations

The factor analyses of the eight evaluation items, shown in Table 6.7, produced three factors. The first factor obtained high loadings for the students' ratings of their schools as having been

TABLE 6.7

Factor Analysis of Student Class and Self-Evaluations

Items	Loadings			h^2
	1	2	3	
How interesting have you found school this year?	.72	.09	-.02	.53
How much fun have you had in school this year?	.63	.18	-.05	.44
How much do you think you have learned in school this year?	.48	.08	.05	.24
How often do kids in this class help each other?	.39	.23	-.25	.26
How many kids in this class would you like to stay close friends with?	.18	.74	-.02	.58
How many of the other kids do you think would like to stay close friends with you?	.15	.71	-.02	.52
How often do kids in this class get mad at each other or fight?	-.12	-.04	.59	.36
How many kids do you think don't have many friends in this class?	.03	.00	.21	.05
Percent of variance	30.1	15.0	14.3	
Eigenvalue	2.40	1.20	1.15	

Source: Compiled by the authors.

"interesting" and "fun" during the year, and moderate loadings for their estimates of the amount they learned during the year and of the helpfulness of the children in the class. The high-loading items were given more weight in naming the factor "enjoyment of class."

Two items, both referring to the student's friendships in the class, determine the second factor which is therefore called "social involvement in class." The primary item on the third factor is "How often do kids in this class get mad at each other or fight?" There is also a small positive loading for the rating of the number of social isolates in the class, and a small negative one for the rating of the amount of interstudent helping. The latter two seem consistent with the primary item, and with a designation of the factor as "perceived class disruptiveness." The analysis of the same items in the pilot study also produced three factors with a quite similar pattern of loadings. The names given the present factors are the same as those used in the pilot study.

Teachers' Ratings of Students

As mentioned earlier, the rating scale which teachers used to present their perceptions of the children's classroom behavior was shortened from the 30-item form (with five-point scales) used in the pilot study to an 11-item form (with four-point scales). While the items were in some cases taken directly from the pilot study and in other cases newly devised, they were intended to represent each of the five factors obtained in that study. It was, then, expected that a similar set of factors would emerge from this shorter version. It can be seen in Table 6.8 that this did not occur; only two factors emerged from this rating scale.

All but two of the items load most highly on the first factor. The strongest of these refer to the child's perseverance, hard work, cooperativeness, self-control, and achievement motivation. This factor is termed "task perseverance, social maturity."

The two items with relatively high loadings on the second factor are "highly active, energetic" and "curious about many things." These seem to represent mutually consistent characteristics. In order to convey this total combination, the factor is called "active, energetic, curious."

While these two factors do seem to represent meaningful combinations of items, a somewhat more differentiated grouping was expected, as in the pilot study. The pilot study results constitute clear evidence that teachers perceive children in terms of more than one or two dimensions. It may be that a scale longer than the 11-item one used in the present study (perhaps as long as 30 items) with

TABLE 6.8

Factor Analysis of Teacher Ratings of Students

Rating Items	Loadings		h^2
	1	2	
Works hard in class	.84	.19	.75
Cooperative, does what is asked	.83	.01	.68
Perseveres with tasks	.82	.28	.75
Self-controlled	.81	-.22	.71
Works well with other children	.74	.13	.56
Not satisfied until good understanding of topic or task is achieved	.70	.40	.66
Learned much this year	.63	.40	.55
Highly involved in class activities	.63	.52	.67
Looked up to by other children	.58	.37	.47
Highly active, energetic	-.12	.66	.45
Curious about many things	.44	.56	.51
Percent of variance	55.2	13.6	
Eigenvalue	6.07	1.50	

Source: Compiled by the authors.

a more specific set of descriptive items, is necessary to bring out the finer discriminations represented by the larger number of factors.

SOME DATA ON CONVERGENT VALIDITY

The more differentiated teacher rating scale used in the pilot study included items which paralleled some of the cognitive, motivational, and attitudinal student measures. Correlations between these scales and the most relevant teacher rating scale items were calculated in the course of analyzing the pilot study data. It was not known whether the teacher ratings represented good criteria for the various qualities represented by these measures. (In fact, prior research and the "folklore" of the field suggested that they would not be.) Therefore, low correlations could not be considered clear evidence of invalidity. Indications of agreement between a teacher rating and a conceptually similar student measure, however, could be considered evidence for the validity of both. Most of these student measures were changed to some degree after the pilot study, as we have indicated, but most of the changes were relatively minor; therefore, the validity correlations should also be relevant to consider in the context of the present study.

The measure of intrinsic motivation was, in the pilot study (Solomon and Kendall 1974, 1976) correlated .29 (p < .01) with the teacher rating "has strong interests in many areas" but -.02 with "works well without rewards or praise"; achievement motivation was correlated .17 with "strong interests in many areas," .12 with "strives to achieve," and .10 with "perseveres with tasks"; democratic values were correlated .21 (p < .05) with "tolerant of differences"; cooperation was correlated .20 with the rating of "cooperative, helpful"; tolerance for differences, .14 with the rating "tolerant of differences"; and self-esteem was correlated .36 (p < .01) with the rating "good self-image." The teachers' ratings of students as being "creative verbally" correlated .32 and .28 (p < .01 for both) with the uses scores and .16 and .15 with the patterns creativity scores, while "skilled at problem solving, inquiry" showed correlations of .30 or greater (significant at p < .01) for four of the five inquiry scores. When the teacher ratings from the pilot study were factor analyzed (Solomon and Kendall 1977), four factors were obtained. The first, "democratic, cooperative behavior" correlated .21 (p < .01) with students' value on cooperation (but not significantly with the other democratic values); a second rating factor, "autonomous intellectual orientation" showed significant correlations with a number of the student scales, including achievement motivation (.22), intrinsic motivation (.29), self-esteem (.18), fear of failure (-.19), I+ (.22), bureaucratic orientation (-.31), generality of strong task preferences (.19), social desirability (-.30), inquiry skill (.18), creativity (.23), value on decision-making autonomy (.20), assertion responsibility (.15), tolerance for differences (.23), and democratic values (.21). The validity evidence seems moderately good for self-esteem, creativity, and inquiry skill, and fair or undetermined for the remaining scales.

LIST OF FACTORS AND INDEXES REPRESENTING CLASSROOM CHARACTERISTICS, CHILD CHARACTERISTICS, AND EDUCATIONAL OUTCOMES

Before proceeding further, it may be useful to present a complete listing of the various dimensions and indexes, described in the preceding chapters, which will be involved in subsequent analyses.

Classroom Dimensions.

1. Warmth, friendliness, involvement, interest versus coldness, hostility, boredom.
2. Teacher control, structure, orderly task orientation versus permissiveness, spontaneity, lack of control.
3. Imposed, common repetitive activities versus student-initiated (and -maintained) varied, simultaneous activities.
4. Individualized teacher-student interaction, teacher consultative role (negatively scored).
5. Energetic teacher promotion of student verbal (academic) participation.
6. Emphasis on student expressiveness, exploration, and creativity.

Child Preferences, Orientations and Motives.

1. Preference for classes with autonomy and personal expression for students (assessed in fall).
2. Compliant, conforming orientation (assessed in fall).
3. Personal control/intrinsic motivation (assessed in fall).
4. Achievement motivation (assessed in fall).
5. Socioeconomic status (SES) (based on family bread-winner's occupation, not a factor score).

Student Academic Achievement and Other Cognitive Outcomes.

1. Prior achievement (from third grade tests).
2. Achievement test performance (from fourth grade tests).
3. Creativity (assessed in fall and spring).
4. Inquiry skill (assessed in fall and spring).
5. Writing quality (not a factor score, assessed in fall and spring).

Student Attitudes and Values.

1. Self-confidence (assessed in fall and spring).
2. Value on interpersonal equality (assessed in fall and spring).
3. Concern for the welfare of others (assessed in fall and spring).
4. Value on self-direction versus group participation (assessed in fall and spring).
5. Self-esteem (not a factor score, assessed in fall and spring).

Student Class and Self-Evaluations.

1. Enjoyment of class (assessed in spring only).
2. Social involvement in class (assessed in spring only).
3. Perceived class disruptiveness (assessed in spring only).

Teachers' Ratings of Students.

1. Task perseverance, social maturity (assessed in spring only).
2. Activity, energy, curiosity (assessed in spring only).

7 IDENTIFYING CLASSROOM "TYPES" AND CHILD "TYPES"

The various child and classroom "dimensions" produced by the factor analyses described in the preceding two chapters appeared to be meaningful and potentially useful; further analyses concerning them will be presented in Chapter 9. It was decided, however, to take these dimensions an additional step in order to see if they could be employed to group the children and the classrooms into small sets of identifiable "types," each type containing members with similar profiles in terms of the selected dimensions. It was hoped that, if empirical groupings which were conceptually meaningful could be obtained, a way would be available to look at the effects on various educational outcomes of entities representing children and classrooms in their natural groupings with much of their natural complexity retained. This was seen as a potentially useful supplement to (and perhaps eventually even a replacement for) the more typical approach which would analyze one or two isolated or abstracted dimensions at a time, looking at their main effects and interactions, while ignoring or attempting to hold statistically constant the simultaneous effects of other significant dimensions. The approach based on natural groupings accepts the complex of dimensions represented in a group profile, and looks at its total effects compared with those of other groupings. Intuitively, this approach seems more likely to represent accurately social (and educational) reality, which is complex, involves multiple simultaneous influences from numerous sources, and (perhaps) actually does form limited numbers of constellations of attributes (natural groupings). Whether it will actually provide for greater theoretical development and greater usefulness in attempts at practical applications, however, has yet to be demonstrated. Some of the discussion in the final chapter will address this issue.

CLUSTER ANALYSIS OF CLASSROOMS

Cluster analysis is a technique which groups cases into "clusters" or "sets" based on the similarity of their profiles (Blashfield 1976, Anderberg 1973). Its purpose is to identify groupings which are maximally differentiated between clusters and maximally similar within clusters. Many cluster analysis methods have been developed; several were tried with the classroom factor profiles. One was a "Q" factor analysis method which factors cases (over items) rather than items or tests (over cases), and produces factors which represent differentiated groupings of cases; one was a "Linear Typal Analysis" method described by Overall and Klett (1972); one was a "cluster buildup" method developed by Lorr and Radhakrishnan (1967); one was McQuitty's (1957) "Elementary Linkage Analysis"; and one was a "hierarchical" method (Ward 1963). In each analysis, the profile of six classroom-factor scores for each classroom provided the basic data. Most of the methods produced six classroom clusters.

Although there was some overlap, these methods produced somewhat different results. A procedure to select a single set of clusters from these was improvised. Several sets of "core clusterings" were developed; each of these started from the vantage point of one of the clustering methods and identified for each cluster those classes which also fell into the same group by at least two of the other clustering methods. A discriminant-function analysis (from SPSS, see Nie et al. 1975) was applied to each of these "core clusterings," and each of the remaining ungrouped classrooms was assigned to the "core cluster" which it most closely resembled by the discriminant-function criterion. A new discriminant-function analysis was then run with the new cluster assignments. Because the new assignments altered the pattern of the total set of clusters, this second discriminant-function analysis invariably identified some new "misplacements." These were reassigned to their "most probable" clusters, and a third discriminant analysis was done. This procedure was continued, iteratively, until all cluster placements were ratified by the discriminant-function criterion. The final clustering, which produced the most meaningful and interpretable group profiles (and which also, in later analyses, most strongly showed differentiation between types of children in their performance with respect to various outcomes), was the one built up from the six "core clusters"—originally involving 24 classrooms—based on the "Q" analysis approach.

Profiles for each of these classroom clusters are presented in Table 7.1 and in Figure 7.1. The profile components are the factor-score means for all the classrooms grouped into a given

TABLE 7.1

Classroom Clusters: Means, Standard Deviations, and F-Ratios for Cluster Components (classroom factor scores)

Classroom Clusters		Classroom Factors					
		Warm, Friendly Vs. Cold	Control, Order Vs. Lack of Control	Common Vs. Varied Activ.	Nonindivid. Vs. Individ. Interact.	Encour. of Verbal Acad. Partic.	Emph. on S. Express.
1 (N = 10)	Mean	.49	-1.29	-.64	-.37	.14	.28
	S.D.	.90	.97	1.31	.88	.65	.77
2 (N = 10)	Mean	-.63	1.11	-.60	.51	-.25	-.05
	S.D.	.54	.54	.73	.84	.66	.63
3 (N = 9)	Mean	-.87	-.29	.91	.27	.32	.58
	S.D.	1.10	.54	.57	1.29	1.10	.99
4 (N = 8)	Mean	.76	.45	-.01	-.09	.15	-.98
	S.D.	.61	.48	.80	.86	.64	.89

5 (N = 6)	Mean	.82	.00	.16	.30	-1.58	.97
	S.D.	.56	.51	.63	1.01	.68	.83
6 (N = 7)	Mean	-.26	.12	.47	-.70	.94	-.79
	S.D.	.73	.48	.70	.75	.75	.55
Total (N = 50)	Mean	.00	.00	.00	.00	.00	.00
	S.D.	1.00	1.00	1.00	1.00	1.00	1.00
F ratios (5, 44 df) (between clusters)		7.29*	15.54*	4.57†	1.88	7.88*	6.84*

*p < .001.

†p < .01.

Note: Probabilities are presented in this table only to give an indication of the discriminative success of the clustering procedure.

Source: Compiled by the authors.

FIGURE 7.1

Factor Score Profiles of Classroom Clusters

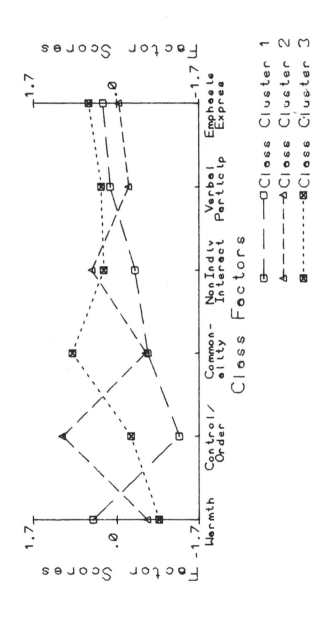

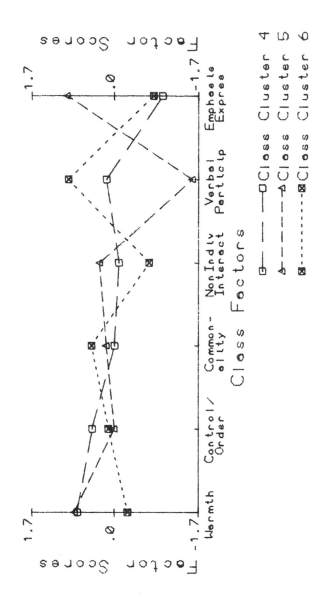

Factor Scores

Warmth · Control/ · Common- · NonIndiv · Verbal · Emphasis
Order · ality · Interact · Particip · Expres

Class Factors

□—□ Class Cluster 4
△——△ Class Cluster 5
⊠······⊠ Class Cluster 6

cluster. Within-group standard deviations and F values showing the degree to which the clusters are differentiated according to each of the components (factors) are also shown in Table 7.1. These indicate that, with the exception of individualized interaction, each of the separate components was strongly differentiated between the clusters. In the following paragraphs, we will describe each of these obtained clusters.

Cluster One

The most salient attribute of the classrooms comprising this cluster was their extreme permissiveness, lack of control, and student autonomy. None of the other clusters approached the position of this one with respect to this component. Cluster 1 classrooms also tended to have varied, student-initiated activities and relatively individualized teacher-student interaction. They were in the moderate range with respect to warmth, energetic encouragement of verbal (academic) participation, and emphasis on student expressiveness. Although these classrooms showed some of the characteristics which have been attributed to "open" classrooms, their extreme lack of control and order was beyond that recommended in the ideal "open" classroom (in most descriptions), where control is shared between teacher and students. It is difficult to provide cluster names which accurately reflect the total complex of components making up the profiles. As a shorthand description, however, cluster one is considered to represent classrooms which are permissive and uncontrolled, with much student autonomy.

Cluster Two

Classrooms in cluster 2 were highly controlled and orderly, but students also had relatively great opportunity to initiate their own, varied, activities. To put it slightly differently, teachers in these classrooms provided for an overall structure and a disciplined approach to tasks, but within this framework, students were free to select and direct their own particular activities. Classrooms in cluster 2 also tended to be somewhat cold, and to have undifferentiated (rather than individualized) interaction between teacher and students. They were moderate with respect to encouragement of verbal participation and emphasis on student expressiveness. These classrooms could be described as providing for a substantial degree of student self-direction within a controlled, disciplined, nonindividualized, and somewhat impersonal setting. The profile gives the impression of a rather serious, businesslike, and, in a certain sense, autonomous orientation to classroom tasks.

Cluster Three

Classrooms in the third cluster tended to be cold and unfriendly and to have common (whole-class) activities. They were also moderately permissive and uncontrolled, and were somewhat oriented toward both student expressiveness and verbal (academic) participation. Teacher-student interaction was slightly nonindividualized. This cluster provides an interesting contrast with cluster 2. Both tended to be cold and somewhat unfriendly (cluster 2 less so, however). But in cluster 2, the juxtaposition of this "coldness" with the other profile components gives the impression of a no-nonsense, serious, and task-oriented setting, whereas in cluster 3, where it is combined with an extreme reliance on common, teacher-directed activities, but also with a fair degree of permissiveness and lack of control, the impression conveyed is rather of a setting which is relatively <u>hostile, arbitrary, and regimented, but also somewhat uncontrolled and disorganized</u>.

Cluster Four

These classrooms were quite warm, friendly, and involving, and were also fairly highly controlled and orderly. They were moderate with respect to individualized teacher-student interaction and energetic encouragement of verbal (academic) participation, but gave the least emphasis of any cluster to student expressiveness and creativity. It is instructive to compare this cluster profile with that of cluster 2. Both of these clusters of classrooms tended to be controlled, orderly, disciplined, and task-oriented, but for cluster 2 these characteristics are combined in a rather cold and impersonal atmosphere, while for cluster 4, where they are combined with warmth and general involvement, the impression conveyed is of an atmosphere which is <u>controlled, disciplined, academically oriented, and supportive</u>. It will be noted that this pattern resembles the definition of "direct instruction" put forth by Rosenshine (1976a and b) (see Chapter 2).

Cluster Five

Three of the component means in the profile for this cluster represented extremes. This was the highest scoring cluster with "warmth, friendliness" and with "emphasis on student expressiveness," and the lowest scoring with "energetic encouragement of verbal (academic) participation." Mean factor scores were in the moderate range for "control, orderliness," "commonality of activities," and "individualized teacher-student interaction." In some respects, this cluster comes closer to the "open class" ideal than does cluster one: the atmosphere is warm, friendly, and involved; there is a strong emphasis on expressiveness, exploration, and creativity, and there is a moderate amount of student autonomy and self-direction (that is, control is shared between teacher and students). However, the teacher-student interaction is not as individualized as one would expect in an open class. In summary, this profile represents classes which are <u>warm and friendly, strongly oriented toward student expressiveness and creativity (rather than traditional academic outcomes), and moderate with respect to teacher control and student autonomy</u>.

Cluster Six

Classrooms in the sixth cluster tended clearly to encourage verbal (academic) participation, and to have individualized teacher-student interaction. They did not emphasize student expressiveness, tended to have common activities, and were moderate on both the control and warmth dimensions. Focusing on the most salient components, we can describe this cluster as containing classrooms which are <u>academically oriented, with much verbal and individualized teacher-student interaction</u>.

It will be noted that none of these profiles corresponds precisely with existing descriptions of what might be expected in "pure" examples of either "open" or "traditional" classrooms, although some components of either or both are found in virtually all the clusters. This corresponds with the initial expectation that the concepts "open" and "traditional" would prove to be too global and that actual classrooms could more usefully be described in terms of observed combinations of attributes than with such terms. It is for this reason that neither of these terms will be used to describe any of these clusters, even those which come closest to resembling classic descriptions. It seems preferable to use designations which are more descriptive, even if also more cumbersome.

It seems desirable to avoid other simple terms which would tend to reduce and muddy the specific meaning of an obtained cluster. Yet it can be pointed out that some of these clusters do resemble "types" which have been identified in previous research in other settings. Thus, for example, the classic Lewin, Lippitt, and White

(1939) designation of children's groups as "autocratic," "democratic," and "laissiz faire" represented characteristics not dissimilar from those seen, respectively, in the present clusters 3, 5 (perhaps), and 1. For another example, Selvin (1959) investigated the effects of four "leadership styles" (in an army setting), which he called, "paternal" (somewhat similar to the present cluster 4), "persuasive" (closest to the present cluster 5), "arbitrary" (possibly similar to cluster 3), and "weak" (not clearly represented here, although in some respects it also resembles cluster 3). A more recent study by Cunningham (1975) used a cluster-analysis methodology similar to that used in the present study, but based it primarily on teachers' beliefs about instructional strategy rather than objective observations. Four clusters were produced in that study which nevertheless show some similarity to those found in the present study. One combined a strong belief in teacher control with high scores on "subject matter integration" and very low scores on "teacher empathy" and "student direction"; this seems to resemble the present clusters 2 and 4. A second cluster in the Cunningham study was low on "subject-centeredness" and moderate on all other components; this does not correspond well with any of the present clusters. The third cluster combined "student-centeredness" and low "teacher control" and "subject integration" with high scores on "teacher empathy" and "student direction"; this seems quite similar to the present cluster 1. The fourth Cunningham cluster was "subject-centered" but low on "teacher control"; this would seem to correspond the most closely to the present cluster 3. Bennett (1976) also clustered classrooms on the basis of teacher questionnaire responses. Although the resulting 12 clusters show combinations of teacher control and student autonomy which resemble some of those found in the present research, too few of the other profile elements are similar to those used here to make detailed comparisons possible.

Moos (1978) found five clusters of high school and junior high school classrooms from an analysis of mean student questionnaire responses. These clusters were called "control-oriented" (probably closest to cluster 2 here), "innovation-oriented" (possibly similar to cluster 1), "affiliation-oriented" (similar to cluster 5), "task-oriented" (most comparable to cluster 4), and "competition-oriented" (not clearly represented in the present clusters).

Thus, the present classroom clusters show some attributes which resemble those seen in other settings. The similarity is not close enough, however, to say that these approach anything like universal "types" of social environments or classroom environments. It does seem to suggest that there are certain fairly common and central dimensions of classroom life (and, more generally, of human group life), and that there are probably certain recurring patterns of combinations of these dimensions. Any single study, involving a particular sample of environments will probably identify some "types" which will closely resemble those found with other samples and some which will be more limited to that sample alone. Only after comparing the results of numerous studies using similar methodologies but varying samples of environments will it be possible to say with some certainty which are the general, recurring "types" and which the more sample-specific ones. For the present, the present set of classroom clusters can be considered to represent the best set of "types" which could be achieved with the present sample. The groupings of components seem to make fairly good sense. If they show meaningful relationships with the various outcome measures, and interactions with individual measures (and clusters), this will provide evidence for the potential usefulness of this set of clusters and this general approach to the problems targeted by this research. Such results will be presented in the following chapters. But first we consider the cluster analysis of the individual measures, parallel to that performed with the classroom measures.

CLUSTER ANALYSIS OF CHILDREN

A large sample is often an advantage, but it created a problem with the plan to cluster analyze the individual children in the study; the number of children for whom data were available far exceeded the maximum number of cases which could be handled by any of the cluster analysis programs available. It was decided to use a procedure followed by Overall and Klett (1972) when faced with the same problem—to cluster random subsamples, and then cluster the clusters. Because this promised to be a rather involved procedure which would require some extensive computer manipulations, it was necessary to select a single clustering technique, rather than to compare the results obtained with several, as was done with the classroom cluster analyses. The Overall and Klett "Linear Typal Analysis" was the most convenient method for us to use in this way and was therefore the one selected.

A computerized "random number generator" was adapted to produce 12 random subsamples from the total sample of 1,292 children. These subsamples ranged in size from 92 to 120. In order to produce clusters which would represent "total" children as closely as possible with the present set of data, it was decided to include, as input into the cluster analyses, variables covering a broad range of dispositions, attitudes, skills, and interests describing the children as they were at the start of the school year. Therefore, in addition to the four preference, orientation, and motive factors, measures of cognitive skills (the prior achievement, precreativity, and pre-inquiry-skill factors plus prewriting quality), and the four "pre-" attitude and value factors were also included as cluster analysis input components.

The cluster analyses of the 12 subsamples produced a total of 62 clusters, ranging from four to six clusters in the various subsamples. These 62 clusters were then entered into a new cluster analysis, using within-cluster means on the various components. This analysis resulted in three clusters. An iterative sequence of discriminant analyses was then undertaken, similar to that done with the classroom cluster analyses, so that the final cluster assignment of each student met the discriminant-function placement criterion. The resulting cluster profiles, composed of the component means (and standard deviations) for the children identified as members of each cluster, are presented in Table 7.2. The F ratios, showing the degree to which each component differentiates the clusters (all highly significant, it will be noted) are also presented in this table. The most clearly differentiated component means are plotted in Figure 7.2.* The total number of children represented in these clusters (1,035) are those for whom none of the measures in any of these components were missing. This number is smaller than the number included in any of the separate factor analyses; therefore, the total sample means and standard deviations for the various factors represented in this table differ slightly from the mean of 0 and standard deviation of 1 originally produced after orthogonal rotations. The three cluster profiles are described below.

Cluster One

Children in this cluster scored low on prior achievement and other cognitive skills (creativity, inquiry skill, and writing quality). They were relatively lacking in self-confidence, and tended not to value interpersonal equality or to be concerned about the welfare of others. They did not believe that they exerted much effective environmental control, had little intrinsic motivation, and expressed a value on compliance. They were, however, moderate with respect to autonomy, self-direction, and achievement motivation. These child-

---

*One of the child indexes shown in Figure 7.2, pre-writing quality, was not a factor score. Scores on this variable were standardized (with a mean of zero and a standard deviation of one) so that they could be presented on the same graph as the factor scores.

TABLE 7.2

Child Clusters: Means, Standard Deviations, and $\underline{F}$ Ratios for Cluster Components (child factor scores)

Child Factors (plus writing quality)	Child Clusters								$\underline{F}$ Ratios (2, 1031 df) (between clusters)*
	1 (N = 383)		2 (N = 462)		3 (N = 190)		Total (N = 1035)		
	Mean	S.D.	Mean	S.D.	Mean	S.D.	Mean	S.D.	
Prior achievement	−.80	.85	.61	.58	.35	.74	.04	.97	422.02
Pre– creativity	−.28	.86	.28	.95	.07	.96	.03	.96	38.77
Pre– inquiry skill	−.45	.71	.33	1.01	.22	.91	.02	.96	87.11
Pre– writing quality	3.99	1.35	5.38	1.20	4.76	1.37	4.75	1.43	121.92
Pre– self-confidence	−.30	.55	.29	.52	.04	.57	.02	.60	124.66
Pre– value on equality	−.26	.66	.11	.72	.39	.64	.03	.72	63.90
Pre– concern for others	−.40	.64	.30	.76	.12	.74	.01	.79	101.39
Pre– self-direction	−.02	.55	−.13	.58	.41	.66	.01	.62	58.50
Preference for class with autonomy	.03	.81	−.32	.70	.78	.87	.01	.87	134.96
Compliant orientation	.48	.69	−.18	.74	−.58	.64	−.01	.81	167.00
Personal control, intrinsic motivation	−.33	.72	.37	.69	−.18	.76	.01	.78	110.97
Achievement motivation	−.05	.63	.14	.64	−.29	.59	−.01	.65	33.15

*p < .001 for each factor.

Note: Probabilities are presented in this table only to give an indication of the discriminative success of the clustering procedure.

Source: Compiled by the authors.

FIGURE 7.2

Factor Score Profiles of Child Clusters

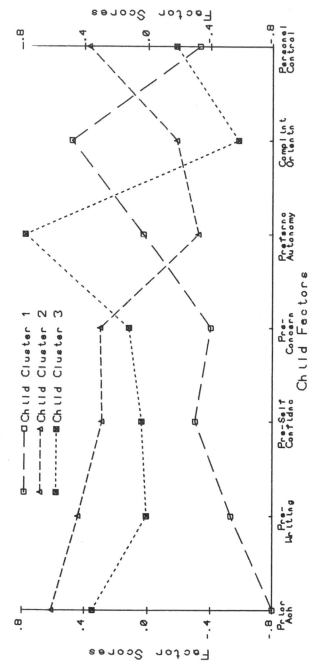

ren feel themselves to be lacking in power. They have relatively little confidence in themselves, their ability to influence their environment, and the value of their own interests (thus the low intrinsic motivation). Their high score on compliance seems a reasonable corollary to this; because they feel that their own efforts lack efficacy and value, they wish to be more guided by conforming to the directives of authorities. Their poor academic performance may be both cause and effect of this composite. They may feel relatively powerless because they do relatively poorly in school (and get persistent negative feedback as a result); at the same time, they may perform poorly academically because they lack the necessary internal motivation and self-confidence. Focusing on the most salient aspects, this cluster represents children who are low prior achievers who value compliance, lack self-confidence and intrinsic motivation, and feel powerless.

Cluster Two

In most respects, this cluster is diametrically opposed to cluster 1. Most of the components which had low mean scores for the children in cluster 1 have high mean scores for those in cluster 2. The cluster 2 children scored high on prior achievement and the other cognitive-skill measures; they also obtained high scores on self-confidence, concern for others, personal control/intrinsic motivation, and achievement motivation. At the same time, their scores were low for both value on task self-direction and preference for class with autonomy (and personal expression), and moderate for both value on equality and compliant, conforming orientation. These are children who perform quite well in school and like a relatively clearly structured, teacher-controlled classroom setting. They are also strongly motivated internally, and feel self-confident and in control of themselves and their environment. They apparently accept the school's academic objectives, work successfully toward achieving them, and do not wish to set their own goals or directions. For a brief description, these children can be considered self-confident, motivated prior achievers who value structure and direction.

Cluster Three

Children in this cluster stated strong preferences for classrooms which provided students with much autonomy and with the opportunity for personal expressiveness. They also valued self-direction in task activities and interpersonal equality; they tended to be noncompliant, and scored low on achievement motivation. With respect to the various cognitive skills and self-confidence, the children in cluster 3 obtained moderate scores (although for achievement-test performance and inquiry skill they were substantially above the total sample mean, while not as high as the cluster 2 children). These children appear to feel the need to be independent, autonomous, self-directing, and self-expressive and to reject external authority and direction. The fact that their scores for achievement motivation and intrinsic motivation are relatively low indicates that their desire for self-direction does not incline them particularly toward task accomplishment (even though their school performance is moderate to good). To summarize, this cluster contains children who value autonomy, self-direction, and the opportunity for self-expression.

Although there has been much more prior research which applies cluster-analytic techniques to the grouping of persons than to the grouping of situations, there has been little which is directly relevant or comparable to this cluster analysis of children. The development of typologies of persons has long been a characteristic activity of personality theorists; while most of these typologies have not been subjected to validation by cluster analysis, there have been studies which clustered psychiatric patients by symptoms into groupings which closely resembled certain standard "syndromes" (see Overall and Klett 1972).

Gordon (1975) reported results of cluster analyses of four different sets of scales representing value orientations and personality characteristics obtained from several different samples of adults. Four clusters emerged which were general and comparable across scales and samples. The first, "control of others" or "enterprising," may be comparable in part to the present cluster 2; the second, "service to others" or "social" does not seem clearly represented by any of the present clusters, although the most relevant components (such as "concern for others") also obtained their highest mean scores in cluster 2. Both the third and the fourth clusters identified by Gordon, called respectively "self-determination" and "institutional restraint versus self-expression," seem contained in the present cluster 3.

Four prior studies have cluster analyzed children in educational situations. Cunningham (1975) did so and found four clusters. The first of his clusters contained high achieving, competent, and advantaged children, similar to cluster 2. The second of his clusters had moderately high achievers who were also extraverted and cooperative; this also seems most closely related to several of the components of cluster 2. The last two Cunningham clusters included children who were low achievers, one combining it with "introversion," the other with alienation and disruptiveness; these both would relate most closely with the present cluster 1. Bennett (1976) clustered children in terms of their personality profiles and produced eight clusters. Several of them seem very similar to those found in the present study. The present cluster 1 seems to correspond closely with one which he called "unmotivated introverts" (and also possibly to another, called "unmotivated extroverts"). The present cluster 2 seems similar to his "Saints" ("stable, extrovert, motivated conformists") and his "motivated stable extroverts." The present cluster 3 probably corresponds to his "sinners" ("contentious nonconformists"). Good and Power (1976) derived five student types from a series of canonical analyses. They labeled these types "success," "social," "dependent," "alienated," and "phantom." The first of these probably parallels the present cluster two, while the third ("dependent") shows some similarity to cluster 1, and the fourth ("alienated") to cluster 3. Finally, in the secondary analysis of data from the pilot study for this research (Solomon and Kendall 1976), a cluster analysis of four preference/orientation factors plus prior achievement produced six clusters of children. The first of these combined high prior achievement with internal motivation, resembling the present cluster 2. Another combined a "preference for open situations" with moderate achievement, similar to cluster 3. None of the clusters in the earlier study duplicated the present cluster 1 very closely, although three of them showed some similar elements (one combined low achievement and low motivation with moderate compliance, another low achievement and high motivation with moderate compliance, and the third high compliance with moderate achievement and motivation). A final cluster in the pilot study does not clearly resemble any of those in the present one, although it probably comes closest to the present cluster 2, since it combines fairly high achievement and "personal-control orientation" with a preference for structured situations.

Although certain similar elements appear to run through all of these studies, it is obvious that much further research needs to be done before a clear, validated, and replicable set of child types with relevance to educational situations is definitively established. As with the classroom clusters, however, the present set of child clusters seems to represent recognizable types and leads to fairly clear expectations about how well (relatively) each "type" of child should perform in each "type" of classroom setting. The next chapter will show how well such expectations are borne out.

8 EFFECTS OF CLASSROOM "TYPES" AND CHILD "TYPES" ON OUTCOMES

Because both sets of clusters (child and classroom) represented discrete qualitative categories, analysis of variance seemed an appropriate and logical method for investigating their separate and joint effects on the various outcome measures. Selecting the appropriate unit of analysis to use with this procedure, however, presented something of a problem. Typically, with analysis of variance, the individual student would constitute the unit of analysis; this would clearly be appropriate for an experiment in which each subject received a "treatment" independently of other subjects. But when the students are organized into ongoing groups (or classrooms), the treatment (or educational experience) of one student cannot be considered to be independent of that of any of the others in the same classroom. Treating the student as the unit of analysis would clearly overestimate any classroom variable main effects, as well as any interactions involving classrooms. Yet, the investigation of child-classroom interactions was a major objective of this research, and means to study such interactions without considering the individual child as the unit of analysis (but, at the same time, using the two sets of cluster designations) were not readily apparent.

One solution to this problem was suggested in an article by Page (1975); a similar procedure was advocated and used in research by Walberg et al. (1972). The essentials of this solution, as stated by Page, were:

> Treat each . . . classroom . . . as if it were a single subject. Then treat the interesting subcategories within the classroom as if they represented repeated measurements of the same subject, made under different pseudoconditions (: 342).

This implies the use of a "repeated-measures" analysis-of-variance procedure, which divides the sources of variance (including error terms) into two general classes: "between-subjects" variance and "within-subjects" variance (or, in this application, "between-classrooms" and "within-classrooms" variance). With respect to a given dependent variable, each classroom would then be represented by a single score (most likely a mean) for each of the within-classroom "subcategories."

In the present instance, the child variables which were to be reconstituted into within-classroom "subcategories" included child cluster membership and sex of child. Therefore, for each dependent (outcome) variable a mean score was derived, within each class, for each child cluster by sex grouping; this produced six repeated-measure scores within each class. The analysis of variance then included "classroom cluster" as a nonrepeated independent variable (with six levels), and "sex" and "child cluster" as repeated-measure independent variables (with two and three levels, respectively). Each classroom, with its "repeated" subcategories, constituted a "replicate" within its classroom cluster. Each cell entry was a subcategory score within a single classroom. These entries were combined across the classrooms in a given cluster to compose a "cell." Because some of the classrooms had few children, it was inevitable that all six of the child "subcategories" would not be represented within some of the individual classrooms. In fact, 8.67 percent of the 300 possible cell entries (6 subcategories within 50 classrooms) were missing; these missing entries were represented by total sample means. The missing entries were distributed so that there were no empty cells however; each of the sex-child cluster subcategories was represented in all or nearly all of the classrooms within any given classroom cluster.

Tables 8.1 and 8.2 show how equally the children were distributed by sex between the different child clusters and classroom clusters (considered separately), before the data were regrouped according to subcategory means within classrooms. The child clusters were differently distributed for the two sexes. Girls were overrepresented in cluster 2, and boys were overrepresented in clusters 1 and 3. The distributions between the classroom clusters, however, were fairly equal for the two sexes, as shown in Table 8.2. Similar distributions were also obtained for the child-cluster by classroom-cluster combinations. Tables 8.3, 8.4, and 8.5 show these for boys, girls, and the total sample. While the distribution for boys did not deviate significantly from chance (as indicated by the chi-square value shown in Table 8.3), the distributions for girls and the total sample did (Tables 8.4 and 8.5).

The analysis method which was used began by assigning a single (mean) value to each child-cluster-by-sex subcategory, within each classroom, for each dependent variable. The distribution dis-

TABLE 8.1

Distribution of Children by Sex within Child Clusters
(N = 1035)

| Sex | Child Cluster | | | Chi^2 Value |
	1	2	3	
Boys	209	184	117	32.30* (2 df)
Girls	174	278	73	

*p < .01.
Source: Compiled by the authors.

TABLE 8.2

Distribution of Children by Sex within
Classroom Clusters (N = 1035)

| Sex | Classroom Cluster | | | | | | Chi^2 Value |
	1	2	3	4	5	6	
Boys	84	102	109	77	50	88	.80 (5 df)
Girls	90	110	103	82	54	86	

Source: Compiled by the authors.

TABLE 8.3

Distribution of Boys in Child Cluster by Class
Cluster Combinations (N = 510)

Child	Classroom Cluster						Chi^2 Value
Cluster	1	2	3	4	5	6	
1	30	45	45	31	16	42	
2	30	41	38	29	20	26	8.75 (10 df)
3	24	16	26	17	14	20	

Source: Compiled by the authors.

TABLE 8.4

Distribution of Girls in Child Cluster by Class
Cluster Combinations (N = 525)

Child	Classroom Cluster						Chi^2 Value
Cluster	1	2	3	4	5	6	
1	28	31	42	24	18	31	
2	54	71	45	43	28	37	19.78* (10 df)
3	8	8	16	15	8	18	

*p < .05.
Source: Compiled by the authors.

TABLE 8.5

Distribution of All Children in Child Cluster by
Class Cluster Combinations (N = 1035)

Child Cluster	Classroom Cluster						Chi^2 Value
	1	2	3	4	5	6	
1	58	76	87	55	34	73	
2	84	112	83	72	48	63	19.36* (10 df)
3	32	24	42	32	22	38	

*p < .05.
Source: Compiled by the authors.

crepancies shown in Tables 8.4 and 8.5 were eliminated with this procedure; all student subcategories were given equal weights in all classes. The only remaining discrepancies were those associated with the classroom clusters (the "nonrepeated" independent variable), which ranged in size from six to ten. The repeated-measures analysis-of-variance procedure which was used was taken from Winer (1971), and used "unweighted means" to handle the unequal classroom-cluster frequencies.

A large number of analyses of variance was computed for this research. Some are reported and discussed in this chapter, others in the following chapter and in Appendix A. Because of this number, it will not be possible to present complete analysis-of-variance tables. Tables summarizing these analyses, themselves limited to the presentation of F-values and probability levels for the various effects, are presented in Appendix B. Tables presenting selected F-values, means, and t-values for differences between means will be presented in the body of the monograph. Graphs displaying some of the obtained effects will also be presented.

Most of these analyses of variance were concerned with 14 outcome measures. For those which included both pre- and posttest measures, residual scores were obtained with a regression analysis. These residuals constituted the deviation of each actual posttest score, for each individual, from that predicted on the basis of the parallel pretest score. The residuals were essentially measures of "gain"; children with positive scores had gained more than "expected," while those with negative scores had gained less than "expected." They were calculated for the measures of achievement test performance (using the factor score from the third grade tests as the predictor), creativity, inquiry skill, writing quality, the four attitude and value factors (self-confidence, value on equality, concern for others, and value on self-direction), and the single score which represented "self-esteem." (Although self-esteem had contributed to the "self-confidence" factor, it was decided also to include it as a separate variable because of general interest in this concept, and also because it did not seem well-represented by that factor, its contribution to it having been relatively weak.) Two other sets of factors had been derived from measures obtained only in the spring: the students' class and self-evaluations (with three factors—enjoyment of class, social involvement, and perceived class disruptiveness) and the teachers' ratings of students (with two factors—perseverance/social maturity, and activity/curiosity); these were used as outcome measures directly.

In the remaining pages in this chapter detailed tables are presented for all main effects and for those interactions which reached significance at the .10 level or better. Because this research had exploratory and heuristic objectives, the .10 probability level was considered appropriate. It was felt, furthermore, that the aggregating procedure, which reduced the number of "cases" from 1,035 (and 1,292 in some instances) to 50, may have been to some degree an overcompensation (particularly with respect to interactions), and thus justified a relatively unconservative probability level.

CLUSTER AND SEX MAIN EFFECTS

Tables 8.6, 8.7, and 8.8 present the main effects for the classroom clusters, child clusters, and sex, respectively. Because the two sets of clusters encompass virtually all of the available information describing classrooms and children (as they were at the outset of the school year) and because each set's effects are relatively independent of those of the other two (except as they are involved in interactions), these main effects can be considered "best estimates." Although the possibility of adding the measure of socioeconomic status as a covariate in these analyses was considered, it was rejected on the grounds that socioeconomic status was correlated with prior achievement and several of the other variables which helped comprise the child clusters (see Table B.3), and that partialling it out would therefore be partialling out some of the effect which was to be investigated. (Socioeconomic status was, however, also included as a separate independent variable, and its interactions with classroom clusters and classroom dimensions investigated; these findings are presented in later sections.)

TABLE 8.6

Means for Classroom Cluster Main Effects on All Dependent Variables

Dependent Variable	Classroom Cluster						$\underline{F}$ (5, 44)	Between–Mean Diff. Req. for Signif. (p < .05)
	1	2	3	4	5	6		
Achievement–test performance	-.16	.11	-.02	.09	.02	-.02	2.52*	.19
Creativity	-.17	.13	-.10	.13	.27	-.09	1.64	
Inquiry skill	-.08	-.06	-.09	.10	-.12	.01	.53	
Writing quality	-.34	.07	.22	.40	-.04	.01	1.50	
Self-esteem	-.27	-.26	-.62	.28	.16	.04	.37	
Self-confidence	-.03	.04	-.03	.01	-.01	.04	.23	
Value on equality	-.04	.05	.05	.03	.05	.07	.39	
Concern for others	.05	.01	-.10	-.06	.06	.03	1.20	
Value on self-direction	.14	-.01	-.02	-.01	.00	.06	.90	
Enjoyment of class	-.08	-.16	-.06	-.12	.02	.05	.45	
Social involvement	.02	.07	-.10	.03	-.03	-.05	.32	
Perceived class disruptiveness	-.01	-.06	.23	-.05	-.18	.07	2.51*	.27
Perseverance, social maturity	.04	-.06	-.17	.15	.13	-.08	.93	
Activity/curiosity	.17	-.08	.05	-.26	.19	.07	2.53*	.33

*p < .05.
Source: Compiled by the author.

151

Table 8.6 presents the classroom-cluster main-effect means for all dependent variables. Those with $\underline{F}$ values of 1.0 or greater are plotted in Figure 8.1. Three of these show significant effects: achievement-test performance, perceived class disruptiveness, and activity/curiosity. In addition, the effect for creativity can be considered to be of borderline significance; it slightly misses an acceptable level of significance in the present analysis, but in some additional analyses (partially presented in Appendix A) which also investigated classroom-cluster main effects, creativity did show significant effects. This suggests that the effect on creativity is not a very strong one but is sufficiently clearly indicated to be worthy of notice.

The effect on achievement-test performance shows high residual scores for clusters 2 and 4, low scores for cluster 1, and intermediate scores for the other classroom clusters. Clusters 2 and 4 were both characterized as being relatively tightly controlled and orderly and as having a disciplined approach to tasks (see Table 7.1). Cluster 4 combined this with warmth while cluster 2 combined it with a fairly cold and businesslike approach, but it appears likely that it is the orderly, disciplined element in common which is important for developing the skills necessary for good achievement-test performance. The classroom cluster which shows the lowest achievement-test scores in the present results, cluster 1, was characterized by extremely low scores on the same component; classrooms in this cluster were permissive, undisciplined, and lacking in control. This finding can be compared with the pilot study results, which found better achievement-test performance for children in "traditional" than in "open" classes (where the traditional were observed to be more controlled and more oriented to academic task performance than were the open classes). Similar results were also obtained in some (but not all) of the relevant prior studies cited earlier, particularly those containing elements which were described as representing "direct instruction."

The highest residual scores for creativity were obtained by class cluster 5, the grouping which combined great warmth and friendliness with a strong emphasis on student expressiveness, exploration, and creativity. It seems altogether reasonable that children in such classes would perform well with respect to creativity. (This finding is also consistent with some of the prior research.) It is interesting to note, however, that the classroom clusters characterized by control and orderliness (2 and 4) also did relatively well with respect to creativity, while the extremely permissive and uncontrolled one (cluster 1) did quite poorly. The extreme lack of control and discipline was apparently harmful to creativity as well as academic achievement.

FIGURE 8.1

Mean Scores for Class Clusters on Selected Dependent Variables

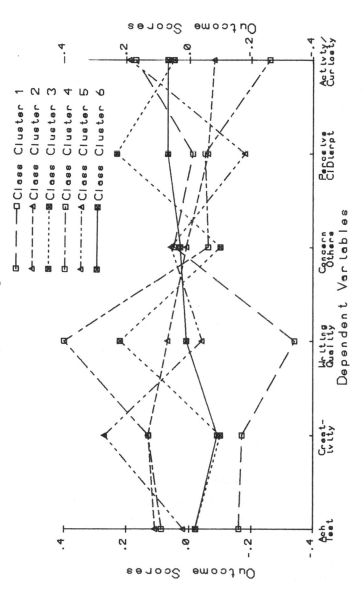

Two classroom clusters demonstrated high scores on the teachers' rating factor, "activity, curiosity": cluster 1, the extremely permissive and varied cluster, and cluster 5, the warm and expressive one. Children in the former were presumably active and curious because they were given a good bit of autonomy and independence with few restrictions; those in the latter were perhaps so as a result of the teacher's active promotion of student exploration within a warm and friendly context.

The other significant class-cluster main effect, on "perceived class disruptiveness," showed high scores for the coldest and most unfriendly cluster (3), and lowest scores for the warmest and friendliest one (5). This is not surprising; in fact, it should probably be considered to be little more than validity information about the classroom-cluster designations. Unfriendly and hostile classes are seen as containing disruptive children, while warm and friendly classes are seen as relatively devoid of them.

The impression derived from examining the results for all outcome measures (including those which did not show statistically significant differentiation) is that the best performance, overall, was shown by students in class clusters 4 and 5. Those in class type 4 (which combined control and orderliness with warmth and supportiveness) did well with respect to academic/cognitive measures, including achievement-test performance, inquiry skill, and writing quality; they also showed high scores for self-esteem and perseverance/social maturity. As mentioned earlier, this cluster seemed to represent most closely the Rosenshine definition of "direct instruction." The present evidence of its general academic effectiveness is thus quite consistent with the integrative hypothesis Rosenshine derived from his summary of the recent research.

Students in cluster 5 (warm and expressive, with moderate student autonomy) also scored high on self-esteem and perseverance, in addition to creativity, concern for others, activity/curiosity, and enjoyment of class; at the same time, they did relatively well on achievement tests and saw their classes as the least disruptive. Cluster 5 classes emphasized different goals and activities from those in cluster 4. Their profiles of outcomes show both similarities and differences; yet they both appear to represent relatively "successful" classes.

Two of the class types, 1 and 3, showed relatively poor performance with respect to the outcome measures, with somewhat different patterns. Students in type 1 (permissive and uncontrolled, with much student autonomy) showed low scores for several cognitive measures, including achievement-test performance, creativity, and writing quality; their scores on self-esteem were also low. At the same time, they obtained high scores for concern for others, value on self-direction, and activity/curiosity. Children in cluster 3 (cold, unfriendly, common activities, relatively permissive) tended also to be low on most of the cognitive measures; they further obtained the lowest scores for self-esteem, concern for others, social involvement, and perseverance and perceived the greatest disruptiveness in their classes.

It is interesting that there were two class types which contained numerous elements of an "open" environment, yet produced different patterns of outcomes. Type 1 classes, which showed a fairly extreme degree of student autonomy and a lack of orderliness and control, did poorly on cognitive measures (including creativity), although their scores on some of the social attitudes and on curiosity were high. It seems likely that the extreme disorganization and lack of control in these classes made it difficult for the children to concentrate on academic tasks. For the students in type 5—in which teacher control and student autonomy were moderate, the atmosphere was "warm," and there was a very strong emphasis on student expressiveness—creativity was maximized, achievement test scores were fairly high, and students thought well of themselves, worked well, and enjoyed their classes.

Child-cluster main effects are presented in Table 8.7. Ten of the fourteen dependent variables were significantly influenced by the child clusters. In general, these differences slightly favored cluster 2, the cluster characterized by high prior achievement, self-confidence, personal control. There were, however, several dependent variables for which child cluster 3 (characterized by student autonomy, self-direction, independence) achieved scores not significantly lower than cluster 2; this occurred for creativity, writing quality, value on equality, concern for others, and activity/curiosity. Cluster 3 children scored highest with respect to residual "value on self-direction." Children in cluster 1 (compliant low achievers) achieved the lowest scores on all dependent variables showing significant child-cluster effects, except for enjoyment of class, which was lowest for cluster 3.

Sex main effects from these analyses are presented in Table 8.8. Ten of the dependent variables demonstrated significant sex effects, most of them favoring girls. Girls obtained higher scores on academic and cognitive skills and various social attitudes and values, while boys were more active and more likely to value self-direction. These differences are in accord with other findings which have been reported concerning differences among pre-adolescent boys and girls (e.g., Maccoby 1966). Parallel findings in the form of correlations, from analyses in which the individual child constituted the unit of analysis, can be seen in Table B.3. The findings from the two analyses are generally similar.

TABLE 8.7

Means for Child-Cluster Main Effects on All Dependent Variables

Dependent Variable	Child Cluster			Between-Cluster t-Values			F (2, 88)
	1	2	3	1 vs. 2	1 vs. 3	2 vs. 3	
Achievement-test performance	.00	.03	−.02				.85
Creativity	−.14	.13	.09	1.75*	NS	NS	7.11‡
Inquiry skill	−.23	.15	−.03	2.58†	NS	NS	13.28‡
Writing quality	−.29	.24	.21	2.37†	2.23†	NS	14.16‡
Self-esteem	−.89	.55	.00	NS	NS	NS	3.33†
Self-confidence	−.05	.04	.02				2.20
Value on equality	−.10	.11	.10	2.00†	1.91†	NS	10.17‡
Concern for others	−.08	.06	.01	NS	NS	NS	3.39†
Value on self-direction	−.03	.01	.10	NS	NS	NS	3.56†
Enjoyment of class	.03	.03	−.26	NS	1.89*	1.92*	9.66‡
Social involvement	.03	.01	−.07				1.20
Perceived class disruptiveness	.05	−.06	−.00				2.20
Perseverance, social maturity	−.34	.37	−.02	4.41‡	1.98†	2.43†	39.10‡
Activity/curiosity	−.28	.24	.11	4.05‡	3.01‡	NS	35.47‡

*p < .10.

†p < .05.

‡p < .01.

Note: t-tests were not calculated if the F-value did not reach the .10 level of significance, that is, not significant (NS).

Source: Compiled by the authors.

TABLE 8.8

Means for Sex Main Effects on All Dependent Variables
(based on class means)

Dependent Variable	Sex		$\underline{F}$ (1, 44)
	Boys	Girls	
Achievement-test performance	-.03	.04	3.48*
Creativity	-.04	.09	5.83‡
Inquiry skill	-.02	-.06	.39
Writing quality	-.10	.21	7.22‡
Self-esteem	-.08	-.15	.04
Self-confidence	-.04	.05	4.22†
Value on equality	-.06	.13	13.41‡
Concern for others	-.08	.08	12.32‡
Value on self-direction	.06	-.01	2.78*
Enjoyment of class	-.24	.11	26.10‡
Social involvement	-.02	.00	.13
Perceived class disruptiveness	-.04	.04	1.87
Perseverance, social maturity	-.17	.17	22.73‡
Activity/curiosity	.23	-.18	33.70‡

*$p < .10$.
†$p < .05$.
‡$p < .01$.
Source: Compiled by the authors.

INTERACTIONS

The next set of tables presents means and significance levels
for the various two- and three-way interactions which manifested
significant effects ($p < .10$ or better) for the analyses which included
classroom cluster and child cluster as independent variables. Table
8.9 shows means for two significant sex-classroom cluster interactions, one affecting "activity/curiosity," the other, "self-esteem."
Although boys' activity levels were generally higher than those of
girls (as seen in the main effect discussed above), the two sexes show
different patterns regarding the type of class in which this characteristic was maximized. Boys were rated as most active and curious
in class cluster 5, the type of class in which curiosity and exploration

TABLE 8.9

Means for Significant Two-Way Interactions between
Sex and Classroom Clusters

Dependent Variable	Sex	Classroom Clusters						F (5, 44)	Between-Mean Difference Required for Significance (p < .05)
		1	2	3	4	5	6		
Activity/curiosity	Boys	.26	.25	.00	.04	.52	.28	3.17*	.42
	Girls	.08	-.40	.09	-.56	-.14	-.14		
Self-esteem	Boys	.04	.25	.21	.47	-.67	-.76	2.30†	1.72
	Girls	-.59	-.78	-1.46	.09	1.00	.84		

*p < .05.
†p < .10.
Source: Compiled by the authors.

TABLE 8.10

Means for Significant Two-Way Interactions between
Sex and Child Clusters

Dependent Variable	Sex	Clusters			Between-Cluster t-Values			F (2, 88)
		1	2	3	1 vs. 2	1 vs. 3	2 vs. 3	
Social involvement	Boys	-.06	-.07	.05	NS	NS	NS	5.91*
	Girls	.13	.09	-.20	NS	3.25*	2.87*	
Between-sex t-values		1.81†	NS	2.52‡				

*p < .01.
†p < .10.
‡p < .05.
Source: Compiled by the authors.

159

are actively promoted by the teacher; girls, on the other hand, tended to be most active in the relatively permissive and uncontrolled classes represented by clusters 1 and 3. The results with self-esteem were somewhat different. Boys' self-esteem showed greatest residual gains in class cluster 4 (warm, controlled, and orderly), while for girls the gains were greatest in clusters 5 (warm and expressive) and 6 (verbal participation-oriented, individualized teacher-student interaction). To the degree that one can generalize from these results, it appears that boys' self-esteem is most enhanced in a warm, but businesslike and task-oriented setting, while girls' self-esteem is enhanced in settings with more personalized teacher-student relationships.

One significant sex by child-cluster interaction was found with these analyses, and is presented in Table 8.10. The cluster 3 (autonomous, noncompliant, self-directing) boys were most socially involved with their classmates, while girls in this cluster were least socially involved.

Two of the dependent variables, activity/curiosity and residual creativity, were influenced by two-way interactions between classroom cluster and child cluster, shown in Table 8.11. The effect on creativity is also shown in Figure 8.2. Both the low achieving, compliant (cluster 1) children and the autonomous, self-directing (cluster 3) children were the most active and curious in the most permissive, least controlled class type (represented by cluster 1), while the high achieving, motivated children were most active and curious in the classes which emphasized expressiveness and exploration and were warm and friendly (cluster 5). Thus, the children who stated a preference for autonomy and self-direction were rated as highly active and curious in classes which provided for much student autonomy, while the children who were achievement-oriented and moderately compliant showed most activity and curiosity in the classes which actively promoted curiosity. All three types of children scored high on creativity in the warm and expressive classes (cluster 5), but children in clusters 2 and 3 also did well in class cluster 4 (warm, controlled, orderly), and cluster 3 children (those preferring autonomy) did well in class cluster 2 (which combined control and orderliness with student initiation of varied activities). This provides some evidence that children who like self-direction are benefited in some respects by a class setting which allows them to initiate their own tasks, and that an orderly, disciplined approach to tasks can help promote creativity as well as academic achievement even for those whose stated preference is for autonomy (but not, apparently, for the children with the lowest levels of prior achievement).

Five dependent variables were influenced by three-way interactions (child cluster by sex by class cluster): self-esteem, self-

TABLE 8.11

Means for Significant Two-Way Interactions between Child Clusters and Classroom Clusters

Dependent Variable	Child Cluster	Classroom Cluster						F (10, 88)	Between–Mean Difference Required for Significance (p < .05)
		1	2	3	4	5	6		
Creativity	1	.00	-.11	-.26	-.29	.11	-.30	2.21*	.30
	2	-.12	.10	.08	.29	.43	.01		
	3	-.39	.39	-.14	.39	.26	.04		
Activity/curiosity	1	.03	-.43	-.16	-.67	-.31	-.14	2.80*	.25
	2	.11	.24	.14	.14	.66	.15		
	3	.38	-.05	.16	-.26	.21	.19		

*p < .05.
Source: Compiled by the authors.

FIGURE 8.2

Interaction Effect of Child Clusters and Class Clusters on Creativity

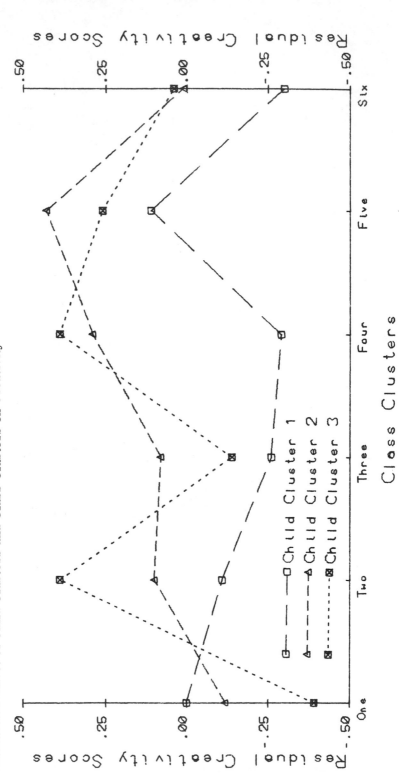

confidence, value on equality, concern for others, and perseverance/
social maturity. The means from these interactions are shown in
Table 8.12. Children of both sexes in the low-achieving, compliant
cluster (cluster 1) showed the greatest residual self-esteem in warm
and friendly classroom environments—boys in classes which combined
this warmth with control and orderliness (cluster 4) and girls in those
which combined it with an emphasis on student expressiveness
(cluster 5). Girls in child cluster 1 also obtained relatively high
self-esteem residual scores in class cluster 6, involving the most
individualized teacher–student interaction. Different effects on self-
esteem were also found for the two sexes in child cluster 2 (personally
controlled, high prior achievers, etc.): the boys did best in class
clusters 5 and 2 (one warm and expressive, the other both controlled
and self-initiating), while the girls did best in clusters 4 and 6 (warm
and controlled, and individualized). The autonomous, expressive
(cluster 3) girls showed greatest self-esteem in the warm and expressive classrooms (cluster 5), while the boys in this cluster showed it
in class cluster 4 (warm, controlled, orderly). The results for self-
confidence were generally similar, as would be expected. The only
clear differences occurred for the cluster 3 children (autonomous,
etc.); boys of this type showed greatest residual self-confidence in
class cluster 1 (permissive, providing for autonomy), while girls
did so in class cluster 2 (combining orderliness with student initiation
of tasks).

Cluster 1 (low-achieving, compliant) children of both sexes
achieved the highest residuals for value on equality in class cluster
5 (warm and expressive); cluster 2 (high-achieving) boys scored
highest in class cluster 4 (warm, controlled, orderly), while cluster
2 girls did so in cluster 6 (involving individualized teacher–student
interaction); autonomous, expressive (cluster 3) boys scored highest
in class cluster 6 (individualized, etc.) while cluster 3 girls did so
in class cluster 3 (involving a relatively high level of permissiveness).

Boys in child cluster 1 achieved their highest "concern for
others" scores in class cluster 5 (warm and expressive), while girls
in this child cluster scored highest in class cluster 1 (extremely
permissive, etc.). Cluster 2 boys and girls alike scored highest in
class clusters 2 and 4 (both relatively controlled and orderly). Cluster 3 boys obtained high scores on concern for others in class clusters
1, 5, and 6 (respectively, permissive, expressive, and individualized), while girls in this cluster did so in clusters 1, 3, and 4 (the
first two relatively permissive, the other, warm and orderly).

Results of the cluster-by-cluster interaction effect on "perseverance, social maturity" are also shown in Figure 8.3. Low-
achieving, compliant (cluster 1) boys were rated high on this variable

TABLE 8.12

Means for Significant Three–Way Interactions among Child Clusters, Sex of Child, and Classroom Clusters

Dependent Variable	Sex, Child Cluster	Classroom Cluster						F (10, 88)	Between–Mean Diff. Req. for Signif. (p < .05)
		1	2	3	4	5	6		
Self–esteem	Boys								
	1	.10	-1.51	-.23	.59	-1.48	-1.59	1.75*	1.27
	2	-.05	1.25	-.28	-.48	1.96	-.15		
	3	.08	1.02	1.14	1.30	-2.50	-.53		
	Girls								
	1	-.88	-3.08	-1.14	-2.41	.55	.40		
	2	.80	.72	-.17	1.55	.56	.85		
	3	-1.70	.02	-3.07	1.14	1.89	1.26		
Self–confidence	Boys								
	1	-.14	-.18	-.14	.07	.04	-.07	1.78*	.14
	2	-.04	.00	-.01	-.16	.04	-.02		
	3	.13	.00	.08	.02	-.29	-.06		
	Girls								
	1	-.10	-.03	.07	-.15	-.03	.09		
	2	.14	.13	.05	.15	.04	.19		
	3	-.17	.30	-.22	.11	.16	.14		
Value on equality	Boys								
	1	-.22	-.31	-.06	-.19	-.04	-.37	2.47†	.15

	1	2	3	4	5	6		
2	-.19	.17	.12	.22	-.16	-.05		
3	.09	.03	-.18	-.32	.05	.40		
Girls								
1	-.17	.07	.00	-.04	.18	-.10		
2	.20	.21	.04	.23	.25	.29		
3	.06	.12	.41	.31	.03	.22		
Concern for others							1.93*	.14
Boys								
1	-.14	-.13	-.17	-.29	.02	-.11		
2	-.19	.09	-.14	.10	-.04	-.01		
3	.21	-.25	-.53	-.30	.22	.22		
Girls								
1	.20	.01	-.09	-.27	.00	-.01		
2	.04	.27	.14	.22	.17	.13		
3	.18	.07	.19	.21	.01	-.05		
Perseverance, social maturity							1.83*	.20
Boys								
1	-.56	-.61	-.51	-.65	-.01	-.74		
2	.07	.25	-.11	.27	.13	.39		
3	-.01	-.16	-.58	.14	-.01	-.31		
Girls								
1	-.06	-.13	-.30	.12	-.43	-.25		
2	.65	.56	.46	.68	.70	.43		
3	.14	-.25	.06	.31	.42	-.02		

*p < .10.
†p < .05.
Source: Compiled by the authors.

FIGURE 8.3

Interaction Effect of Child Clusters, Sex, and Class Clusters on Perseverance/Social Maturity

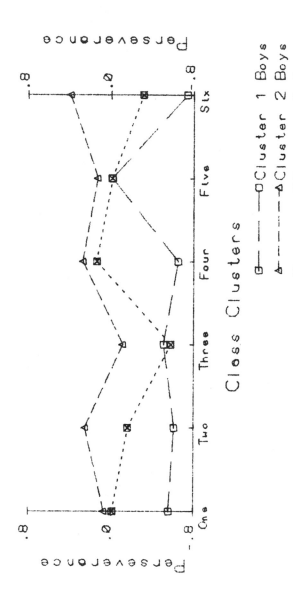

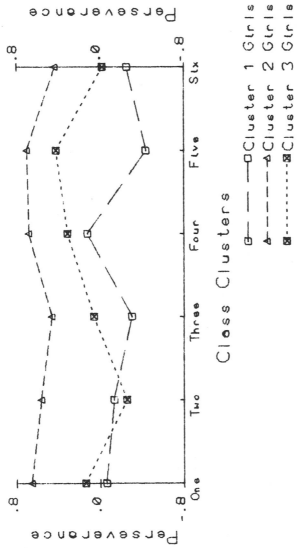

Class Clusters

Perseverance

Perseverance

□ Cluster 1 Girls
▲ Cluster 2 Girls
⊠ Cluster 3 Girls

One Two Three Four Five Six

in class cluster 5 (warm and expressive), while girls of this type persevered most in class cluster 4 (warm, controlled, orderly). High-achieving motivated (cluster 2) boys persevered most in class cluster 6 (characterized by individualized teacher-student interaction); girls in this child cluster were rated as persevering in just about every type of class, with highest scores for clusters 1 (permissive), 4 (warm and controlled), and 5 (warm and expressive). Autonomous, expressive (cluster 3) boys scored highest on perseverance in class cluster 4 (warm and orderly), while girls in this cluster did so in clusters 4 and 5 (warm and expressive).

SUMMARY OF INTERACTIONS INVOLVING CHILD CLUSTERS AND CLASSROOM CLUSTERS

Although there were some differences between the results for the different dependent variables in the three-way interactions, the major trends can be summarized as follows: On the whole, the low-achieving, compliant (cluster 1) boys did best in warm and expressive classes with moderate control (class cluster 5); the motivated, high-achieving boys (cluster 2) did best in classes which were controlled and orderly but also allowed for student initiative and varied activities (cluster 2); and the boys who valued autonomy and personal expression (cluster 3) did best in classes which were permissive and provided for much autonomy and student initiation of activities (class cluster 1). At the same time, the cluster 1 (low-achieving) girls performed well in both the warm, expressive (cluster 5) and the individualized (cluster 6) classes; the cluster 2 (high-achieving, motivated) girls did best in cluster 4 classrooms (combining warmth with control and orderliness), and the cluster 4 (autonomous-expressive orientation) girls did best in class cluster 5 (combining warmth with an emphasis on student expressiveness).

The major differences between the sexes in these interactions were (1) low-achieving, compliant girls did relatively well in classes which provided for individualized teacher-student interaction, in addition to the warm, expressive classes favored by both sexes in this child cluster; (2) the motivated, high-achieving children of both sexes did well in classes which were controlled and orderly; however, boys did best in classes which combined this orderliness with student-initiated activities, girls in those which combined it with warmth and friendliness; (3) the boys who were oriented toward autonomy and personal expression showed more of a tendency to do well in the classes which provided for much student autonomy, while the girls so oriented did best in classes which emphasized greater student expressiveness.

Concerning the effects which held across the sexes, the low-achieving (cluster 1) children scored highest on both activity/curiosity and creativity in the most permissive (cluster 1) classrooms; the cognitively proficient, motivated (cluster 2) children did well on both these variables in warm and expressive (cluster 5) classrooms, and on creativity also in cluster 4 (warm and controlled); and the autonomy-preferring (cluster 3) children were most active and curious in permissive (cluster 3) classrooms, but most creative in clusters 2 and 4 (both characterized by relatively high levels of control and orderliness, among other things).

The interactions involving sex seem to show girls doing somewhat better in classes which allow for more personalized relationships and expressiveness, boys in those which allowed for more autonomy. More generally, the class types which appeared to be the most beneficial for the children with low initial levels of cognitive skill and motivation (in child cluster 1) were those characterized by great permissiveness and variety of activities (class cluster 1) and by the combination of warmth and a strong emphasis on student expressiveness (cluster 5). It may be suggested that these classroom environments, which encourage the children's development of self-direction and self-expression, may have helped children to develop (or discover) motivation for task performance which may initially have been lacking. The cluster 2 children (well motivated, with initially high levels of cognitive skill), on the other hand, generally did best in class clusters 2 and 4, both characterized by high levels of control and orderliness and relatively high levels of student initiation of activities. They also did relatively well in class cluster 5, particularly with respect to activity/curiosity and creativity; this, of course, was the cluster in which student expression and exploration were strongly emphasized, and which produced generally high creativity scores for all types of children. The importance of controlled and orderly classes to the performance of the most proficient and motivated children was not anticipated. But, to build on the explanation presented for the cluster 1 children, it would seem that these children, being well motivated to begin with, would not require external stimulation and varied opportunities to motivate them. A controlled and orderly task orientation (within a context which also allows them the opportunity to initiate their own tasks) may be what they require to help them further develop from an already high level of proficiency. Furthermore, a preference for structured classrooms was one of the components making up this cluster; these children are therefore performing well in the types of class which they prefer (and they may prefer them, of course, because they help them progress with tasks efficiently).

The pattern of results obtained for the autonomy-preferring, expressive, noncompliant children (cluster 3) was somewhat more varied. Perhaps the most interesting aspect is that evident in the two-way interactions, showing that children's activity and curiosity are maximized in the most permissive classrooms (cluster 1), but creativity is maximized in clusters 2 and 4 (both characterized by high levels of control and orderliness). It is possible that permissive classrooms can increase the activity level and expressed curiosity of children oriented toward autonomy because the environment allows (and perhaps welcomes) what the children are inclined to do. But the development of a specific cognitive skill (such as creativity) may require that the children's expressive and autonomous inclinations be tempered somewhat. A relatively structured setting, with an orderly approach to tasks, may provide these children with a framework which they lack and may thereby help them to develop their expressive motives in productive directions.

9 EFFECTS OF CLASSROOM "DIMENSIONS" AND CHILD "DIMENSIONS" ON OUTCOMES

In addition to the analyses of the main effects and interactions of the child and classroom "types" represented by clusters and presented in the preceding chapter, parallel analyses were also done with the individual components of the clusters, generally factor scores. The major concern was again with child-classroom interactions; therefore, a number of analyses were performed, each investigating the interaction of one child dimension with one classroom dimension. The classroom dimensions included in these analyses were the six classroom factor scores; the child dimensions were the four orientation/motive factor scores, plus socioeconomic status. The same fourteen dependent variables used in the preceding analyses were also used in these (including residual scores for all measures which had had pre- and posttest administrations). The same repeated-measures analysis-of-variance procedure which was used to investigate the cluster main effects and interactions, with the classroom as the unit of analysis, was also used for these analyses. In order to do this, it was necessary to "block" the independent variables into categorical groupings, since they represented continuous measures. This was done before the data were aggregated into within-class subgroup means. Each of the child and classroom independent variables was trichotomized into approximately equal thirds, according to the distributions obtained for the total sample. Each classroom measure was blocked so that the low, medium, and high groups contained, respectively, 17, 16, and 17 classrooms.

CLASSROOM AND CHILD-DIMENSION MAIN EFFECTS

Earlier, reasons were discussed for selecting the repeated measures approach as a means for investigating interactions while still using the classroom as the unit of analysis. With the analyses using clusters, this also provided a reasonable means for investigating the main effects as well. However, the analyses using blocked dimensions were not considered to give the "best estimates" of their main effects, because the blocking necessarily discarded some of the information contained in the data. This seemed unavoidable in the investigation of interactions, but not in the investigation of the main effects. The best estimates of the effects of the child preference and orientation factors and SES are probably the correlations with the outcome measures presented in Table B.3. These indicate (1) generally positive effects for "personal control, intrinsic motivation" (with significant correlations for residual achievement-test performance, inquiry skill, writing quality, self-esteem, self-confidence, value on equality, concern for others, enjoyment of class, perseverance, and activity level), and (2) generally negative effects for "compliant, conforming orientation" (with significant correlations for creativity, inquiry skill, writing quality, value on equality, concern for others, value on self-direction, and activity level but also a significant positive correlation with "enjoyment of class"). A few scattered significant correlations were also obtained with the other two orientation/motive factors—"preference for class with autonomy" and "achievement motivation"—but they were nowhere near as pervasive as those for the two factors mentioned above. Socioeconomic status showed modest positive correlations with the measures of cognitive skills and some of the residual value and attitude measures (none of the correlations were above .13, however), and showed slightly higher positive correlations with the teacher rating factors. It also obtained significant correlations with the two orientation/motive factors which were related to the bulk of the outcome measures, compliant conforming orientation (a negative correlation) and personal control, intrinsic motivation (a positive one).

To determine the degree to which the factor-analysis-derived classroom dimensions were independent of or related to modal aggregated individual attributes of the children in the classrooms, mean scores were derived for the four individual orientation/motive factors and for socioeconomic status within each classroom. These mean scores were then correlated with the six obtained classroom dimensions. These correlations are shown in Table 9.1. They show classroom warmth to be correlated with the average level of student compliance, with girls' personal control, and with SES; control and orderliness fairly strongly (negatively) related to the average preference for classes allowing autonomy; energetic encouragement of verbal (academic) participation related to boys' achievement motivation; and emphasis on student expressiveness correlated with girls' personal control and with SES (fairly weakly).

TABLE 9.1

Correlations between Class Means on Individual Variables (Orientations and SES) and Second-Order Classroom Factor Scores

Individual Variables		Second-Order Classroom Factors					
		Warm, Friendly, vs. Cold.	Control, Order vs. Lack of Control	Common vs. Varied Activ.	Nonindivid. vs. Individ. Interac.	Encour. Verbal Partic.	Emph. on S Express.
Pref. for aut.	Boys	.02	-.50*	-.09	-.05	-.08	.04
	Girls	.05	-.36*	.07	.04	-.14	.00
	Total	.02	-.52*	-.02	.02	-.12	.02
Comp. orient.	Boys	-.27†	-.07	-.01	-.05	.16	-.17
	Girls	-.19	-.02	-.03	.07	-.15	-.05
	Total	-.24†	-.02	-.03	-.02	.00	-.11
Pers. cont./ intrins. motiv.	Boys	-.06	.08	.08	.17	-.01	.10
	Girls	.24†	.04	-.19	.00	-.12	.30‡
	Total	.17	.09	-.03	.08	-.08	.29‡

(continued)

173

Table 9.1 (continued)

Individual Variables		Second-Order Classroom Factors					
		Warm Friendly, vs. Cold.	Control, Order vs. Lack of Control	Common vs. Varied Activ.	Nonindivid. vs. Individ. Interac.	Encour. Verbal Partic.	Emph. on S Express.
Ach. motiv.	Boys	-.20	-.13	-.01	.09	.29‡	-.04
	Girls	-.17	.01	-.06	-.13	.04	.09
	Total	-.19	-.08	-.05	-.03	.24†	.05
SES	Boys	.29‡	-.10	.01	.07	.08	.21
	Girls	.21	-.13	.02	.15	-.06	.21
	Total	.29‡	-.14	.01	.13	.04	.24†

*p < .01.
†p < .10.
‡p < .05.
Source: Compiled by the authors.

A multiple regression approach was used to obtain estimates of the classroom dimension main effects without altering the "continuous" character of these dimensions. Separate three-stage hierarchical regression analyses were performed with each of the fourteen dependent variables. In each case, the classroom was the unit of analysis and the dependent variables were class means. In order to control for differences between classes in the average (or "composite") individual characteristics of the children within them, class mean scores on the four preference and orientation factors and on SES were entered as the first stage of the regression analysis. The six class factors were then entered, together, as the second stage. Finally, in order to investigate possible quadratic effects of these classroom factors (it was anticipated that moderate positions would be optimal in some instances), squared terms for each of the classroom factors were entered as the third stage in each of these analyses. These regression analyses were done separately for boys, girls, and the total sample. It should be noted that the six classroom factors are orthogonal (uncorrelated). Their respective regression coefficients can therefore be considered to represent the independent contributions of each, uncontaminated by problems of collinearity.

A summary of the regression analyses done with the cognitive outcome residuals and self-esteem is presented in Table 9.2. Each column represents a single regression analysis, with a single dependent variable. The entries after each independent variable are the standard partial regression coefficients (beta weights), with the significance levels of their contributions to the dependent variables. At the bottom of each column is the multiple correlation and its square, which indicates the portion of the total variance in that dependent variable accounted for by the combination of the independent variables.

The upper portion of this table (and the following two), representing the effects of the aggregated individual orientations and SES, are included only as controls; they show the influence of class averages (or "compositional" effects) but should not be considered in any way to represent individual level effects (which, as mentioned, are shown most clearly by the individual-level correlations presented in Appendix B). These compositional effects are presented here primarily so that they may be discounted in considering the class-dimension main effects, in the bottom portions of the tables.

Each of these classroom dimensions shows one or more significant relationships with the outcome measures presented in Table 9.2. (A graphic representation of the class-factor regression weights for the total sample is shown in Figure 9.1.) To a significant degree warmth is positively related to creativity for girls, and to writing quality and self-esteem for boys. Control/orderliness shows strong positive linear relationships with achievement-test performance and

TABLE 9.2

Regression Coefficients (Betas) and Multiple Regression Coefficients from Multiple Regression Analyses Showing Class-Level Main Effects on Cognitive Skills and Self-Esteem

| | Dependent Variables (Residuals) | | | | | | | | | | | | | | |
| | Achievement Test Performance | | | Creativity | | | Inquiry Skill | | | Writing Quality | | | Self-Esteem | | |
Independent Variables	Boys	Girls	Total	Boys	Girls	Total	Boys	Girls	Total	Boys	Girls	Total	Boys	Girls	Total
Aggregated Ind. Orients. and SES (Controls)															
Pref. for aut.	-.28	.07	-.08	-.35†	-.25*	-.38†	-.30*	.14	-.12	-.14	.12	.01	.18	.21	.22
Comp. orient.	.00	-.17	-.07	-.34†	-.30	-.28*	-.38†	-.33	-.25	-.32*	-.02	-.21	-.12	-.03	-.14
Pers. contr. intr. motiv.	-.01	.17	.00	-.01	-.28	-.22	-.07	.20	-.02	-.12	.04	-.34*	.04	.23	-.20
Ach. motiv.	.07	-.31†	-.08	-.09	-.05	-.14	.19	.24	.26	.19	.00	.18	.42†	.05	.43†
SES	.15	-.27	.04	-.04	.15	.13	.15	-.15	.04	-.17	.33	.12	-.07	.14	.22
Class Factors (Linear Effects)															
Warmth	.23	.14	.21	.17	.30*	.19	.07	.13	.19	.39†	-.06	.26	.50†	.00	.44†
Cont., order	.35*	.53†	.54†	.30*	.26	.25*	.30	.28	.38*	.45†	.43†	.60†	.34	.09	.32*
Commonality	.28*	.00	.21	.11	-.01	.06	.29†	.23	.32*	.41†	-.07	.24	.20	.03	.18
Nonindivid.	.16	.09	.11	-.13	-.02	-.10	-.30*	.01	-.15	-.06	-.22	-.15	.06	-.13	.01
Enc. of verbal partic.	-.20	-.16	-.23*	-.28†	-.45†	-.41†	-.26*	-.01	.17	.02	-.01	-.09	.06	-.04	-.06
Emph. S. express.	-.06	-.18	-.11	.04	.09	.12	.11	.07	.14	-.01	-.17	-.02	.20	.06	.25
Squared Class Factors (Quadratic Effects)															
Warmth, sq.	-.01	.12	-.02	-.11	-.09	-.16	-.33	-.09	-.24	-.03	-.06	-.03	.15	-.17	.01
Control, sq.	.01	-.24*	-.11	.09	.01	.02	.13	-.11	.07	.45†	.30	.45†	.16	.19	.24
Common., sq.	-.04	.24	.10	.14	.19	.17	.19	.13	.20	.19	-.05	.14	-.06	-.23	-.17
Nonind., sq.	.11	.28†	.19	.33†	.21	.26*	.09	.20	.16	-.01	.19	.09	.00	.02	-.07
Partic., sq.	-.09	-.01	-.09	.01	.17	.09	-.11	-.35†	-.33*	-.04	.03	-.01	-.38†	.04	-.30*
Express., sq.	-.13	-.49†	-.26*	.00	-.05	-.02	.16	.16	.20	.22	.27	.30*	-.01	.28	.27
Mult. R	.77	.83	.80	.79	.73	.80	.74	.67	.68	.68	.59	.66	.62	.53	.69
Mult. R²	.59	.68	.64	.62	.54	.64	.55	.44	.47	.46	.35	.44	.38	.28	.48

*p < .10.
†p < .05.
‡p < .01.

Note: Positive signs for betas of squared terms indicate higher outcome scores for the high and low extremes than for the middle range of the independent variable; negative signs indicate higher outcome scores for the middle range than for the extremes. The former represent U-shaped, the latter, inverted-U-shaped relationships.

writing quality, and somewhat weaker, but still significant, relationships with the other outcome measures represented in this table
(girls' self-esteem being the only exception). Control also demonstrates some quadratic effects; girls' achievement-test performance
was highest with moderate control, while boys' writing quality was
enhanced at both extremes of control. These control effects, while
not entirely expected, are generally consistent with the implications
which seemed to emerge from the cluster results presented in the
preceding chapter and with some of the prior research summarized
in Chapter 2 which relates, as stated earlier, to the concept of "direct
instruction." It appears that various cognitive skills are enhanced
in classrooms which provide for an orderly and disciplined approach
to tasks.

Boys' achievement-test performance, inquiry skill, and writing
quality were highest in classes with greatest commonality of activities,
while this variable showed no significant effect for girls. Boys' inquiry skill was also highest in classes with the most individualized
teacher-student interaction. There was, in addition, some indication
that achievement and creativity were enhanced by both extremes of
individualization.

Teachers' energetic encouragement of verbal (academic)
participation related negatively to creativity residual scores, an
unsurprising finding suggesting that the development of creativity
may be inconsistent with a strong academic emphasis, and with
devoting much time to public, verbal discussions of academic material.
The same independent variable, however, also showed some weak
negative relationships with achievement-test performance and boys'
inquiry skill; findings which are somewhat more difficult to explain,
but may indicate than an overemphasis on verbal teacher-student
interaction may detract from the time which students have to practice
directly the skills being learned. A moderate position on this same
variable related to maximal inquiry skill development (for girls) and
maximal self-esteem (for boys). The major result which was expected for emphasis on student expressiveness, a positive relationship with creativity, was not found. In fact, the only relationships
shown with this variable are quadratic ones: an inverted U-shaped
relationship with achievement test performance for girls, and a
U-shaped one with writing quality

Regression analyses relating the classroom factors to the
four attitude and value factor residuals are presented in Table 9.3.
Warmth was significantly related to girls' value on equality, both
linearly and quadratically, and to value on self-direction (quadratically, with highest scores for the moderately warm classes). Control
related negatively to value on self-direction, indicating that classes
which provided for greater student autonomy and self-direction helped

FIGURE 9.1

Main Effects (Betas) of Class Factors on Cognitive Skills and Self-Esteem

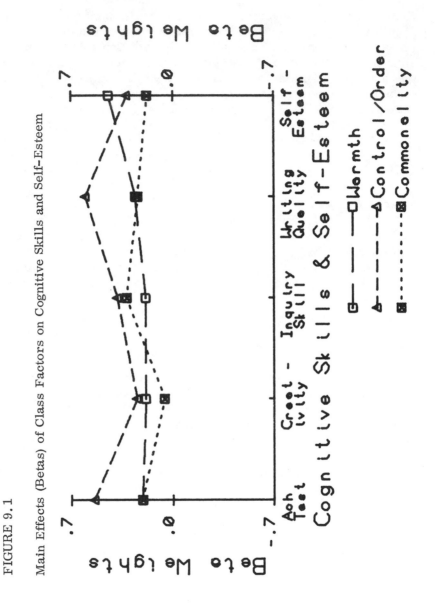

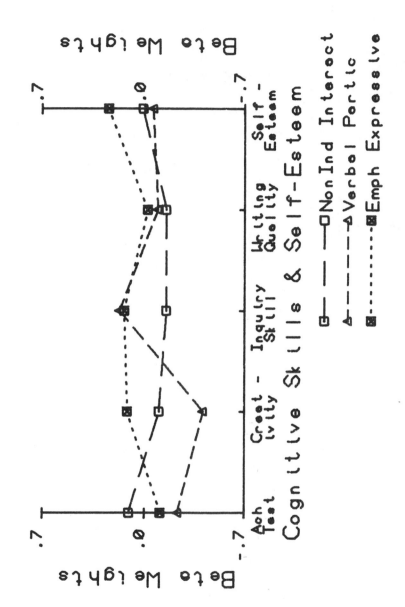

TABLE 9.3

Regression Coefficients (Betas) and Multiple Regression Coefficients from Multiple Regression Analyses Showing Class-Level Main Effects on Residual Attitudes and Values

Independent Variables	Dependent Variables (Residuals)											
	Self-Confidence			Value on Equality			Concern for Others			Value on Self-Direction		
	Boys	Girls	Total	Boys	Girls	Total	Boys	Girls	Total	Boys	Girls	Total
Aggregated Ind. Orients. and SES (Controls)												
Pref. for aut.	-.13	.21	.15	.12	.14	.25	-.11	-.03	-.07	.17	.00	-.03
Comp. orient.	-.37†	-.25	-.24	-.04	-.38*	-.18	-.33*	-.35*	-.53‡	-.28*	-.39*	-.34*
Pers. contr. intr. motiv.	.28	.19	.20	-.18	-.11	-.30	.03	.14	.15	.61‡	-.09	.43†
Ach. motiv.	.13	.22	.20	.30	.59‡	.66‡	.17	.54‡	.42†	-.26	-.22	-.28
SES	-.18	.04	-.18	-.08	.03	.03	.22	-.14	-.23	-.07	.26	-.10
Class Factors (Linear Effects)												
Warmth	.18	.00	.23	.03	.29*	.19	.05	.17	.16	-.11	-.27	-.24
Cont., order	.15	.14	.25	.29	.24	.54†	.13	-.03	.13	-.23	-.21	-.40†
Commonality	.29*	.03	.25	.12	.06	.19	-.02	.08	.11	-.11	.05	.01
Nonindivid.	-.14	.27	.16	.05	.21	.12	-.05	.18	.07	-.29*	-.07	-.18
Enc. of verbal partic.	.01	.03	.02	-.12	-.26*	-.34†	-.15	-.10	-.16	.11	-.15	-.01
Emph. S. express.	-.07	-.03	-.03	.14	.00	.16	.19	.07	.24	-.04	.21	.05
Squared Class Factors (Quadratic Effects)												
Warmth, sq.	-.07	.19	.17	-.21	.40*	-.02	-.09	.19	.00	-.37*	-.32	-.41†
Control, sq.	.32*	-.01	.20	.07	.15	.24	-.16	.06	-.01	.00	.15	.02
Common., sq.	.19	.05	.21	.28	.03	.19	.22	.29	.36*	-.01	-.16	-.02
Nonind., sq.	.31*	-.13	.13	.14	-.16	.02	-.01	-.08	-.05	.34*	.12	.34†
Partic., sq.	-.16	-.02	-.18	-.43†	-.05	-.42†	-.03	.13	.04	.17	-.14	-.01
Express., sq.	-.10	.01	-.15	-.07	.09	.06	.16	-.24	-.11	-.08	.03	-.15
Mult. R	.65	.48	.52	.47	.70	.65	.65	.72	.71	.69	.72	.72
Mult. R²	.42	.23	.27	.22	.49	.42	.42	.52	.51	.48	.52	.52

*p < .10.
†p < .05.
‡p < .01.
Source: Compiled by the authors.

180

to develop values favoring such options on the part of the students. Control also showed a positive relationship with value on equality, and a quadratic (U-shaped) relationship with boys' self-confidence.

Commonality of class activities showed two significant effects; a positive one with boys' self-confidence, and a U-shaped one with concern for others. Classes characterized by individualized teacher-student interaction produced the greatest gains in boys' value on self-direction, although significant quadratic effects with the same independent variable indicated that boys' value on self-direction and self-confidence were maximal in classrooms at the upper and lower extremes of individualization.

Encouragement of verbal (academic) participation showed two significant effects, both influencing value on equality residual scores; for girls, there was a negative relationship, while for boys the scores were maximized in classrooms in the moderate range. Classrooms' emphasis on student expressiveness did not relate significantly to any of the value and attitude residual scores.

Relationships of these classroom dimensions to students' class and self-evaluations, and to the two factors representing teachers' ratings of students' classroom behavior, are presented in Table 9.4. These dependent variables, having been obtained only once, at the end of the school year, are the only ones which are not residuals. Classroom warmth appeared to have its major effect on these dependent variables for boys. Boys in warm classes were rated as persevering by their teachers and expressed enjoyment of the classes (although the latter variable also demonstrated a quadratic effect, with high scores on self-rated enjoyment obtained in classes at both extremes of the warmth dimension). Classrooms which were controlled and orderly also showed relatively high ratings for boys' perseverance (suggesting that they were responding to an emphasis on an industri-ous, disciplined approach to tasks in these classes), and for children's self-rated enjoyment of class (a fairly weak effect, however). A stronger quadratic effect on class enjoyment was found for girls: they stated greatest enjoyment in classes which were moderate with respect to the permissiveness versus control dimension. Boys also showed the greatest social involvement in such classes.

Girls tended to persevere most in classes which were highly or moderately varied; with boys' enjoyment of class, the same vari-able (commonality of activity) showed both a positive, linear relation-ship and a quadratic one (with a U-shaped relationship). Boys also tended to perceive the greatest classroom disruptiveness in the least individualized classrooms; while children (girls, in particular) stated greatest enjoyment for classes in which there was much energetic encouragement of verbal (academic) participation. Boys' activity and curiosity showed a U-shaped relationship with this classroom

TABLE 9.4

Regression Coefficients (Betas) and Multiple Regression Coefficients from Multiple Regression Analyses Showing Class-Level Main Effects on Student- and Teacher-Rating Outcomes

	Dependent Variables														
	Student Class and Self-Evaluations									Teacher Ratings of Students					
	Enjoyment of Class			Social Involvement			Perc'd. Disrupt.			Perseverance			Activity, Curiosity		
Independent Variables	Boys	Girls	Total	Boys	Girls	Total	Boys	Girls	Total	Boys	Girls	Total	Boys	Girls	Total
Aggregated Ind. Orients. and SES (Controls)															
Pref. for aut.	.10	.53*	.53*	.06	.05	.15	.23	-.11	.01	.09	.38‡	.39†	-.08	.10	.08
Comp. orient.	.31‡	.26	.37†	.16	.23	.28	.11	.17	.10	-.05	.10	-.09	-.10	.11	-.08
Pers. contr. intr. motiv.	.28	.51*	.13	.03	-.11	.23	.19	-.25	.07	.12	.02	-.06	.13	.09	.19
Ach. motiv.	.09	.19	.26	.32	-.23	.28	-.09	-.01	-.11	.24	.17	.39‡	.19	-.18	.18
SES	-.22	.05	.08	-.03	.04	-.06	-.55*	-.34	-.61†	.09	.32	.09	.39‡	.16	.13
Class Factors (Linear Effects)															
Warmth	.57*	.04	.43†	.20	.18	.20	.00	.06	-.01	.48†	.09	.46†	-.05	-.16	-.03
Cont., order	.20	.12	.36‡	.25	.00	.14	.01	-.21	-.17	.40‡	.10	.41†	-.21	-.21	-.16
Commonality	.42†	-.20	.20	.09	-.11	-.05	.11	.23	.18	.12	-.41†	-.09	-.26	-.18	-.18
Nonindivid.	.06	-.10	-.01	.08	.04	.13	.32‡	.06	.24	.05	.04	.11	-.16	-.14	-.07
Enc. of verbal partic.	.14	.26†	.24‡	.05	-.03	.08	.24	-.02	.12	-.01	.09	.01	-.16	.20	-.01
Emph. S. express.	.07	-.12	.02	.06	-.10	-.17	-.16	.12	-.05	.10	.02	.11	.12	.47†	.26
Squared Class Factors (Quadratic Effects)															
Warmth, sq.	.43†	-.08	.30	.27	-.10	.22	.14	.10	.09	.29	-.10	.17	-.14	.02	.01
Control, sq.	.01	-.47‡	-.26	-.36‡	.14	-.22	.08	-.03	-.03	.26	.11	.20	-.06	.01	-.03
Common., sq.	.32‡	-.07	.10	.21	-.27	-.08	.26	.14	.27	-.06	-.39‡	-.19	-.19	-.30	-.12
Nonind., sq.	.03	.06	.00	-.09	.14	-.06	-.13	.13	.04	-.06	-.01	-.04	.28	-.16	-.10
Partic., sq.	-.05	-.09	-.12	-.12	-.05	-.06	.01	-.11	-.06	-.06	-.11	-.16	.30‡	.11	.24
Express., sq.	-.12	.10	.03	.06	-.09	-.07	-.11	-.06	-.13	.36‡	.36‡	.38‡	.09	-.02	.07
Mult. R	.66	.81	.74	.63	.53	.57	.70	.68	.66	.67	.64	.66	.68	.58	.63
Mult. R²	.44	.66	.55	.40	.29	.32	.48	.46	.43	.45	.41	.44	.47	.34	.40

*p < .01.
†p < .05.
‡p < .10.

Note: Positive signs for betas of squared terms indicate higher outcome scores for the high and low extremes than for the middle range of the independent variable; negative signs indicate higher outcome scores for the middle range than for the extremes. The former represent U-shaped, the latter, inverted-U-shaped relationships.

Source: Compiled by the authors.

variable. Girls' activity/curiosity was maximal in classes with a strong emphasis on student expressiveness and exploration, while for children of both sexes there was a clear U-shaped relationship between this classroom variable and the teachers' ratings of perseverance and social maturity; children were seen as persevering most in classes which were at the high and low extremes in emphasizing student expressiveness. This may indicate that the children in the different types of classrooms represented by these two extremes were persevering at different types of tasks; possibly creative, exploratory tasks in the most expressive classes and more rote, academic tasks in the least expressive.

To summarize these classroom-dimension main effects: classroom warmth and friendliness showed main effects primarily with boys; boys in warm classrooms wrote well, thought well of themselves, persevered, and enjoyed the classes; girls' creativity and value on equality were enhanced in warm classes. Classrooms which were controlled and orderly produced the greatest gains in cognitive skills, achievement-test performance and writing quality, in particular. This permissiveness versus control dimension was also involved in some quadratic effects; for example, girls' enjoyment of class and boys' social involvement were highest in classrooms at the moderate position on this dimension. Commonality of class activities showed a few scattered main effects, relating most clearly to the development of boys' cognitive skills. The significant effects of individualization of teacher-student interaction were also fairly scattered; boys' inquiry skill and value on self-direction were most enhanced in the most individualized classrooms. The clearest effect of the classroom factor, "energetic encouragement of verbal (academic) participation," was a negative relationship with the creativity residuals: the greater the scores on this classroom variable, the lower the creativity scores. Emphasis on student expressiveness produced a few significant main effects, the clearest a quadratic (U-shaped) relationship with perseverance/social maturity.

CLASSROOM DIMENSION BY CHILD DIMENSION INTERACTIONS

Means, F values, and significance levels for classroom dimension by child dimension interactions which reached the .05 level or better are presented in Tables 9.5 to 9.16. (Although a cut-off point of .10 was used to identify F-values representing interactions worthy of examination and interpretation in the cluster by cluster interactions discussed in the preceding chapter, the .05 level was used with the present large set of analyses merely in order to reduce the number of relationships to be investigated, and to limit them to the strongest interaction effects.) Interaction results for each classroom factor are presented in two adjacent tables, the first showing means for significant two-way interactions (including a child dimension), the second showing means for three-way interactions (with sex of child as the third independent variable).

Interactions With Classroom Warmth

Significant two-way interactions between classroom warmth and child factors are presented in Table 9.5. Three of the interactions with warmth reached the .05 level of significance, two of them involving socioeconomic status. The high-SES children showed greater residual gains in value on equality and concern for others in relatively cold and unfriendly classrooms, while the low-SES children showed a slight tendency to score higher on these dependent variables in warmer classrooms. Children at the high and low extremes of the compliant, conforming orientation distribution tended to be most socially involved in warm classes, while those in the moderate range were more socially involved in the colder classrooms.

Three-way interactions, involving classroom warmth, various child factors, and sex, are shown in Table 9.6. The interaction with SES, relating to achievement-test performance, is also shown in Figure 9.2. There were nine of these significant interactions, three involving SES, three involving achievement motivation, two involving personal control, and one involving compliant, conforming orientation. Low-SES boys scored highest in residual achievement-test performance and in enjoyment of class in classes scoring high on warmth dimension; their self-esteem was maximized in moderately or very warm classes. High-SES boys, on the other hand, tended to do better with respect to the same three outcome variables in relatively cold classes. For girls, the pattern was somewhat different: they tended to do best in classes which were either moderate or high on warmth at all SES levels. It seems likely that warm classrooms are especially beneficial to low-SES boys because they help acclimatize them and make them feel more comfortable in classroom situations which they may find relatively difficult and unfamiliar. This may be particularly true in a social setting such as that of Montgomery County where families on the whole are relatively affluent, and where, therefore, the lower-SES children may feel more atypical and distant from their school peers than they might in other school settings. This may be especially the case for low-SES boys, who have often been found to have a greater degree of difficulty with school than low-SES girls. The better performance of high-SES boys

TABLE 9.5

Means for Significant Two-Way Interactions between Child Factors (plus SES) and the Class Factor, "Warmth and Friendliness Versus Coldness"

Dependent Variable	Child Variable	Levels	Levels of Class Var.			Between-Class-Level t-Values			$F_{(4, 94)}$
			Low	Med	High	L vs. M	L vs. H	M vs. H	
Value on equality	SES	Low	-.11	-.02	.02	NS	1.78*	NS	2.61†
		Med	.05	.07	-.03	NS	NS	NS	
		High	.12	-.11	-.02	3.33‡	2.04†	NS	
Concern for others	SES	Low	-.07	-.03	-.02	NS	NS	NS	2.57†
		Med	-.05	.06	.02	1.90*	NS	NS	
		High	.19	.03	-.01	2.54†	3.24‡	NS	
Social involvement	Compliant orientn.	Low	-.20	-.10	.10	NS	3.24‡	2.22†	2.84†
		Med	.09	-.01	-.10	NS	2.07†	NS	
		High	.02	-.09	.16	NS	NS	2.63‡	

*p < .10.
†p < .05.
‡p < .01.
Source: Compiled by the authors.

185

TABLE 9.6

Means for Significant Three-Way Interactions Among Child Factors (plus SES), Sex, and the Class Factor, "Warmth and Friendliness Versus Coldness"

Dependent Variable	Child Variable	Sex, Levels	Levels of Class Var.			Between-Class-Level t-Values			F (4, 94)
			Low	Med	High	L vs. M	L vs. H	M vs. H	
Achievement Test Performance	SES	Boys							2.95†
		Low	-.14	-.12	-.01	NS	2.87*	2.38†	
		Med	-.15	-.03	.01	2.57†	3.44*	NS	
		High	.12	-.14	.02	5.87*	2.18†	3.69*	
		Girls							
		Low	-.09	-.04	-.03	NS	NS	NS	
		Med	.12	.01	.18	2.52†	NS	4.03*	
		High	-.09	.13	.16	4.98*	5.62*	NS	
Creativity	Achievement Motivation	Boys							2.56†
		Low	-.13	-.11	.20	NS	6.16*	5.74*	
		Med	-.39	-.12	.00	5.07*	7.30*	2.23†	
		High	-.22	-.06	-.21	3.02*	NS	2.88*	
		Girls							
		Low	-.20	.14	.16	6.24*	6.55*	NS	
		Med	-.05	.12	.28	3.02*	5.98*	2.96*	
		High	-.15	.25	.43	7.34*	10.65*	3.32*	

Variable								
Inquiry Skill								
Personal Control, Intrinsic Motivation	Boys							
		Low	−.22	−.37	−.26	2.10†	NS	NS	2.90†
		Med	−.13	−.05	.14	NS	3.63*	2.61†	
		High	.05	.35	.28	4.01*	3.12*	NS	
	Girls								
		Low	−.43	.24	.00	8.90*	5.75*	3.15*	
		Med	.00	.08	−.03	NS	NS	NS	
		High	.22	.20	.14	NS	NS	NS	
Self-Esteem								
SES	Boys							
		Low	−1.59	.29	.05	4.82*	4.21*	NS	2.74†
		Med	−.83	.39	1.21	3.14*	5.24*	2.10†	
		High	1.49	−.76	.24	5.77*	3.19*	2.58†	
	Girls								
		Low	−1.77	−.67	−1.09	2.81*	1.73‡	NS	
		Med	−.24	.38	−.97	NS	1.86‡	3.47*	
		High	−.12	1.37	1.25	3.80*	3.51*	NS	
Value on Equality								
Compliant, Conforming Orientation	Boys							
		Low	−.05	.01	.03	NS	1.88‡	NS	2.69†
		Med	−.02	−.06	−.33	NS	7.07*	6.20*	
		High	−.19	−.25	−.17	NS	NS	1.74‡	
	Girls								
		Low	.33	.14	.12	4.52*	4.94*	NS	
		Med	.11	.01	.11	2.26†	NS	2.37†	
		High	.07	.00	−.04	1.73‡	2.55†	NS	

(continued)

Table 9.6 (continued)

Dependent Variable	Child Variable	Sex, Levels	Levels of Class Var.			Between-Class-Level t-Values			F (4, 94)
			Low	Med	High	L vs. M	L vs. H	M vs. H	
Value on Self-Direction	Personal Control, Intrinsic Motivation	Boys							
		Low	.09	.04	.05	NS	NS	NS	3.53*
		Med	-.16	.05	.10	4.66*	5.93*	NS	
		High	-.05	.18	.10	5.21*	3.47*	1.74‡	
		Girls							
		Low	-.27	-.04	-.02	5.24*	5.68*	NS	
		Med	.10	.02	-.06	1.76‡	3.61*	1.85‡	
		High	-.08	-.04	.09	NS	3.64*	2.72*	
Enjoyment of Class	Achievement Motivation	Boys							
		Low	-.40	-.25	-.07	2.10†	4.56†	2.45†	2.57†
		Med	-.37	-.08	-.28	4.08*	NS	2.83*	
		High	-.20	-.24	.25	NS	6.38*	6.98*	
		Girls							
		Low	-.04	-.02	-.13	NS	NS	NS	
		Med	.06	.35	.41	4.09*	4.88*	NS	
		High	.10	.44	.19	4.85*	NS	3.57*	
Enjoyment of Class	SES	Boys							
		Low	-.39	-.09	-.02	4.48*	5.60*	NS	3.00†
		Med	-.31	-.19	.00	1.70‡	4.51*	2.81*	
		High	.07	-.30	-.13	5.58*	3.06*	2.52†	

188

Perceived Disruptive-ness	Girls	Low	.00	.11	.29	1.64‡	4.37*	2.73*
		Med	.02	.33	-.01	4.66*	NS	5.14*
		High	-.07	.24	.23	4.74*	4.49*	NS	2.51†
Achieve-ment Motivation	Boys	Low	.03	.15	-.17	2.83*	4.76*	7.59*
		Med	.07	.01	-.22	NS	6.79*	5.30*
		High	.18	.09	-.19	2.05†	8.51*	6.46*
	Girls	Low	.15	-.05	.02	4.70*	2.97*	1.73‡
		Med	-.15	.07	.08	5.20*	5.25*	NS
		High	.14	-.09	-.11	5.30*	5.94*	NS

*p < .01.
†p < .05.
‡p < .10.
Source: Compiled by the authors.

189

FIGURE 9.2

Interaction Effect of SES, Sex, and Class Warmth on Achievement-Test Performance

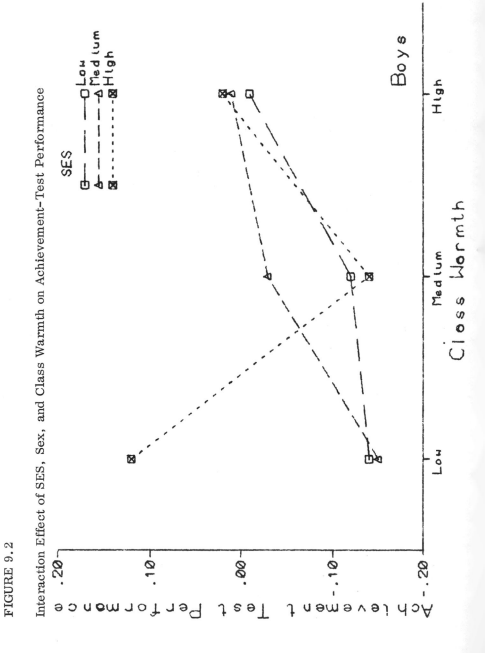

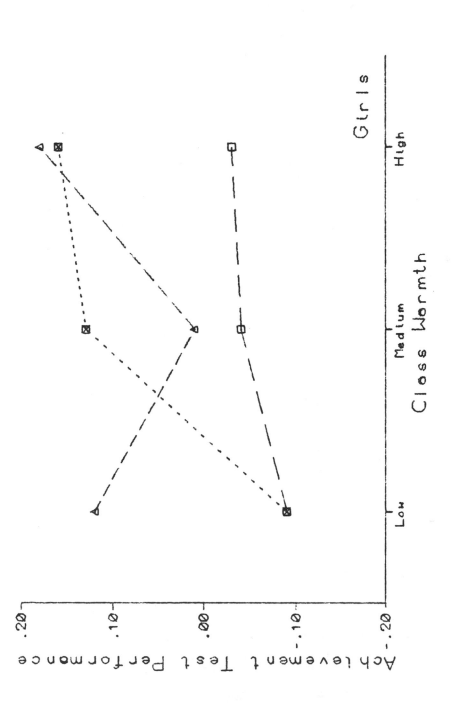

in the "cooler" classrooms is not easy to account for but may relate to a preference for a more businesslike, less "personal" approach to academic tasks. The preference of girls at all SES levels for classrooms which are at least moderately warm is consistent with numerous other research findings which have shown girls (in this culture, at least) to be more socially oriented, more interested and involved in interpersonal relationships, and the like (see Maccoby 1966). The similar U-shaped trends shown for high-SES boys and medium-SES girls are difficult to account for, however.

Achievement motivation was involved in three-way interactions (along with classroom warmth and sex) affecting creativity, enjoyment of class, and perceived disruptiveness. Boys who were low in achievement motivation were most creative in, and most enjoyed, classrooms which were high on warmth and friendliness; they tended to see most disruptiveness in moderately warm classrooms. Highly achievement-motivated boys were the most creative in moderately warm classrooms (perhaps they supplied for themselves some of the motivation which classroom—and teacher—warmth provided to the boys who were not themselves well motivated). At the same time, the highly motivated boys stated greatest enjoyment of the classes which were very warm, while those with moderate achievement motivation preferred classes which were moderate on warmth. Boys who scored in the low or moderate achievement-motivation groups tended to perceive high levels of class disruptiveness in the coldest classes. Girls again generally favored classes which were either highly or moderately warm. The highest creativity cell mean for girls combined highly motivated girls with very warm classrooms; at the same time, the most motivated girls reported the greatest enjoyment in moderately warm classes (while moderately motivated girls enjoyed classrooms which were either moderate or high on warmth, and the relatively unmotivated girls showed no differentiation in enjoyment between classrooms differing in warmth). Girls at both extremes of achievement motivation saw relatively cold classrooms as containing the greatest disruptiveness, while moderately motivated girls saw the greatest disruptiveness in classes which were moderately or highly warm.

Personal control was involved in two significant interactions with classroom warmth, one affecting inquiry skill, the other, value on self-direction. Boys who scored low on personal control/intrinsic motivation showed only slight variation between classes varying with respect to warmth, but with a slight trend in favor of the "colder" classes; boys with moderate or high scores on personal control did best with respect to creativity and self-direction in classes which were highly or moderately warm. It may be that the more intrinsically motivated boys felt freer to explore their own interests (and thereby also developed their inquiry skills) in classes which were warm, friendly, and interpersonally involved. For girls, the patterns represented in these two interactions were somewhat different. The only significant differentiation with respect to girls' inquiry skill occurred for those scoring low in personal control/intrinsic motivation; they did best in classes which were moderate with respect to warmth. The highest value on self-direction scores for girls occurred in warm classes for those scoring high on personal control and in cold classes for those with moderate personal-control scores.

Value on equality was influenced by one three-way interaction involving "compliant, conforming orientation," classroom warmth, and sex. Noncompliant boys stated their greatest value on equality in warm classes, while noncompliant girls did so in cold classes. Compliant boys developed a value on interpersonal equality equally in both warm and cold classes, while compliant girls did so primarily in the colder classes. The major sex difference in this interaction occurred for the noncompliant children, with the boys valuing equality in warm, and girls, in cold classes. No ready explanation for this difference can be offered.

Interactions with Control/Orderliness

Significant two-way interactions involving classroom control and orderliness (versus lack of control) are presented in Table 9.7. Three of these interactions were with the child factor, "preference for class with autonomy"; the outcome measures affected were self-esteem, value on task self-direction, and enjoyment of class. There was some similarity in the shapes of these three interactions. Generally, the children who stated the least preference for autonomy scored highest on these dependent variables in the least controlled (most permissive and autonomous) classrooms, while those with greater preference for autonomous situations tended to have higher scores in moderately or highly controlled and orderly classrooms. This is approximately the opposite of what was expected for the interactions between these variables. It is possible that some sort of a "compensation" mechanism is reflected in these results. Children without a strong orientation towards individual autonomy may find an unexpected benefit from classrooms in which such autonomy is pervasive and relatively unavoidable; children with stronger orientations toward autonomy may similarly be benefited by being in situations which teach them some of the advantages of more disciplined, orderly, and controlled approaches to tasks. To put this more generally, children with certain needs and preferences may derive some advantage from situations which force them to explore options and activities which their own inclinations would lead them to avoid.

TABLE 9.7

Means for Significant Two-Way Interactions between Child Factors (plus SES) and the Class Factor, "Control and Orderliness Versus Lack of Control"

Dependent Variable	Child Variable	Levels	Levels of Class Var.			Between-Class-Level t-Values			F (4, 94)
			Low	Med	High	L vs. M	L vs. H	M vs. H	
Creativity	Compliant Orientation	Low	−.22	−.06	.32	1.85*	6.25†	4.40†	3.24‡
		Med	−.24	−.11	.17	NS	4.65†	3.22†	
		High	.00	−.02	.02	NS	NS	NS	
Self-Esteem	Preference for Class with Autonomy	Low	.10	.06	−.27	NS	NS	NS	2.56‡
		Med	−1.02	−.85	.95	NS	3.34†	3.04†	
		High	−.20	.83	−.17	1.75*	NS	1.69*	
Value on Self-Direction	Preference for Class with Autonomy	Low	.06	−.04	−.08	NS	2.06‡	NS	2.85‡
		Med	.00	.00	−.10	NS	NS	NS	
		High	.05	.03	.24	NS	2.64†	2.99†	
Enjoyment of Class	Preference for Class with Autonomy	Low	.17	.04	.01	NS	1.77*	NS	4.20†
		Med	−.05	.14	.01	2.11‡	NS	NS	
		High	−.09	.10	−.45	2.12‡	3.96†	6.08†	
Perseverance, Social Maturity	Compliant Orientation	Low	−.05	.01	.33	NS	4.07†	3.43†	2.94‡
		Med	−.02	−.12	.07	NS	NS	2.05‡	
		High	.14	−.19	−.02	3.48†	NS	1.84*	

*p < .10.
†p < .01.
‡p < .05.

Source: Compiled by the authors.

194

The other two interactions shown in Table 9.7 involve class control and orderliness and children's compliant, conforming orientation. These show fairly similar effects on residual creativity and on the teacher-rating factor "perseverance, social maturity." For both of these outcome measures, children in the low or medium compliance groups show their highest scores in the most controlled and orderly classrooms. The level of class control did not differentially influence creativity for the highly compliant children; they did, however, persevere most in the least controlled and orderly classrooms. Here again, a compensation mechanism seems to offer the most likely explanation: noncompliant children are benefited by a controlled situation in which a fair amount of compliance is required, while relatively more compliant children derive some advantage (at least with respect to perseverance) in situations which force them to be more self-directing and self-reliant. These results for children's compliance and preference for autonomy are comparable to those found with the cluster-by-cluster analyses presented in Chapter 8, particularly with respect to child clusters 1 and 3 (each containing these two child factors as central components).

Three-way interactions, involving classroom control, various child factors, and sex, are presented in Table 9.8. Children's preference for classes with autonomy appeared with three of these interactions, affecting residual achievement-test performance, value on self-direction, and perseverance. The interactions relating to the first two of these outcome measures showed some indications of the "compensation" mechanism discussed with regard to the last table (also involving the same major independent variables). Achievement-test performance was generally highest in the most controlled and orderly classrooms (consistent with the main effect findings reported earlier); the one exception was for boys with a low preference for autonomy, who showed better achievement in moderately and highly controlled classrooms. This interaction is also shown in Figure 9.3. With value on self-direction, children of both sexes who stated preferences for more highly structured classrooms scored highest in the least structured (most autonomous) classrooms, while girls who preferred autonomy scored highest in the most structured classrooms (scores were not differentiated between classrooms for boys with high or moderate preferences for autonomy). Thus, for each of these two outcome measures, there was some indication that children oriented toward autonomy actually did better in classes which imposed a fair amount of external discipline on them, while children oriented toward more external control were benefited by classrooms which required them to be somewhat more autonomous and self-directing. The interaction with which the same independent variables influenced children's perseverance took a somewhat differ-

TABLE 9.8

Means for Significant Three-Way Interactions among Child Factors (plus SES), Sex, and the Class Factor, "Control and Orderliness Versus Lack of Control"

Dependent Variable	Child Variable	Sex, Levels	Levels of Class Var.			Between-Class-Level t-Values			F (4, 94)
			Low	Med	High	L vs. M	L vs. H	M vs. H	
Achievement Test Performance	Preference for Class with Autonomy	Boys							
		Low	.01	.07	-.05	1.79*	1.90*	3.69†	4.12†
		Med	-.03	-.16	.15	3.96†	5.28†	9.24†	
		High	-.21	.03	.10	7.56†	9.64‡	2.08‡	
		Girls							
		Low	-.03	.09	.15	3.53†	5.61†	2.08‡	
		Med	-.10	.05	.16	4.56†	7.82†	3.26†	
		High	.03	.01	.17	NS	4.26†	4.69†	
Inquiry Skill	Achievement Motivation	Boys							
		Low	-.10	-.15	.19	NS	5.13†	5.95†	2.79‡
		Med	-.16	.01	.12	2.86†	4.80†	1.94*	
		High	-.07	-.27	.30	3.62†	6.36†	9.98†	
		Girls							
		Low	-.01	-.29	.06	5.01†	NS	6.13†	
		Med	.03	.09	.19	NS	2.73†	1.68*	
		High	.04	.30	.13	4.55†	NS	2.97†	

Self-Esteem								
Achievement Motivation	Boys							
	Low	-1.08	.19	.62	3.07†	4.12†	NS	2.94‡
	Med	-.55	-.32	.76	NS	3.17†	2.63†	
	High	.89	-.90	.40	4.36†	NS	3.17†	
	Girls							
	Low	-1.16	-1.67	-.34	NS	1.99‡	3.23†	
	Med	.00	-.12	-.05	NS	NS	NS	
	High	-.48	2.35	.14	6.89†	NS	5.38†	
Value on Self-Direction								
Preference for Class with Autonomy	Boys							
	Low	.10	.01	-.13	2.17‡	5.66†	3.49†	2.79‡
	Med	-.01	-.04	-.04	NS	NS	NS	
	High	.13	.13	.15	NS	NS	NS	
	Girls							
	Low	.03	-.09	-.03	3.01†	1.69*	NS	
	Med	.01	.05	-.17	NS	4.47†	5.41†	
	High	-.02	-.08	.33	NS	8.88†	10.25†	
Compliant Orientation								
Perceived Class Disruptiveness	Boys							
	Low	.06	.05	-.20	NS	5.45†	5.27†	2.50‡
	Med	.14	-.06	-.16	4.10†	6.17†	2.08‡	
	High	-.04	.04	.16	1.68*	4.13†	2.45‡	
	Girls							
	Low	.09	-.03	-.13	2.48‡	4.56†	2.08‡	
	Med	.06	.13	-.17	NS	4.92†	6.45†	
	High	.00	.18	-.19	3.76†	4.05†	7.82†	

(continued)

Table 9.8 (continued)

Dependent Variable	Child Variable	Sex, Levels	Levels of Class Var.			Between-Class-Level t-Values			F (4, 94)
			Low	Med	High	L vs. M	L vs. H	M vs. H	
Perseverance, Social Maturity	Preference for Class with Autonomy	Boys							
		Low	.11	-.12	.14	3.73†	NS	4.12†	2.66‡
		Med	-.24	-.64	-.01	6.51†	3.72†	10.24†	
		High	-.40	-.34	-.06	NS	5.57†	4.59†	
		Girls							
		Low	.29	.31	.38	NS	NS	NS	
		Med	.20	.12	.37	NS	2.76‡	3.98‡	
		High	.40	.04	.01	5.85†	6.38‡	NS	
Perseverance, Social Maturity	Personal Control, Intrinsic Motivation	Boys							
		Low	-.39	-.64	-.26	3.89†	1.92*	5.81†	3.60†
		Med	-.27	-.33	-.15	NS	1.79*	2.76†	
		High	.13	.04	.42	NS	4.48†	5.82†	
		Girls							
		Low	-.38	.03	.15	6.38†	8.22†	1.84*	
		Med	.39	.00	.20	6.15†	3.05†	3.10†	
		High	.67	.44	.47	3.48†	3.04†	NS	

*p < .10.
†p < .01.
‡p < .05.
Source: Compiled by the authors.

198

ent shape. Boys generally persevered most in the most highly controlled classes, whatever their level of preference for autonomy (although the low-low cell also showed a high score). Girls, however tended to persevere best when there was an approximate match between their preference for autonomy and the classroom's provision for autonomy; those with a strong preference for autonomy persevered most in the least controlled classrooms, and those with a moderate preference did so in the most controlled classrooms. A generally similar finding was obtained in the pilot study.

Achievement motivation appears in two of the three-way interactions shown in Table 9.8, influencing inquiry skill and self-esteem. Children of both sexes who scored low on achievement motivation (and also, in most cases, those who scored moderately) did best in highly controlled and orderly classes with respect to both of these outcome measures; girls with high achievement-motivation scores did best in moderately controlled classrooms, while boys in this grouping obtained the highest self-esteem scores in the least controlled (most permissive) classrooms, but obtained their highest inquiry scores in the most controlled ones. It may be suggested that children with low achievement motivation require the close external direction and supervision provided in the more controlled classrooms, while the highly motivated children are more able to provide these functions themselves and thus, on the whole, do well in classrooms which allow for relatively more student autonomy and self-direction.

A similar process appeared to be involved in the interaction, also shown in Table 9.8, which included children's personal control/ intrinsic motivation and influenced perseverance/social maturity. The relationship again appeared to hold primarily for girls; those with low personal control and intrinsic motivation persevered most in the most controlled classes, while those with high or moderate scores on this variable did so in the least controlled classes. Boys, however, tended to persevere most in the most controlled classes at all levels of personal control. For girls, then, it again appears that they work best in externally controlled classrooms when they are relatively lacking in internal direction, and best in classes which allow for self-direction when they are oriented toward providing it.

The remaining interaction shown in Table 9.8 related children's compliant, conforming orientation (along with classroom control and sex) to their perceptions of classroom disruptiveness. The general trend, which occurs for both sexes (but more clearly for boys), is for the relatively noncompliant children to see most disruptiveness in the least controlled classrooms, and for compliant children to see it in more controlled classrooms. It may be that the compliant children were in each case more likely to accept general classroom norms and standards, including tolerance of a wider range of behaviors in

FIGURE 9.3

Interaction Effect of Preference for Class with Autonomy, Sex,
and Control–Orderliness on Achievement–Test Performance

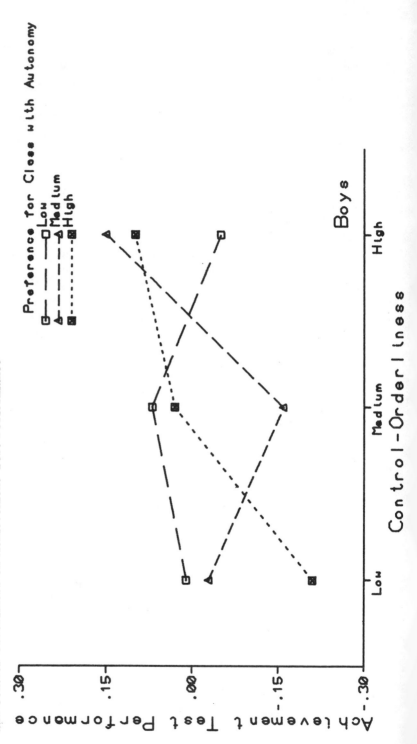

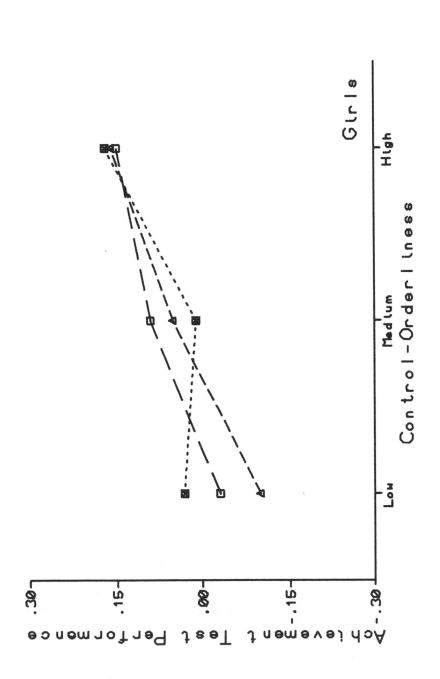

the more permissive classrooms (see Solomon and Kendall 1975).
Thus, they may see more disruptiveness in controlled classrooms
(where the setting implicitly defines more behaviors as being inappropriate), and less in permissive classrooms (where fewer are defined
as inappropriate).

Interactions with Commonality Versus
Variety of Activities

Two of the two-way interactions represented in Table 9.9,
showing the joint effect of children's personal control/intrinsic
motivation and classroom commonality of activity on creativity and
enjoyment of class, show patterns which suggest a process similar
to one which was suggested to account for some of the results seen
in Table 9.8. (The interaction effect on creativity is also shown in
Figure 9.4.) Although the shapes of these two interactions are not
precisely the same, in each case there is a slight trend for children
with lower personal-control and intrinsic-motivation scores to do
best with respect to these outcome measures in classrooms with
more common, externally imposed activities, and for children with
higher personal-control scores to do best in classrooms which are
more characterized by varied, student-initiated activities. Thus,
those children who are motivated to provide their own control and
direction show most enjoyment and creativity in classrooms which
allow for the exercise of this motivation, those with little such
motivation show most when they are provided with more external
direction. Some evidence of similar processes, relating to different
dependent variables, was found with "personal-control orientation"
in the pilot study.

The other interaction in Table 9.9 relates children's compliant,
conforming orientation and commonality of class activities to perceived class disruptiveness. Relatively noncompliant children saw
the most disruptiveness in classrooms with the greatest commonality
of activities, while the moderately compliant children did so in
moderately varied classrooms; for children high in compliance,
there was no difference across levels of the class variable in perceived disruptiveness. It is possible that the relatively more compliant children feel less comfortable in classes with less commonality
of activity and, therefore, perceive more disruptiveness in these
classrooms. This explanation, however, is inconsistent with that
offered to account for the interaction involving compliant orientation,
class control, and perceived disruptiveness, shown in Table 9.8.

The two significant three-way interactions involving commonality versus variety of classroom activities, shown in Table 9.10,

TABLE 9.9

Means for Significant Two-Way Interactions between Child Factors (plus SES) and the Class Factor, "Commonality Versus Variety of Activities"

Dependent Variable	Child Variable	Levels	Levels of Class Var.			Between-Class-Level t-Values			$F_{(4, 94)}$
			Low	Med	High	L vs. M	L vs. H	M vs. H	
Creativity	Personal Control, Intrinsic Motivation	Low	-.18	-.09	-.04	NS	1.84*	NS	2.94†
		Med	.06	-.14	-.05	2.64‡	NS	NS	
		High	.07	.15	-.07	NS	1.70*	2.76‡	
Enjoyment of Class	Personal Control, Intrinsic Motivation	Low	-.09	-.14	-.15	NS	NS	NS	3.63‡
		Med	-.14	-.14	.18	NS	3.54‡	3.51‡	
		High	-.06	.23	.04	3.18‡	NS	2.07†	
Perceived Class Disruptiveness	Compliant Orientation	Low	-.04	-.12	.08	NS	1.72*	2.93‡	3.09†
		Med	-.02	.10	-.11	1.84*	NS	3.09‡	
		High	-.01	.02	.06	NS	NS	NS	

*p < .10.
†p < .05.
‡p < .01.
Source: Compiled by the authors.

FIGURE 9.4

Interaction Effect of Personal Control and Commonality of Activities on Creativity

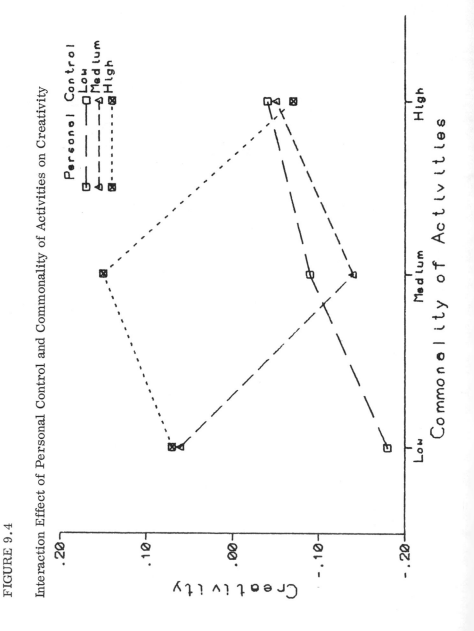

TABLE 9.10

Means for Significant Three-Way Interactions among Child Factors (plus SES), Sex, and the Class Factor, "Commonality Versus Variety of Activities"

Dependent Variable	Child Variable	Sex, Levels	Levels of Class Var.			Between-Class-Level t-Values			F (4, 94)
			Low	Med	High	L vs. M	L vs. H	M vs. H	
Value on Equality	Achievement Motivation	Boys							3.15†
		Low	-.12	-.04	-.21	NS	NS	3.02*	
		Med	-.23	-.06	-.04	3.17*	3.45*	NS	
		High	-.07	-.11	-.02	NS	NS	NS	
		Girls							
		Low	-.04	.03	.16	NS	3.76*	2.44†	
		Med	.38	.13	.03	4.70*	6.50*	1.80‡	
		High	-.01	.12	.13	2.40†	2.67*	NS	
Activity, Curiosity	Personal Control, Intrinsic Motivation	Boys							2.53†
		Low	.17	.07	-.05	NS	3.46*	1.95‡	
		Med	.23	.20	.17	NS	NS	NS	
		High	.28	.34	.33	NS	NS	NS	
		Girls							
		Low	-.34	-.48	-.08	2.29†	4.11*	6.40*	
		Med	-.02	-.22	-.22	3.17*	3.15*	NS	
		High	.26	-.09	-.16	5.50*	6.60*	NS	

*$p < .01$.
†$p < .05$.
‡$p < .10$.

Source: Compiled by the authors.

205

demonstrate different directions of relationship for the two sexes. The two child variables represented in these interactions are both measures of internal motivation, "achievement motivation" and "personal control, intrinsic motivation." For girls, the trend is for those with greater internal motivation to score higher on the outcome measures (value on equality and activity/curiosity) in the classrooms with more student-initiated, varied activities. (Girls with high achievement motivation, who gain most in value on equality in classrooms with more common activities, constitute an exception to this trend.) The trend is generally reversed for boys; it is primarily those with low (or moderate) motivation who score highest in the classrooms with more varied activities. It appears, at least with regard to these outcomes, that boys with low motivation are encouraged by situations in which they are allowed to explore and initiate their own tasks, while girls with low motivation are helped by more structured situations with common activities, and without the necessity of supplying their own directions.

Interactions with Individualized
Teacher-Student Contact

The two internal motivation factors are also involved in the two significant two-way interactions (influencing self-esteem and value on equality) presented in Table 9.11. Children high in achievement motivation gain the most in self-esteem in the least individualized classrooms (while their gains in the highly individualized classrooms were moderate); low achievement-motivated children showed the highest self-esteem in moderately individualized classrooms; and moderately achievement-motivated children scored highest in the most individualized classrooms. Although the trend is not really clear-cut, it shows some tendency for self-esteem scores to be higher with increasing levels of achievement motivation in classrooms with less individualized teacher-student interaction. Perhaps a greater degree of individualization is particularly enhancing for those starting with a low or moderate level of achievement motivation; the added interaction with the teacher may serve to build up their self-images.

With respect to value on equality, the shape of the interaction (obtained, in this instance, with child personal control) is somewhat different. Children in moderately individualized classrooms scored highest on this outcome measure if they were either high or low on personal control/intrinsic motivation, while those in nonindividualized classrooms scored highest if they were moderate with respect to personal control.

TABLE 9.11

Means for Significant Two-Way Interactions between Child Factors (plus SES) and the Class Factor, "Nonindividualized Versus Individualized Teacher-Student Interaction"

Dependent Variable	Child Variable	Levels	Levels of Class Var.			Between-Class-Level t-Values			F (4, 94)
			Low	Med	High	L vs. M	L vs. H	M vs. H	
Self-Esteem	Achievement Motivation	Low	-.59	-.04	-1.05	NS	NS	1.91*	3.97†
		Med	.84	-.10	-.88	1.77*	3.26†	NS	
		High	.37	-.54	1.30	1.71*	1.77*	3.48†	
Value on Equality	Personal Control, Intrinsic Motivation	Low	-.16	-.03	-.18	1.75*	NS	2.02‡	2.99‡
		Med	-.05	-.11	.16	NS	2.70†	3.49†	
		High	.04	.17	.07	1.71*	NS	NS	

*$p < .10$.
†$p < .01$.
‡$p < .05$.

Source: Compiled by the authors.

Achievement motivation and personal control/intrinsic motivation were also involved in the significant three-way interactions with individualized teacher-student interaction, influencing writing quality and self-confidence. These are shown in Table 9.12. The effect on writing quality is plotted in Figure 9.5.

For boys, the trend is for those with low motivation to do best in classes with greater individualization of teacher-student interaction, while those with higher levels of motivation do better in less individualized classrooms. This is similar to some effects discussed earlier; apparently, the individualized interaction provides an impetus to boys who are relatively lacking in a strong internal motive, while those with stronger motivation require less external encouragement and actually do better with less of it. While some evidence of this trend is also apparent with respect to girls' self-confidence (with the exception of those low in personal control, who show greatest self-confidence in the least individualized classrooms), it is not seen for girls in the writing-quality effect; their scores on this variable are generally highest in the most individualized classes for all levels of achievement motivation (although those with low motivation obtained high writing-quality scores in classrooms manifesting both high and low levels of individualization).

Interactions with Verbal (Academic) Participation

Seven significant two-way interactions were obtained with the classroom factor, "energetic encouragement of verbal (academic) participation." These are presented in Table 9.13. Three of these, relating to self-esteem, self-confidence, and value on self-direction, involved the children's socioeconomic status as the second independent variable. With self-esteem and self-confidence (partially overlapping variables, it should be remembered), the shapes of the interactions are quite similar—with no differentiation across class level for the low-SES children, highest scores in the least "energetically encouraging" classrooms for the moderate-SES children, and highest scores in conjunction with moderate or high levels of the class variable for children at the high-SES level. These interactions indicate that it is the high-SES children who are most benefited by a very energetic emphasis on student verbal (academic) participation. It may be that these children are more academically inclined; correlations shown in Table B.3 indicate that the high-SES children obtained higher scores on prior achievement test performance and on the prior measures of the other cognitive skills as well. Thus it seems possible that their self-esteem may be particularly buoyed in classes with an active, energetic, verbal-academic emphasis because they

TABLE 9.12

Means for Significant Three-Way Interactions among Child Factors (plus SES), Sex, and the Class Factor, "Nonindividualized Versus Individualized Teacher-Student Interaction"

Dependent Variable	Child Variable	Sex, Levels	Levels of Class Var.			Between-Class-Level t-Values			$F_{(4, 94)}$
			Low	Med	High	L vs. M	L vs. H	M vs. H	
Writing Quality	Achievement Motivation	Boys							2.50†
		Low	.13	.09	-.43	NS	5.80*	5.40*	
		Med	-.12	-.44	-.08	3.30*	NS	3.68*	
		High	-.31	-.18	-.37	NS	NS	1.94‡	
		Girls							
		Low	.31	-.14	.32	4.64*	NS	4.73*	
		Med	.73	.12	.12	6.24*	6.21*	NS	
		High	.48	.06	.17	4.24*	3.20*	NS	
Self-Confidence	Personal Control, Intrinsic Motivation	Boys							3.90*
		Low	.01	-.23	-.21	6.24*	5.82*	NS	
		Med	-.07	-.12	.04	NS	2.84*	4.03*	
		High	.05	.08	.10	NS	NS	NS	
		Girls							
		Low	-.22	-.01	.01	5.31*	5.99*	NS	
		Med	.15	.09	.03	NS	3.13*	NS	
		High	.08	.10	.15	NS	1.78‡	NS	

*$p < .01$.
†$p < .05$.
‡$p < .10$.

Source: Compiled by the authors.

FIGURE 9.5

Interaction Effect of Achievement Motivation, Sex, and Nonindividualized
Teacher-Student Interaction on Writing Quality

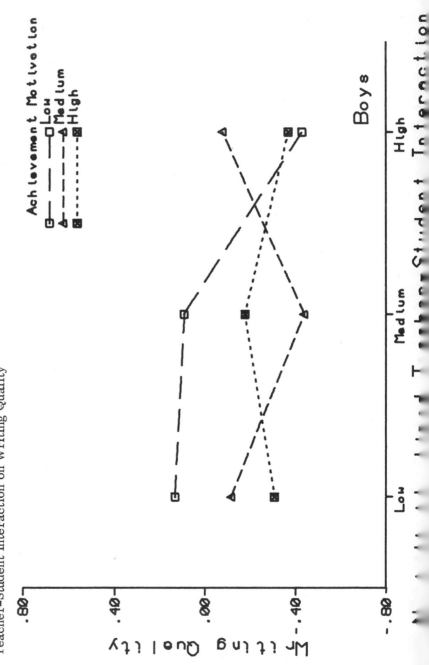

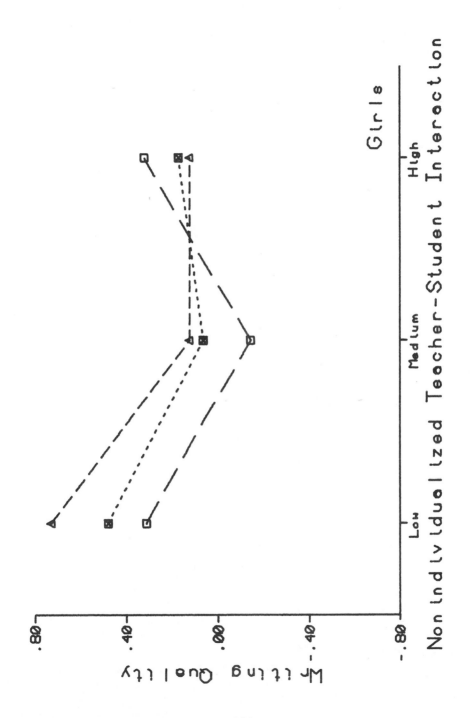

Girls

Nonindividualized Teacher-Student Interaction

Writing Quality

TABLE 9.13

Means for Significant Two-Way Interactions between Child Factors (plus SES) and the Class Factor, "Energetic Encouragement of Verbal (Academic) Participation"

| Dependent Variable | Child Variable | Levels | Levels of Class Var. | | | Between-Class-Level t-Values | | | $F_{(4, 94)}$ |
			Low	Med	High	L vs. M	L vs. H	M vs. H	
Creativity	Personal Control, Intrinsic Motivation	Low	-.02	-.16	-.13	1.85*	NS	NS	3.02†
		Med	.22	-.02	-.32	3.15‡	6.97‡	3.82‡	
		High	.28	-.02	-.12	3.91‡	5.17‡	NS	
Self-Esteem	SES	Low	-1.08	-.93	-.42	NS	NS	NS	3.53‡
		Med	1.01	-.49	-.60	2.91‡	3.12‡	NS	
		High	-.23	.82	1.17	2.03†	2.71‡	NS	
Self-Confidence	SES	Low	-.11	-.09	-.07	NS	NS	NS	2.78†
		Med	.08	.02	-.05	NS	2.48†	NS	
		High	-.03	.02	.12	NS	3.21‡	2.11†	

Value on Equality	Compliant Orientation	Low	.06	.18	.05	NS	NS	NS	2.68†
		Med	-.03	.02	-.08	NS	NS	NS	
		High	.09	-.18	-.20	3.56‡	3.87‡	NS	
Concern for Others	Personal Control, Intrinsic Motivation	Low	-.07	-.16	-.07	NS	NS	NS	2.80†
		Med	-.07	.11	-.10	2.81‡	NS	3.20‡	
		High	.19	.10	.16	NS	NS	NS	
Value on Self-Direction	SES	Low	.06	.01	.03	NS	NS	NS	2.66†
		Med	-.09	.05	-.04	2.52†	NS	1.75*	
		High	.08	-.07	.05	2.86‡	NS	2.26†	
Perseverance, Social Maturity	Preference for Class with Autonomy	Low	.07	.20	.29	NS	2.31†	NS	2.99†
		Med	.14	-.25	.02	3.98‡	NS	2.70‡	
		High	-.08	-.04	-.05	NS	NS	NS	

*p < .10.
†p < .05.
‡p < .01.
Source: Compiled by the authors.

perform well and receive rewards and praise in such classrooms. However, this trend did not occur for the other SES interaction shown in Table 9.13, that influencing value on self-direction.

Children's personal control/intrinsic motivation is involved in another two of the interactions: one relating to creativity, the other, to concern for others. With respect to creativity, children at all levels of personal control showed highest scores in the classrooms lowest on verbal (academic) emphasis (consistent with the main effect for this variable shown earlier). Within these classrooms, the scores increase with increasing levels of children's personal control, so that the highest score shown in this subtable is obtained by children who score high in personal control/intrinsic motivation, in classrooms which are least characterized by energetic encouragement of verbal (academic) participation. The "concern for others" residual scores are also highest in the same cell (but barely); it is only the children with moderate personal control scores, however, who show significant differentiation across the levels of the class variable. For them, scores on the dependent variable are highest in classrooms which are moderate with respect to encouragement of academic participation.

Children's compliant, conforming orientation and preference for classes with autonomy are the variables involved in the other two interactions represented in Table 9.13. For the former interaction—which relates to children's value on equality—the most compliant children demonstrated the highest equality value scores in classrooms in the lower third of the verbal participation distribution (the differentiation across levels of the class variable was not significant for children in the other two compliance groupings). For the interaction involving preference for class with autonomy, which relates to the teachers' ratings of perseverance/social maturity, there is a slight trend for children with higher levels of preference for autonomy to persevere more in classes with lower levels of encouragement of verbal (academic) participation. It is likely that a strong, teacher-imposed emphasis on verbal-academic participation precludes the provision of many opportunities for children to follow their own interests under their own direction, which is a primary aim of those with autonomous orientations. Thus, those lacking such an orientation respond well to a strong academic emphasis by persevering at the tasks set.

Significant three-way interactions involving the same classroom factor are presented in Table 9.14. Two of these, affecting creativity and inquiry skill, include children's personal control/ intrinsic motivation as an independent variable. The shape of the relationship with creativity is similar to that obtained in the two-way interaction relating the same child and classroom factors to creativity

TABLE 9.14

Means for Significant Three-Way Interactions among Child Factors (plus SES), Sex, and the Class Factor, "Energetic Encouragement of Verbal (Academic) Participation"

Dependent Variable	Child Variable	Sex, Levels	Levels of Class Var.			Between-Class-Level t-Values			F (4, 94)
			Low	Med	High	L vs. M	L vs. H	M. vs. H	
Creativity	Personal Control, Intrinsic Motivation	Boys							5.61*
		Low	.01	-.40	-.22	7.20*	4.01*	3.20*	
		Med	.04	-.06	-.33	1.71†	6.43*	4.72*	
		High	.09	.08	-.35	NS	7.59*	7.41*	
		Girls							
		Low	-.06	.08	-.04	2.32‡	NS	2.10‡	
		Med	.40	.01	-.30	6.59*	11.92*	5.34*	
		High	.46	-.12	.11	10.11*	6.03*	4.07*	
Creativity	Achievement Motivation	Boys							4.77*
		Low	.19	-.05	-.18	4.48*	7.00*	2.52‡	
		Med	.04	-.30	-.26	6.52*	5.67*	NS	
		High	-.01	.01	-.49	NS	9.27*	9.57*	
		Girls							
		Low	.25	-.11	-.06	7.04*	5.91*	NS	
		Med	.29	.18	-.12	2.14‡	7.71*	5.57*	
		High	.55	-.10	.07	12.55*	9.18*	3.38*	

(continued)

Table 9.14 (continued)

Dependent Variable	Child Variable	Sex, Levels	Levels of Class Var.			Between-Class-Level t-Values			F (4, 94)
			Low	Med	High	L vs. M	L vs. H	M vs. H	
Inquiry Skill	Personal Control, Intrinsic Motivation	Boys							
		Low	-.35	-.15	-.33	2.70*	NS	2.44‡	2.64‡
		Med	.11	-.27	.10	4.95*	NS	4.85*	
		High	.33	.05	.29	3.72*	NS	3.15*	
		Girls							
		Low	.02	-.24	.00	3.31*	NS	3.09*	
		Med	-.11	.07	.09	2.44‡	2.74*	NS	
		High	.08	.31	.18	3.03*	NS	1.72†	
Self-Esteem	Preference for Class with Autonomy	Boys							
		Low	.46	.29	-.29	NS	1.69†	NS	3.03‡
		Med	-.54	-1.97	1.17	3.18*	3.82*	7.01*	
		High	.83	-.14	.39	2.17‡	NS	NS	
		Girls							
		Low	-1.39	-.41	1.09	2.19‡	5.53*	3.34*	
		Med	.30	.22	-1.01	NS	2.92*	2.75*	
		High	.31	-.87	.23	2.63*	NS	2.45‡	
Enjoyment of Class	SES	Boys							
		Low	-.37	-.06	-.07	4.66*	4.60*	NS	2.74‡
		Med	-.07	-.50	.05	6.40*	1.85†	8.25*	
		High	-.27	-.23	.14	NS	6.12*	5.52*	

	Girls	Low	.21	−.06	.25	4.00*	NS	4.70*	2.57‡
		Med	.12	.10	.12	NS	NS	NS	
		High	.01	.08	.30	NS	4.27*	3.25*	
Perceived Class Disruptiveness	Boys	Low	−.13	−.10	.06	NS	4.42*	3.80*	
Preference for Class with Autonomy		Med	−.03	.06	−.02	1.94†	NS	1.88†	
		High	−.06	.10	−.14	3.73*	2.11†	5.84*	
	Girls	Low	−.08	.07	−.17	3.55*	2.22‡	5.76*	
		Med	.05	.01	−.07	NS	2.97*	1.96‡	
		High	−.10	.05	.00	3.47*	2.28‡	NS	
Perseverance, Social Maturity	Boys	Low	−.49	−.44	−.46	NS	NS	NS	2.63‡
SES		Med	−.06	−.34	.04	4.37*	NS	5.91*	
		High	.08	−.18	.10	3.95*	NS	4.28*	
	Girls	Low	−.19	.00	.16	2.98*	5.40*	2.43‡	
		Med	.20	.43	.01	3.45*	2.96*	6.41*	
		High	.41	.33	.53	NS	1.89†	3.13*	

*p < .01.
†p < .10.
‡p < .05.

Source: Compiled by the authors.

(shown in Table 9.13). Again, creativity is generally highest in the classrooms with the least verbal (academic) participation emphasis (with the exception of girls with low personal control, who were more creative in the moderate classrooms); within these classrooms, creativity scores are highest for the children with the highest levels of personal control/intrinsic motivation. The interaction which relates the same independent variables to inquiry skill presents a pattern which is rather difficult to interpret. Boys in the low personal-control group show greatest inquiry skill in classes with moderate verbal participation emphasis, while boys with moderate or high personal-control scores show the greatest inquiry skill in classes at the two extremes of the verbal participation distribution. For girls, on the other hand, the pattern is almost reversed; those with low personal control show the greatest inquiry skill in classrooms at the extremes of that variable, while those with moderate or high personal control do so in classrooms showing moderate or high levels of academic encouragement.

The three-way interaction in which children's achievement motivation (along with sex and classroom emphasis on verbal-academic participation) relates to creativity also shows a slight reversal between the patterns obtained for boys and for girls. While for both sexes creativity residual scores were generally highest in the classrooms with the least encouragement of verbal-academic participation (again, consistent with the previously discussed main effect), the creativity scores within the classrooms at this level were greatest for boys with low achievement motivation, but for girls with high achievement motivation. That this achievement-motivation factor represents a somewhat different characteristic for boys than it does for girls is indicated by the fact, shown in Table B.3, that the patterns of correlations with various other measures were generally different between the sexes. For girls, it was positively correlated with prior achievement, self-confidence, and enjoyment of class; for boys, it was not. Girls with high achievement motivation appear to have been more attuned to the norms, expectations, and activities of the classrooms than boys with high achievement motivation. Such girls may then have been particularly influenced toward creativity in classes with a low level of verbal, academic emphasis because they were responding to other emphases and expectations which may have characterized those classes. Boys with low achievement motivation may have been most responsive to such classes because they allowed them an acceptable, somewhat non-academic alternative direction for their classroom activities.

Children's preference for class with autonomy participates in two of the significant interactions shown in Table 9.14. The dependent variables affected in these interactions, self-esteem and perceived class disruptiveness, show approximately parallel results; cells in which self-esteem scores are high also tend to have low scores in perceived disruptiveness, and vice versa. This is particularly true for boys. The patterns in these interactions are also somewhat different between the sexes. Focusing on self-esteem, the trend for girls is to some degree consistent with a "matching" explanation, with those with less preference for autonomous classrooms showing higher scores in classrooms with more externally imposed emphases on verbal, academic participation (those which do not allow for much student autonomy). A similar explanation could account for results obtained for boys at the moderate and high levels of preference for autonomy, but high self-esteem scores obtained in the low and moderate classrooms by those with the lowest preference for autonomy might be more consistent with a "compensation" mechanism similar to those discussed earlier. While it is possible that different mechanisms may be involved in producing the results for children at different levels of a given independent variable, further speculation along these lines seems premature at this time.

The remaining two interactions portrayed in Table 9.14 both involve socioeconomic status as the child factor. For both of the dependent variables in these interactions, enjoyment of class and perseverance, the classrooms with the most energetic encouragement of verbal (academic) participation generally produced the highest scores; apparently, the combination of teacher energy and flamboyance with an emphasis on active verbal participation was in general enjoyable and stimulated children's striving behavior as well. Some exceptions to this generalization occurred (accounting for the interactions), but lead to no clear conclusions.

Interactions with Emphasis on Student
Expressiveness

The classroom factor, "emphasis on student expressiveness," participated in five two-way interactions, shown in Table 9.15, three of them involving children's achievement motivation. The dependent variables affected by these three interactions were achievement-test performance, value on equality, and concern for others. For the first two of these, the trend is for children with higher levels of achievement motivation to do best in classrooms with less emphasis on expressiveness; this is seen particularly clearly in the relationship with value on equality. With concern for others, children at the higher levels of achievement motivation were undifferentiated across levels of the classroom variable, but the low achievement-motivated children expressed most concern for others in the most

TABLE 9.15

Means for Significant Two-Way Interactions between Child Factors (plus SES) and the Class Factor, "Emphasis on Student Expressiveness"

Dependent Variable	Child Variable	Levels	Levels of Class Var.			Between-Class-Level t-Values			F (4, 94)
			Low	Med	High	L vs. M	L vs. H	M vs. H	
Achievement Test Performance	Achievement Motivation	Low	.00	.09	-.05	NS	NS	2.51*	2.87*
		Med	.10	-.04	-.03	2.56*	2.39*	NS	
		High	.07	-.10	.03	3.02†	NS	2.28*	
Value on Equality	Achievement Motivation	Low	-.15	-.07	.11	NS	3.24†	2.25*	2.49*
		Med	.04	.09	-.01	NS	NS	NS	
		High	.08	-.05	-.02	1.67‡	NS	NS	
Concern for Others	Achievement Motivation	Low	-.19	-.15	.10	NS	4.35†	3.76†	2.64*
		Med	.03	-.02	.02	NS	NS	NS	
		High	.12	.13	.11	NS	NS	NS	
Social Involvement	Preference for Class with Autonomy	Low	-.09	.10	-.17	2.29*	NS	3.23†	3.66†
		Med	-.02	-.10	.05	NS	NS	1.79‡	
		High	.08	-.14	.05	2.68†	NS	2.27*	
Perseverance, Social Maturity	Personal Control, Intrinsic Motivation	Low	-.36	-.43	.04	NS	3.88†	4.65†	2.64*
		Med	.07	-.17	.02	2.31*	NS	1.82‡	
		High	.34	.36	.39	NS	NS	NS	

*p < .05.
†p < .01.
‡p < .10.

Source: Compiled by the authors.

expressive classrooms. It may be suggested that an emphasis on student expressiveness helps provide children low in achievement motivation with some of the interest and involvement in classroom activities which their own internal resources do not provide; those having stronger achievement motivation may be somewhat distracted or put off by the provision of external encouragement which they do not require and, hence, perform better in classes with less of an emphasis on student expressiveness.

Children's social involvement was influenced by a significant interaction between preference for class with autonomy and the classroom emphasis on student expressiveness (also seen in Table 9.15). Children low in preference for autonomy were most socially involved in highly expressive classrooms, and those with high preference for autonomy were most socially involved in classrooms at the two extremes of expressiveness.

The last interaction shown in Table 9.15 indicates a joint effect of emphasis on student expressiveness and children's personal control/intrinsic motivation on perseverance and social maturity. Children with low personal-control scores persevere most in the most expressive classrooms perhaps, as suggested with regard to some other interactions involving this and other variables, because such classrooms provide these children with the impetus and motivation which they generally cannot provide from within themselves; children with moderate scores on the personal-control factor persevere most at the two extremes of classroom expressiveness, and those with high scores show no significant differentiation across levels of class expressiveness.

Table 9.16 presents the significant three-way interactions involving the same classroom factor ("emphasis on student expressiveness"), sex, and three different child variables, "personal control/intrinsic motivation," "preference for class with autonomy," and socioeconomic status. These interactions affected three outcome measures: "creativity," "value on equality," and "value on self-direction." The interaction effect on creativity is also shown in Figure 9.6. Although it had been expected that classrooms characterized by an emphasis on student expressiveness and exploration would generally promote creativity, the interaction shown here represents the only instance in which these two variables were involved in a significant relationship. The main effect (shown in Table 9.2) was not significant; however the emphasis on expressiveness did form an important part of classroom cluster five, which obtained the highest creativity scores, as seen in Table 8.6 and Figure 8.1. The interaction shown in the present table and figure indicates that the relationship between these variables was mediated by the children's personal control/intrinsic motivation and by sex. The effect

TABLE 9.16

Means for Significant Three-Way Interactions among Child Factors (plus SES), Sex, and the Class Factor, "Emphasis on Student Expressiveness"

Dependent Variable	Child Variable	Sex, Levels	Levels of Class Var.			Between-Class-Level t-Values			$F_{(4, 94)}$
			Low	Med	High	L vs. M	L vs. H	M vs. H	
Creativity	Personal Control, Intrinsic Motivation	Boys							
		Low	-.39	-.31	.09	NS	7.87*	6.60*	2.78†
		Med	-.06	-.30	.00	3.84*	NS	4.86*	
		High	-.04	-.06	-.09	NS	NS	NS	
		Girls							
		Low	.03	-.07	.01	NS	NS	NS	
		Med	.02	.02	.08	NS	NS	NS	
		High	.17	-.06	.34	3.72*	2.85*	6.57*	
Value on Equality	Preference for Class with Autonomy	Boys							
		Low	-.07	-.05	-.03	NS	NS	NS	2.54†
		Med	.02	-.10	-.10	2.14†	2.21†	NS	
		High	-.17	-.05	-.15	2.18†	NS	1.84‡	
		Girls							
		Low	.18	.00	.06	3.19*	2.18†	NS	
		Med	-.01	.21	.26	4.12*	5.07*	NS	
		High	.34	.07	.08	4.95*	4.69*	NS	

Value on Self-Direction	SES							
		Boys						3.89*
		Low	.00	.15	.04	3.86*	NS	2.85*
		Med	.00	.13	-.05	3.57*	NS	4.66*
		High	.02	-.07	.18	2.28†	4.31*	6.59*
		Girls						
		Low	-.05	.22	-.14	6.94*	2.22†	9.15*
		Med	-.15	-.11	.00	NS	3.90*	2.87*
		High	-.08	.12	-.04	5.34*	NS	4.27*

*$p < .01$.
†$p < .05$.
‡$p < .10$.
Source: Compiled by the authors.

FIGURE 9.6

Interaction Effect of Personal Control, Sex, and Expressiveness Emphasis on Creativity

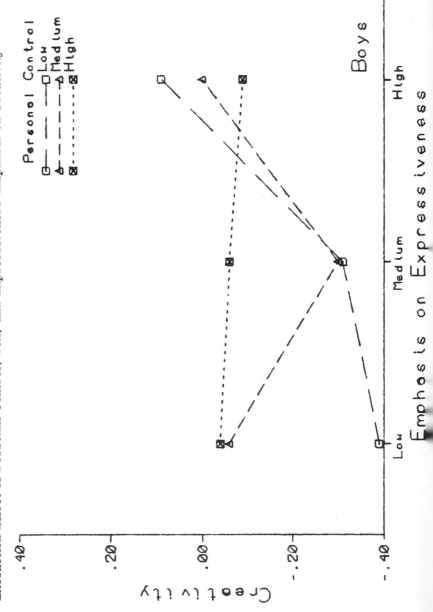

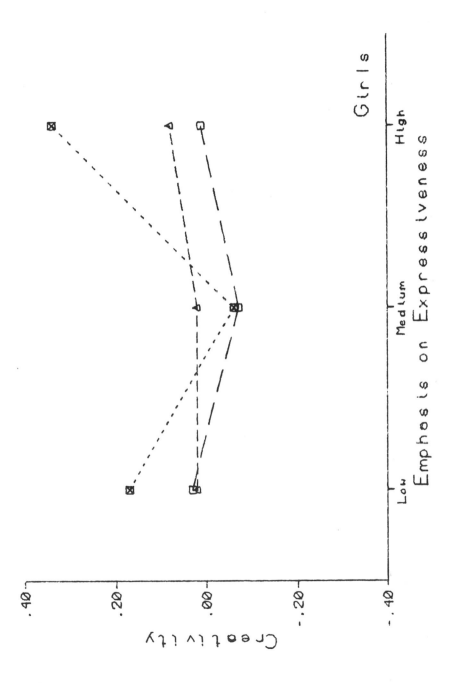

Girls

Emphasis on Expressiveness

Low   Medium   High

Creativity

.40
.20
.00
-.20
-.40

of classroom expressiveness was most pronounced for boys with low personal control (who were most creative in the most expressive classrooms), and for girls with high personal control (who were also most creative in the most expressive classrooms, but scored highly in the least expressive as well). The compensation mechanism proposed on several earlier occasions can again be suggested as a possible explanation of the results obtained for the low personal-control boys and for the high personal-control girls in the relatively unexpressive classrooms. In the former case, the classroom emphasis may provide encouragement and direction to children who are unable to provide these for themselves; in the latter case, some of the girls who do have such inner resources may use them to develop directions not emphasized in their classrooms. A different explanation is required for the high personal-control girls who scored very high on creativity in expressive classrooms; here an additive effect seems to be involved. The classroom atmosphere and their internal dispositions both would seem to impel them toward creativity, hence the highest scores for this combination. It is not clear, however, why the major effect of class expressiveness should occur for low-control boys and high-control girls.

In the next interaction shown in Table 9.16—relating class expressiveness, sex, and preference for autonomy to value on equality—the results for boys and girls are approximately the reverse of each other; cells which show high scores for girls show low scores for boys, and vice versa. The highest cell score for girls occurs for the combination of low class expressiveness and high autonomy preference; the parallel cell shows the lowest mean score for boys. It will be remembered that preference for classrooms with autonomy also involves a preference for situations which provide children the opportunity for personal expression. Thus, it was expected that children with higher scores on this preference would do better in the more expressive classrooms. For girls, there is a trend in this direction for the low and moderate preference groups but a reversal for the high-preference group (possibly again reflecting a compensation mechanism); for boys, the differences are slighter but, to the degree that a trend exists, it does show the expected direction between the moderate- and high-preference groups.

The last interaction shown in Table 9.16 reveals children's value on self-direction to be generally highest for the moderately expressive classes, except for the high-SES boys and the medium-SES girls, who score highest in the most expressive classes. With the exception of the high-SES girls, the trend generally shows high self-direction scores with increasing SES levels as the emphasis on student expressiveness also increases, perhaps indicating that higher-SES children (especially boys) feel more comfortable with a greater emphasis on student expression.

SUMMARY OF DIMENSION-BY-DIMENSION
INTERACTIONS

In this summary, the results just presented are organized by each child variable in sequence, and some of the general trends which appear to be involved are discussed.

Children's "preference for class with autonomy" was involved in interactions with three classroom variables; control/orderliness, energetic encouragement of verbal (academic) participation, and emphasis on student expressiveness. A compensation mechanism was suggested to account for the interactions with class control which affected self-esteem, self-direction, enjoyment of class, and (for boys) achievement-test performance. Children who stated that they preferred more structured situations scored higher on these variables in the less controlled, more permissive classrooms, while those preferring greater autonomy scored higher in the more controlled classrooms. It was suggested that the experience of a situation some- what opposed to their self-perceived inclinations may have been bene- ficial for these children perhaps because it required them to utilize modes of activity which they would otherwise avoid (disciplined order- liness for the autonomy-preferring children, self-direction, independ- ence, and so forth for the control-preferring children). With one other dependent variable, teacher-rated perseverance, there was some evidence of the reverse (or "matching") type of effect for girls; girls who preferred autonomy persevered best in the classes which most allowed for it presumably because they felt most comfortable in such classes.

The other trends involved in the interactions obtained with children's preference for classrooms with autonomy were somewhat less clear but were suggested to show some evidence of both the "compensation" mechanism (low autonomy-preference boys in the interaction with verbal-academic emphasis affecting self-esteem), and the "matching" mechanism (autonomy-preferring children per- severing somewhat more in classrooms with less imposed verbal- academic emphases, and structure-preferring girls showing greater self-esteem in classes with greater academic emphasis). Children's preference for autonomy also participated in two interactions with the classroom factor, "emphasis on student expressiveness." The first of these (relating to social involvement) was difficult to interpret, the second (relating to value on equality) generally showed a "match- ing" effect, where children with a greater autonomy preference (which also involves a preference for self-expression) scored highest in classes with greater emphasis on student expressiveness (with the exception of a reversal for the high-autonomy girls).

The student factor, "compliant, conforming orientation" appeared in interactions with four of the classroom factors, warmth, control, commonality, and emphasis on verbal (academic) participation. In the clearest of these, noncompliant children tended to be most creative, to persevere most, and to perceive least disruptiveness in the most controlled classrooms, again perhaps reflecting the "compensation" mechanism.

The two child factors which directly represented motivational dispositions, "personal control/intrinsic motivation" and "achievement motivation," were involved in the largest numbers of interactions with the classroom factors. In fact, each of them appeared in at least one significant interaction with each of the class dimensions. Boys scoring high on "personal control/intrinsic motivation" showed the greatest inquiry skill and value on self-direction in classes which were relatively warm and friendly, perhaps because these classes gave them more opportunity to explore their own intrinsic interests. Girls scoring high on personal control/intrinsic motivation persevered most in the least controlled, most permissive classrooms, presumably also because they were most free to explore their own interests and set their own directions in these classrooms.

With respect to class commonality of activities, a largely consistent set of interaction patterns, involving children's personal control, was obtained. In general, higher scores on the affected outcome measures (creativity, enjoyment of class, activity/curiosity) were obtained by children with increasing levels of personal control/ intrinsic motivation in classrooms with increasing levels of student-initiated, varied activities. Here again, a matching explanation seems to apply; children oriented toward following their own interests do best in classrooms in which they have the opportunity to initiate and carry out their own activities.

The interactions between children's personal control and individualization of teacher-student interaction were somewhat less clear; the most interpretable trend showed boys with low levels of personal control and intrinsic motivation to score highest on self-confidence in the most individualized classrooms (perhaps helping to supply them with an otherwise lacking impetus and involvement).

The same child variable was involved in three interactions with energetic encouragement of verbal (academic) participation, with effects on creativity, concern for others, and inquiry skill. The clearest effects were obtained with creativity; high personal-control children were most creative in classes with the least verbal (academic) emphasis. It may be suggested that in such classes, children with the inclination were freer to develop skills in directions not strictly academic.

At the same time, there was a trend for children scoring lowest on the personal-control factor to show the highest creativity and perseverance scores in classrooms which most strongly emphasized student expressiveness (with the exception of girls with creativity). A "compensation" mechanism was again invoked here, suggesting that the classroom emphasis provides students the impetus which they are unable to provide for themselves.

Children's "achievement motivation" participated in three interactions with classroom warmth, affecting creativity, enjoyment of class, and perceived class disruptiveness. Although creativity and enjoyment were generally greatest in the warmest and friendliest classrooms, this was especially pronounced for boys with low achievement motivation; here again, it was suggested that the warmth of the classroom atmosphere helped to provide these boys some of the motivation in which they were (relatively) lacking. A somewhat similar mechanism was used to account for the finding that children low in achievement motivation obtained their highest inquiry-skill and self-esteem scores in highly controlled and orderly classrooms (suggesting that the imposed direction and supervision in such classrooms were especially beneficial to children deficient in internal direction and motivation).

Interactions involving achievement motivation and individualization of teacher-student interaction indicated that self-esteem and writing quality (for boys) were generally highest for the relatively unmotivated children in the more individualized classrooms. Such children perhaps are in greatest need of the encouragement and instruction provided by more intense interaction with the teacher.

Creativity scores were generally highest in classes with low levels of encouragement of verbal (academic) participation; this was particularly true for low achievement-motivated boys and high achievement-motivated girls. Children's achievement motivation was also involved in three interactions with classroom emphasis on student expressiveness, affecting achievement-test performance, value on equality, and concern for others. One general trend showed the highly motivated children to score high in the classes with least emphasis on expressiveness (perhaps because they do not require the motivation and impetus of the more expressive classes) while the less motivated children did better in the more expressive classrooms (because they did require such external impetus).

A comparison of the results obtained in these analyses with the two motivation factors—achievement motivation and personal control/intrinsic motivation—with those obtained in the cluster by cluster analyses, is instructive. While the interactions involving achievement motivation were generally consistent with the proposed "compensation" mechanism, there was also some evidence of a "matching" mechanism with respect to its interactions with class control/orderliness. In addition, the results involving personal control/intrinsic motivation (and particularly those also involving

the variety of student-initiated activities as the classroom factor)
tended to be still more consistent with the "matching" mechanism.
In the analyses with clusters, where these two motivational variables
were contributing components, the results were interpreted as being
largely consistent with the "compensation" mechanism. This perhaps
indicates a value in including both these types of analysis. When
combined into clusters, a composite of dimensions can show results
which could not be predicted from knowledge of results with the
individual dimensions alone. If the analyses were limited to the
clusters, information about the effects of the individual factors would
be obscured or lost.

Socioeconomic status participated in interactions with three
classroom factors; warmth, encouragement of academic participation, and emphasis on student expressiveness. A general trend
involving classroom warmth, which occurs in two-way interactions
affecting value on equality and concern for others, and (for boys)
in three-way interactions affecting achievement test performance,
enjoyment of class, and self-esteem, is for high-SES children to
perform best in relatively "cold" classrooms and low-SES children
to do so in relatively "warm" ones. It was suggested that the low-
SES children may be helped to feel more comfortable and confident
in the warmer and friendlier classes, while high-SES children may
prefer a more businesslike approach. In the cases where the trend
did not occur for girls, they generally performed better in the warmer
classes at all SES levels.

SES was also involved in several interactions with energetic
encouragement of verbal (academic) participation; these related to
self-esteem, self-confidence, self-direction, enjoyment of class,
and perseverance. In almost every instance in these interactions,
high-SES children obtained high scores on the dependent variables
in the most academically oriented classrooms, while low-SES children were somewhat mixed across levels of the class variable. It
was suggested that high-SES children may be more academically
inclined and, therefore, perform well more consistently in classes
with a clear academic orientation. A single interaction obtained
between SES and emphasis on student expressiveness, influencing
self-direction, suggested that high-SES children (particularly boys)
may also feel most comfortable in the more expressive classes.
Analyses of interactions between these classroom factors and the
child clusters, and of interactions between the classroom clusters
and the child factors, are presented in Appendix A.

10 SUMMARY, CONCLUSIONS, AND IMPLICATIONS

GENERAL SUMMARY

The purpose of this research was, in general terms, to identify sets of child characteristics and of classroom characteristics which, in combination, would maximize learning by children. It was based on the assumptions that the effects of a particular educational program are mediated through the preferences, orientations, and needs of the children experiencing it, and that a program which is very effective for one child may be ineffective for another, depending on the relevance of the program to each child's particular needs and preferences. It was hoped that, if such sets of "matching" characteristics could be identified, applications could be made to suggestions for classroom assignments in instances where options were available. The possibility that some classroom characteristics or "types" might produce particularly pervasive effects, independent of variations in student attributes, was also explored.

Initially, a pilot study was conducted primarily to develop and try out instruments and procedures but also to make preliminary investigations of substantive issues. This pilot study (summarized in Chapter 3) was conducted in three "open" and three "traditional" classrooms. In the later, "main," study, a broad sampling of classrooms at the fourth grade level was obtained so that the important classroom characteristics and classroom "types" could be arrived at as a result of objective empirical observation rather than by prior designation.

Each of the 50 fourth grade classrooms (in 26 schools distributed throughout a county school system), was observed on eight separate one-hour occasions, spread over a school year, by eight different trained observers. The observers used a structured observation system to tally the occurrence of a large number of specific classroom activities, teacher behaviors, and student behaviors; they also made a set of global ratings, at the end of each visit, concerning the general classroom atmosphere and the quality of the teacher and student activities. Separate factor analyses were conducted with each section of the observation form (with scores for each item in each class summed across the eight observers who had visited the class). These factor analyses reduced a large number of items into a much smaller number of relatively stable underlying "dimensions." A questionnaire with which the teachers described their classroom organization and activities was also factor analyzed. There were eight classroom factor analyses in all, each rotated obliquely, producing a total of 33 factors. Factor scores from these factors were then used as input in a "second-order" factor analysis. This analysis produced six factors (rotated to orthogonal simple structure) which were considered to represent basic dimensions of classroom organization and activity. These factors were given the following names:

1. Warmth, friendliness, involvement, interest versus coldness, hostility, boredom.
2. Teacher control, structure, orderly task orientation versus permissiveness, spontaneity, lack of control.
3. Imposed, common, repetitive activities versus student-initiated (and -maintained), varied, simultaneous activities.
4. Nonindividualized versus individualized teacher-student interaction, teacher consultative role.
5. Energetic teacher promotion of student verbal (academic) participation.
6. Emphasis on student expressiveness, exploration, and creativity.

Next, the 50 classrooms were "cluster-analyzed" into groups with similar profiles in terms of their factor scores on these six factors. This was done so that classroom "types" could be identified, in addition to the individual classroom dimensions. Each "type" is defined by the average profile of all the classes which fell into a single cluster. Six clusters were produced in this way, ranging in size from six to ten classrooms. The following descriptions are based on the profile of mean factor scores for each cluster:

Cluster 1 classrooms were extremely permissive, lacked control and orderliness, had varied student-initiated activities, were moderately warm, and tended to have individualized interaction between teacher and student. Although they showed some of the characteristics which have been attributed to "open" classrooms, their extreme lack of control and order was beyond that recommended in the ideal open classroom (where control is shared between teacher and students).

Cluster 2 classrooms were highly controlled and orderly, but students also had relatively great opportunity to initiate their own, varied, activities. These classes were nonindividualized and tended to be relatively cold. Students tended to direct their own activities in them but in a structured and somewhat cold and impersonal setting.

Classrooms in cluster 3 tended to be cold and unfriendly and to have common (whole class) activities. They were also moderately permissive and moderately oriented toward both verbal-academic participation and student expressiveness.

Classrooms in cluster 4 tended to be warm and also fairly orderly and tightly controlled. They tended not to emphasize student expressiveness and creativity, and were moderate with regard to student initiation of activities, individualized interaction, and encouragement of verbal (academic) participation.

Cluster 5 classrooms were very warm and friendly, showed a strong emphasis on student expressiveness and a very low level of encouragement of verbal (academic) participation. They were moderate on control, student initiation of activities, and individualization of teacher-student interaction. This set of characteristics also seemed close, in several respects, to most descriptions of open classrooms.

Classrooms in cluster 6 tended clearly to encourage verbal (academic) participation, and to have individualized teacher-student interaction. They did not emphasize student expressiveness, tended to have common activities, and were moderate on both the control and warmth dimensions.

There were about 1300 fourth graders in these 50 classrooms. They were administered sets of parallel questionnaires at the beginning and end of the school year measuring creativity, inquiry skill, self-esteem, and several school-related attitudes and values. At the end of the school year they were also asked to evaluate their classes and their benefits from them. An achievement test was also administered at the end of the school year. Scores from another achievement test taken a year earlier (at the end of third grade) were obtained from school records. Questionnaires measuring various motives, preferences, and orientations were also administered in the fall. At the end of the school year, the teachers made ratings concerning the classroom behavior of each of the children in their classes.

Each of these sets of child measures was factor analyzed. The achievement-test subscores all contributed to a single factor, in both pre- and posttest analyses, as did the creativity measures and the inquiry measures. The value and attitude measures produced four factors in both the fall and spring administrations. These were called "self-confidence," "value on equality," "concern for others," and "value on task self-direction." The orientation and motive measures also produced four factors, called "preference for class with

autonomy and personal expression for students," "compliant, conforming orientation," "personal control, intrinsic motivation," and
"achievement motivation."

The next step was to derive clusters of children according to
similarity between them in the profiles of their individual characteristics. Eleven factors (plus one additional measure), representing
status at the beginning of the school year, comprised these profiles:
the four orientation and motive factors, the four attitude and value
factors (from the fall administration), the prior achievement-test
factor, the pretest inquiry and creativity factors, and a measure of
writing quality (rated from the responses to the pretest inquiry skill
items). This cluster analysis produced three clusters of children
with distinctly different profile component means: Members of cluster
1 were low prior achievers who were not intrinsically motivated, not
oriented toward others, lacked self-confidence, scored high on "compliant, conforming orientation," and moderately on "achievement
motivation" and "self-direction." Children in cluster 2 tended to be
highly motivated, self-confident prior achievers. They also scored
low on self-direction and preference for autonomy and were moderately compliant. Cluster 3 members stated strong preferences for
autonomy, personal expression, and self-direction. They scored
quite low on "compliant orientation." Their prior achievement and
motivation scores were moderate, except for "achievement motivation" which was low.

Analysis of variance was the primary method of data analysis
used to ascertain significant effects of the various measured classroom characteristics and classroom types, of the child characteristics and types, and of the interactions between the two. (Sex of
child was also included as a third independent variable in these analyses.) Because it seemed most appropriate for the classroom to be
the unit of analysis, a mean score was derived, within each classroom, for each sex by child-cluster cell, for each dependent variable.
Repeated-measures analyses of variance were then run, with classroom cluster as a nonrepeated independent variable, and child cluster
and sex as repeated independent variables (within classrooms).

There were fourteen outcome measures which served as dependent variables in these analyses. For those which had parallel pre-
and postscores, the outcome measure used was the posttest score
adjusted for between-child differences in the pretest score (using
"residual gains" as calculated by a regression analysis). These
included the measures of achievement, creativity, inquiry skill, and
writing quality, the four attitude and value factors, and a measure
of self-esteem (included separately because of its general interest,
although it also contributed—but fairly weakly—to the "self-confidence"
factor). Two factors derived from the teachers' ratings of the stu-

dents (called "perseverance, social maturity" and "activity/curiosity") and three factors derived from the students' class and self-evaluations (called "enjoyment of class," "social involvement," and "perceived disruptiveness in class") were also included as outcome measures in the analyses of variance.

The use of child and classroom clusters to investigate child-classroom interactions represented something of a methodological departure from most previous related work. It was expected that there could be great advantages in employing a cluster-analytic approach for this purpose because it allows one to compare the effects and combinations of naturally occurring types in their multivariate complexity; this seemed an advantage over looking at the effects of abstracted individual dimensions alone, particularly if practical applications of the results were envisaged. Since measures of the individual dimensions (for both children and classrooms), as well as cluster (or "type") designations, were available it was decided to do the analyses both ways—to investigate both the child cluster by classroom cluster interactions and the child dimension by classroom dimension interactions. (The other combinations—child cluster by classroom dimension and child dimension by classroom cluster— were also investigated; these analyses are presented in Appendix A.) It was anticipated that this might give some notion of the relative utility of the two approaches. Furthermore, it was thought that the comparison of the results obtained by the two methods would lead to a more complete understanding of the data than might be achieved by the limitation to one or the other method alone.

Many of these analyses of variance were carried out. Some main effects were also investigated with other analyses: correlation analyses for the individual child-dimension effects and multiple regression analysis for the class-dimension effects. In general, the characteristics with which the child entered the class showed the strongest overall effects on the outcome measures (the contents of these effects are not summarized here as this was not a major concern of this research). Some of the classroom characteristics showed quite strong effects on outcomes while, for others, the effects were negligible. The classroom characteristic by child characteristic interactions showed a variety of effects, mostly moderate, involving various combinations of independent variables and various outcome measures.

Main Effects

Three of the six classroom dimensions showed significant linear main effects on outcome measures which held for both sexes of children. Classroom control/orderliness showed the most intense of these. It strongly and significantly influenced children's achievement-test performance and writing quality (in both instances children obtained higher scores in the more controlled and orderly classrooms). Similar positive relationships with control, slightly less strong, were also found for creativity, inquiry skill, and value on equality; while a negative relationship with value on self-direction was found. In addition, children's creativity was negatively influenced by the energetic encouragement of verbal (academic) participation, and inquiry skill was enhanced by class commonality of activity.

The classroom clusters (or "types") significantly influenced three of the outcome measures: achievement-test performance, perceived class disruptiveness, and activity/curiosity. Class clusters 2 and 4 (both characterized by high levels for control/orderliness) produced the highest achievement-test scores consistent with the effect obtained with the control dimension analyzed separately. Children in class cluster 3, containing classes which were both cold and relatively uncontrolled, perceived the greatest degree of disruptiveness, while those in clusters 1 (permissive and varied) and 5 (warm and expressive) evidenced the highest levels of activity/curiosity. In addition, a borderline effect upon creativity was obtained, with highest scores in warm and expressive classrooms which deemphasized verbal-academic participation (cluster 5).

Cluster-by-Cluster Interactions

A vast number of specific interaction effects were obtained in the various analyses of variance. In this summary, the major trends which emerged from all these analyses are sketched out. A summary of cluster-by-cluster interaction effects is presented in Table 10.1. Figure 10.1 is derived from this table and shows the number of dependent variables participating in significant interactions which obtained their highest scores (for given child clusters) in each of the child cluster by classroom cluster cells. (Variables which appeared in two-way interactions are arbitrarily given double weight in this figure.) Cluster 1 children, relatively unmotivated, and with low levels of prior achievement and cognitive skill, tended to do their best in permissive and varied classrooms (cluster 1) and in those which combined warmth with an emphasis on expressiveness (cluster 5). It was suggested that such classes may have helped to provide (or develop) motivation which was initially lacking in these children. Cluster 2 children on the other hand—those characterized by high initial levels of motivation and cognitive skill—achieved their best performance in class clusters 2 and 4, both characterized by

TABLE 10.1

Summary of Significant Cluster-by-Cluster Interaction Effects, Showing
Outcome Measures which Obtained Highest Scores for Different Combinations

	Child Clusters								
	1 (Low prior ach. and cog. skills, low pers. cont./ intrin. motiv., high comp.)			2 (High prior ach. and cog. skills, high motiv., low self-dir. and aut., moderate comp.)			(High aut., self-dir., and val. on equal., moderate ach., cog. skills, and pers. cont., low ach. motiv.)		
Classroom Clusters	Boys	Girls	Total	Boys	Girls	Total	Boys	Girls	Total
1 (Permiss-var.)		Conc. for oth.	Activ./ cur., Creat.		Persever.		Self-conf., conc. for oth.	Conc. for oth.	Activ./ cur.
2 (Cont., cold, S-init. of var. activs., nonindivid.)				Self-est., self-conf., Val. on equal. Conc. for oth., Persever.	Conc. for oth.		Self-est.	Self-conf.	Creat.

(continued)

237

Table 10.1 (continued)

	Child Clusters								
Classroom Clusters	1 (Low prior ach. and cog. skills, low pers. cont./intrin. motiv., high comp.)			2 (High prior ach. and cog. skills, high motiv., low self-dir. and aut., moderate comp.)			(High aut., self-dir., and val. on equal., moderate ach., cog. skills, and pers. cont., low ach. motiv.)		
	Boys	Girls	Total	Boys	Girls	Total	Boys	Girls	Total
3 (Cold, com. activs., moderate permiss.)	Val. on equal.	Self-conf.					Self-est., Self-conf.	Val. on equal., Conc. for oth.	
4 (Warm, cont.)	Self-est., Self-conf.	Perse-ver.		Val. on equal., Conc. for oth., Perse-ver.	Self-est., Self-conf., Conc. for oth., Perse-ver.	Creat.	Perse-ver.	Conc. for oth., Perse-ver., Val. on equal.	Creat.

238

5 (Warm, express., low emph. on partic., moderate cont.)	Val. on equal., Conc. for oth., Perse-ver.	Self-est., Val. on equal.	Creat.	Self-est., Self-conf.	Val. on equal., Perse-ver.	Activ./cur., Creat.	Conc. for oth.	Self-est., Perse-ver.
6 (Energ., verbal-acad., individ.)		Self-est., Self-conf.		Perse-ver.	Self-conf., Val. on equal.		Val. on equal., Conc. for oth.	

Note: The "total" columns in this table reflect the results of significant two-way interactions, the "Boys" and "Girls" columns, three-way interactions. The entries in each cell are those dependent variables which obtained their highest scores for a given child cluster in that classroom cluster. Thus, cluster 1 children scored highest in "activity/curiosity" in class cluster 1, and in "creativity" in both class clusters 1 and 5.

Source: Compiled by the authors.

239

FIGURE 10.1

Cluster–Cluster Interaction Cells Showing High Scores on Outcome Measures

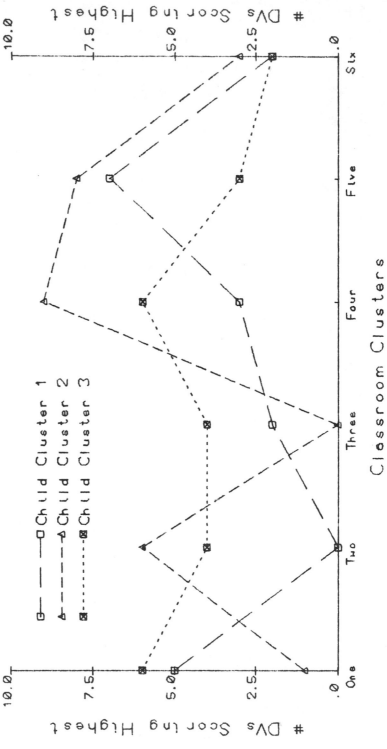

high scores on the "control/orderliness" dimension, and moderate to high scores on "student initiation of varied activities." Here the suggestion was that such children did not require extra spurs to their motivation but were benefited by an environment which allowed them to progress with the mastery of relatively advanced academic skills in an orderly way and in a context which also allowed them a degree of self-direction. (They also did relatively well in class cluster 5, the warm and expressive type of setting, particularly with respect to activity and creativity.) The cluster 3 children, who were non-compliant, valued self-direction, and preferred situations allowing for student autonomy and self-expression, showed varied results among which was the finding that their activity and curiosity were maximized in the most permissive classrooms (cluster 1), while their creativity was maximized in relatively controlled and orderly classrooms (clusters 2 and 4). It seemed possible that their general activity level could be most promoted in situations which allowed them to express their inclinations, but that for the development of a specific cognitive skill, such as creativity, it was necessary to temper these inclinations by providing a relatively structured and orderly framework.

Dimension-by-Dimension Interactions

The interactions produced by the analyses involving child and classroom dimensions are summarized in Table 10.2 and Figure 10.2. This figure shows the number of clear positive trends (in the upper part of the figure) and negative trends (in the lower part) in the significant interactions between the various pairings of child and classroom factors. Trends from two-way interactions are again given double weight. Effects on "perceived disruptiveness" are omitted because there is some doubt as to how best to interpret this variable in this context. These interactions showed trends which, in a number of respects, paralleled those obtained with the analyses involving clusters. The clearest and most numerous set of interactions obtained with children's preferences for classrooms allowing autonomy involved this variable with classroom control and orderliness. These interactions—which related to self-esteem, self-direction, enjoyment of class, and achievement-test performance—generally showed autonomy-preferring children scoring highest in the more controlled and orderly classrooms and structure-preferring children scoring highest in the more permissive classrooms. It was suggested that children apparently benefited from being required to experience modes of activity which their own inclinations would lead them to avoid (at least with respect to these dimensions) and that

TABLE 10.2

Summary of Significant Dimension-by-Dimension Interaction Effects,
Indicating Relationship Directions Obtained with Different Outcomes

Classroom Dimensions	Child Dimensions														
	Preference for Class with Autonomy			Compliant, Conforming Orientation			Personal Control/ Intrinsic Motiv.			Achievement Motivation			Socioeconomic Status		
	Boys	Girls	Total	Boys	Girls	Total	Boys	Girls	Total	Boys	Girls	Total	Boys	Girls	Total
Warmth vs. Cold.				Val. on equal. (m)	Val. on equal. (low)	Soc. involv. (m)	Inquiry (m), Self-dir. (m)	Inquiry (m), Self-dir. (m)		Creat. (-), Enjoy. class (m), Perc. disrupt. (-)	Creat. (high), Enjoy. class (-), Perc. disrupt. (m)		Ach. test (-), Enjoy. class (-), Self-est. (-)	Ach. test (m), Enjoy. class (m), Self-est. (med)	Val. on equal. (-), Conc. for oth. (-)
Cont., Order. vs. Lack of Cont., Permiss.	Ach. test (+) Self-dir. (m) Per-sev. (high)	Ach. test (high), Self-dir. (+), Per-sev. (-)	Self-est. (+), Self-dir. (+), Enjoy. class (+)	Perc. disrupt. (+)	Perc. disrupt. (m)	Creat. (high), Per-sever. (-)	Per-sever. (high)	Per-sever. (-)		Inquiry (high), Self-est. (-)	Inquiry (-), Self-est. (-)				
Com. vs. Var., S-Init. Activs.						Perc. disrupt. (-)	Activ/cur. (low)	Activ/cur. (-)	Creat. (-), Enjoy. class (-)	Val. on equal. (+)	Val. on equal. (m)				

Independent variable												
Nonindivid. vs. Individ. T-S. Interac.				Val. on equal. (m)	Self-conf. (+)	Self-conf. (m)	Val. on equal. (m)	Writ. qual. (m)	Writ. qual. (m, low)			Self-est. (m, +)
Encour. Verbal (Acad.) Partic.	Self-est. (m), Perc. disrupt. (-)	Self-est. (m), Perc. disrupt. (+)	Per-sev. (m)		Creat. (low), Inq. (m)	Creat. (-), Inq. (m)	Creat. (low), Conc. for oth. (m)	Creat. (low)	Creat. (low)	Enjoy. class (high), Per-sev. (m)	Enjoy. class (m), Per-sev. (m)	Self-est. (m, +), Self-conf. (+), Self-dir. (m)
Emph. on S. Express.	Val. on equal. (+)	Val. on equal. (m)	Soc. involv. (m)		Creat. (m)	Per-sev. (m)	Ach. test (m), Val. on equal. (-), Conc. for oth. (m)			Self-dir. (+)	Self-dir. (m)	

Note: The cell entries in this table are the dependent variables influenced by interactions, and descriptions of the effects embodied in those interactions. The symbols in parentheses indicate the direction of effects: "(+)" indicates a generally positive trend, so that high outcome scores occur when high levels of the child variable are combined with high levels of the class variable, and vice versa; "(-)" indicates a negative trend, so that high outcome scores occur when high levels of the class variable are combined with low levels of the child variable, etc.; "(m)" refers to a mixed or varied trend; "(high)," "(med)," and "(low)" refer to levels of the class variable which produce highest scores at all levels of the child variable.

Note: The "total" columns in this table reflect the results of significant two-way interactions; the "Boys" and "Girls" columns, three-way interactions.

Source: Compiled by the authors.

243

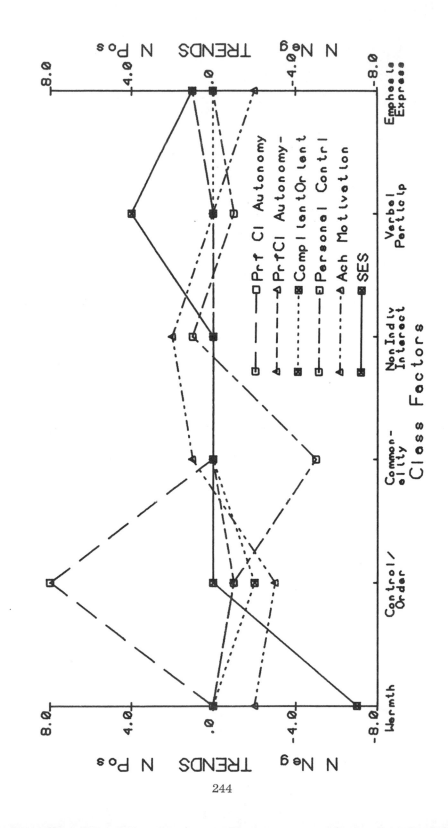

children strongly inclined toward autonomy and freedom perhaps needed to have this inclination tempered somewhat by a relatively structured and orderly setting, while those preferring structure would obtain a parallel advantage through experiencing autonomy, freedom, and variety. These findings, of course, were similar to some of those obtained for the cluster 3 children in the cluster-by-cluster interactions.

The clearest set of findings obtained with the child factor "compliant, conforming orientation" also was comparable to the results with cluster 3 (which, it will be recalled, included both preferences for autonomy and noncompliance as major components). In these interactions, the least compliant children performed best with respect to several measures (including creativity and perseverance) in the most controlled and orderly classes, perhaps again, it was suggested, showing that a noncongruent environment can be valuable to temper one-sided inclinations.

Children characterized by a high degree of personal control/ intrinsic motivation did best with respect to several outcomes (creativity, enjoyment of class, activity/curiosity) in classes in which they were given the opportunity to initiate their own varied activities, while children who were relatively low on this motivational factor did better in classes characterized by more common teacher-directed activities; in these instances, children seemed to benefit from the opportunities to follow their own inclinations.

Several findings suggested that poorly motivated children are helped by supportive, stimulating, and encouraging classroom atmospheres. Children low in achievement motivation (1) were most creative in, and enjoyed most, the warmest and friendliest classrooms, (2) scored highest in self-esteem and writing quality in classrooms with relatively high levels of individualized teacher-student interaction, and (3) scored highly on value on equality and concern for others in classes which strongly emphasized student expressiveness and exploration. In some of these interactions (particularly those involving emphasis on student expressiveness), the highly motivated children did best with classes at the other pole of the dimension presumably because they did not require the added external impetus. There was also a trend showing children with low achievement-motivation scores doing best (with respect to inquiry skill and self-esteem) in the most controlled classrooms, while those at the highest motivation levels did well with less controlling classrooms.

Children's socioeconomic status (based on the family bread-winner's occupation) also served as an independent variable in some of these analyses. It showed numerous significant interactions with two of the classroom dimensions. Low-SES children generally did best, with respect to a number of outcome measures, in the "warm-est" classrooms, while high–SES children (particularly boys) did so in relatively "cold" classrooms. The explanation for these findings was that the low–SES children, who were also somewhat less motivated and less skilled academically, may have felt more comfortable, and been more stimulated and involved, in the warmer classes, while the high–SES boys, already highly motivated and more skilled, may have preferred a more businesslike approach. The other classroom factor which interacted with SES was "energetic encouragement of verbal (academic) participation." High–SES children obtained high self-esteem, self-confidence, class enjoyment, and perseverance scores in the most academically oriented classrooms (perhaps be-cause such children tended to be relatively academically inclined), while the low–SES children showed some variation in results with respect to this class variable.

GENERAL CONCLUSIONS

Interactions

Salomon (1972) has provided a useful framework for research and theory concerning "aptitude-treatment interactions." He describes three basic "heuristic models" called "remedial," "compensatory," and "preferential." The "remedial" model predicts optimal results when an educational program focuses on teaching an individual pre-requisite skills in which he is deficient; the "compensatory" model focuses on treatments which bypass the student's deficiencies either by supplying external substitutes for them or by circumventing the need for them altogether through changing the situation so that the lacking skills will not be required; the "preferential" model attempts to "match" the student's skills and motives to provide a setting which capitalizes on his strengths and inclinations.

Although the initial expectations for this research were most consistent with the "preferential" model, and both the results of the pilot study and many of those in the present study have been generally in line with such an approach, numerous of the present study's find-ings also appear to be compatible with the "remedial" or "compensa-tory" models; many of the explanations which have been offered have, in fact, been framed in terms similar to these.

Thus, it has been suggested that children of low SES, or those who are low on prior achievement, cognitive skills, or achievement-related motivation tended in many instances to perform best in classes which were warm and/or expressive because they were either being supplied with an external motivation to substitute for that which they lacked (a compensatory explanation) or were actually helped to improve their motivation and hence their performance in these classes (a remedial explanation). (The data was not available to determine which of these two related explanations obtained. If motivational measures had been collected at a second point—near the end of the school year—rather than only at the beginning, more specific evidence on this point would have been available.)

A compensatory explanation was also provided to account for many of the findings obtained for the children in the autonomous, self-directing, noncompliant cluster and for those at both poles of the preference-for-autonomy dimension. Particularly with respect to cognitive measures, children with the strongest expressed preferences for autonomy and self-expression, performed best in the more controlled and orderly classrooms, while those whose stated preference was for more structure showed greater gains in classrooms which allowed more student autonomy and self-direction. The general explanation offered was that children at each extreme benefited from a setting which required them to experience a mode of activity which they might otherwise avoid, thus providing them with something which they lacked (greater discipline in their approach to tasks for the autonomous/expressive children; greater experience with choice, freedom, and self-direction for those more oriented toward external control and structure). Another set of findings which demonstrated that the activity level and curiosity of the autonomy-preferring children were highest in permissive classrooms, was explained with a matching, or "preferential," model. Thus, it was suggested, their activity was apparently stimulated in the setting which they preferred, but their cognitive development was best served by that which they needed.

Results for the achieving, well-motivated children of cluster 2, showing that they generally performed best in the most controlled and orderly classrooms (or in clusters containing this control dimension as a common element) were accounted for, in part, with a matching or preferential explanation—that is, that the structure and discipline of these classes helped them to progress from an already high level of proficiency by providing the orderly framework which they needed for this task.

In a few instances, the same child factors appeared to be involved in "compensatory" relationships when combined with other factors into clusters, but in "preferential" relationships when considered individually. Thus, the two motivational factors—achievement motivation and personal control/intrinsic motivation—both contributed high mean scores (along with prior achievement and cognitive skills) to the profile of cluster 2, the cluster which showed generally good performance in controlled and orderly classrooms. When considered separately, each of these motivational characteristics showed some tendency to interact negatively with class control; that is, children scoring high on these variables tended to perform best in moderate or low-control classes. Thus, the composite represented by the cluster produces effects which in some cases could not be predicted from knowledge of the effects of its individual components. In applications to particular cases, this suggests the necessity of considering both types of results; especially in instances where a child's profile does not clearly resemble one of the three "types" identified in this research, it would then be possible to make predictions and recommendations based on the results for the individual dimensions.

The major trends which emerged from the results of the present study were only partially in agreement with those obtained in the pilot study. The main effects were generally similar between the studies, while the interactions were partially similar and partially dissimilar. The differences are difficult to account for specifically, but it should be noted that the pilot study was conducted primarily to develop instruments and procedures, included only six classrooms (compared to 50 in the present study), and did not include pretest measures of the various outcome variables—with the exception of achievement test performance—while the present study included pre- and posttest measures of most of the outcome variables. Thus, although more complete agreement between the two studies would increase the confidence in the reliability and stability of the findings and explanations, it is apparent that, where there are differences, the results of the later study are more likely to be valid and replicable.

Additional support for the validity of some of these findings is provided by comparing them with those reported in other recent studies. In a study by Ward and Barcher (1975), carefully matched groups of children were compared between "open" and "traditional" classroom settings. High-IQ children scored higher on measures of reading and creativity in traditional than in open classrooms. Low-IQ children were not significantly differentiated between settings, but the trend was for their scores to be higher in the open classrooms. If we assume that low- and high-IQ children are represented, respectively, in the present child clusters 1 and 2 and that classroom "openness" is most closely represented by the "control/orderliness versus permissiveness/child autonomy" classroom dimension, the Ward and Barcher results are clearly similar to those obtained in the present study, including, but not limited to, those involving the same dependent variables. (Similar results for reading achievement are shown in Appendix A.) Their explanation of the reading results for the high-IQ children is similar to one which has been offered on several occasions to account for results obtained for the cluster 2 children:

> The structure of the traditional approach could well
> include mastery of the proper sequences of skills in
> reading which are necessary to help bright children
> progress, while the open class's tendency to concen-
> trate upon the enjoyment and usefulness of reading
> may not take the bright child to his optimum level
> (: 690).

Some of Bennett's results, showing low-achieving boys to perform
best in "informal" classrooms, while high-achieving boys (and all
girls) did best in more "formal" ones, are also at least partially
consistent with these findings (1976).

Cantrell et al. (1977), in other results similar to those in the
present study, found that low- and middle-IQ students achieved more
with positive, supportive, and praising teachers than with "authoritarian" ones, while the reverse was true (but less clearly) for
high-IQ students. Stallings and Kaskowitz (1974) also found praise
particularly effective (for math achievement) with low-ability students.
Teacher praise, support, and patience were found to be beneficial
for low-SES students by Brophy and Evertson (1976), who considered
low SES to correspond, generally, with relatively great anxiety and
poor motivation in the classroom situation. St. John (1971) also
found warm and supportive teachers most effective with disadvantaged
black students.

Some of the prior research, however, has also obtained findings
which seem somewhat inconsistent with one major trend of the present
interactional results. That is, the present evidence—particularly
with the findings relating to the clusters—indicates that well-motivated,
high-achieving students did well in relatively structured classrooms,
and poorly motivated, low-achieving students benefited from classrooms with more student autonomy and less of an academic emphasis;
but other research, cited in Chapter 2, has shown "direct instruction"
to be particularly effective for poorly motivated and disadvantaged
students.

It is possible that this discrepancy is due to a difference in the
ages of the students investigated. The studies which found direct
instruction related to academic gains of disadvantaged students (e.g.,
Brophy and Evertson 1976, Stallings and Kaskowitz 1974, Abt Associates 1977) were generally limited to students in the lower elementary
grades, while this study focused on fourth graders. Differences between the studies may reflect a higher-level interaction between
student age, student motivation and ability, the nature of the learning
task (less complex and abstract at the lower grades), and the kinds
of teacher behavior and classroom atmosphere which are motivating
and stimulating to students of different ages and entering characteristics.

When we consider the results obtained for the separate student dimensions in the present study, however, some of these apparent discrepancies are reduced. There is some evidence (shown in Appendix A) that low-achieving boys benefit from classes at <u>both</u> ends of the permissiveness-control dimension, while both low- and high-achieving girls do well in controlled and orderly classrooms. Further, while there was little evidence of clear interactive trends between student SES and classroom control/orderliness (the dimension closest to "direct instruction"), some evidence indicated that students with relatively strong internal motivation performed well in classes which allowed them a measure of autonomy and self-direction, while those with weak internal motivation benefited from more structured and controlled situations. If Brophy and Evertson were correct in assuming a correspondence between SES and motivation, these results would be consistent with the implications of their findings with regard to SES (even though SES itself did not appear in such an interaction in the present research). The interactions obtained with the present motivational variables are also consistent with previous ATI research, summarized by Cronbach and Snow (1977), which indicates that individuals high in "constructive motivation" perform best in settings which allow them to be active, spontaneous, and self-directing.

In addition to these achievement-related motives, it may be suggested that additional motives, relating to students' needs for comfort, security, support, and reassurance, were also operating in these classroom settings. It is assumed that there are often emotional concomitants of low academic skill and motivation and disadvantaged socioeconomic status. Consistent with the observations of Brophy and Evertson (1976) regarding SES differences, it may be suggested that students with the above characteristics may feel uncertain and uncomfortable in competitive classroom situations. These feelings represent hindrances to the students' ability to perform competently on academic tasks and therefore, it seems, must be remedied in some way before their performance can improve. At several points, this study has provided indirect and suggestive evidence that warm, supportive, expressive, and varied classroom settings may help to remedy some of these motivational-emotional deficiencies.

A hierarchical ordering of needs to be met (or compensated for) by the classroom setting is implicitly proposed here. For those with low levels of skill, motivation, or performance, a motivational impetus (to provide support and encouragement) may be the most important need. Before their cognitive skills can advance, they may require encouragement to explore and come to feel comfortable with a particular academic area, or with classroom activities in general. For those who are already well-motivated and proficient, additionally reassuring circumstances may not be required; in fact, in some instances they apparently impede performance. What these students require are more orderly and disciplined approaches to tasks to help them to advance in their academic skills. A setting which gives them some opportunity for initiating and directing their own tasks, within this disciplined framework, also appears to be beneficial for this group of children.

Main Effects of Classroom Variables

Although this research was begun with a strong commitment to an interactive approach (a commitment which has not been abandoned), and several interesting interactive trends have emerged, it must be admitted that some of the strongest and clearest findings occurred with classroom characteristics main effects—both with the clusters and with the individual classroom dimensions. The classroom dimension, "teacher control, structure, orderly task orientation versus permissiveness, spontaneity, lack of control" showed several strong and positive effects on outcomes, particularly cognitive-academic ones. As mentioned earlier, this set of findings is quite consistent with those reported in a number of the studies discussed in Chapter 2, including the large-scale naturalistic studies of Brophy and Evertson, McDonald, Stallings and Kaskowitz, Soar and Soar, the "Follow Through" evaluation report by Abt Associates, the ESAA evaluation, and some of the more recent studies comparing open and "traditional" education. The concept of "direct instruction," as applied to the effective teacher behaviors found in several of these studies by Rosenshine (1976a, 1976b), appears descriptive of this control/orderliness dimension as well. The classroom-cluster main effects, similarly, showed the most positive overall trend for cluster 4, described as being "controlled, disciplined, academically oriented, and supportive." This cluster approaches even more closely Rosenshine's definition of "direct instruction," since it combines control with teacher supportiveness and warmth.

These results do not mean that teachers should immediately abandon all other styles and try to become controlling and directive, or to develop classroom atmospheres which approximate the pattern represented by cluster 4. Although these do seem to represent generally effective patterns of teacher behavior and classroom atmosphere, there are limitations on their generality which should be clearly recognized. In the first place, these main effects are largely limited to cognitive-academic dependent variables (similar to the results for the Follow Through evaluation and the various other studies discussed earlier). The most striking results were for achievement-test performance and writing quality. While the noncognitive outcome measures were not predicted clearly or consistently by any of the other classroom and teacher variables, the evidence suggests that they may not be particularly well promoted by control/orderliness either.

With respect to the clusters, furthermore, there was suggestive evidence that different patterns of teacher behavior and classroom atmosphere may serve to maximize different patterns of outcomes. For example, cluster 5 (combining warmth with an emphasis on expressiveness) also achieved generally positive results, but appeared particularly strong regarding creativity and activity/curiosity. Further evidence on this point is provided by data from a more recent study concerning classroom atmosphere and teacher behavior in desegregated settings (Serow and Solomon 1978). In that study, a strong positive relationship with a factor representing friendly contacts between minority students and white students was found for "teacher warmth," while significant negative trends were found relating "direct business-like teaching" and "teacher-student verbal-academic interaction" to the same measure of general positive interaction. The "direct teaching" factor is, of course, similar to factors and variables which were, in general, positively related to cognitive-academic outcomes in the present study and in much of the other research cited. This seems to suggest that an overly great emphasis on some goals may have a detrimental effect on others. A teacher with a clear priority on academic goals should probably structure a class differently from one with a greater emphasis on social goals. Methods which combine elements of the different approaches may be necessary to realize student gains in several different areas simultaneously (for instance, academic, social, affective, and so forth).

It is also true, as suggested by Kennedy (1978) and others, that nonacademic outcomes (those not measured by achievement tests) are not as yet well represented by measures with demonstrated reliability and validity. Programs whose major objectives include such areas as problem-solving skills, creative thinking, interpersonal sensitivity, self-directing abilities, and so on should not be faulted if their students' performance on standard achievement tests is less than that of students in programs which strongly stress the specific skills and abilities measured by such tests. Yet many of the "nonacademic" programs have been assessed by such achievement tests. It is hoped that progress will soon be made in developing equally reliable tests to represent some of the other "nonacademic" outcomes, and that such measures will be used more widely in evaluations of programs with various nontraditional goals. An attempt was made to represent a broad variety of outcomes in the present research, but much more work will be needed before the measurement of the nonacademic outcomes can match the reliability and validity of the standardized achievement tests.

Probably the most important reason for qualifying or limiting any statements about the generality of direct or main effects of these classroom dimensions and types is the fact that they also combine with student characteristics to produce interaction effects on the various outcomes. The very strong main effect on achievement-test performance of classroom control/orderliness was moderated by a three-way interaction involving students' sex, and preference for autonomy, for example (see Table 9.8). The position on a given classroom dimension which is optimal (in terms of a given outcome) for a student with one set of characteristics is, in many instances, different from that which is optimal for a student with another set of characteristics. This is the major thesis which the present study was designed to explore and which, it is argued, was amply demonstrated by the numerous interactions presented and discussed in this and the previous two chapters (as well as in Appendix A).

Clusters and Dimensions

As stated earlier, the use of the cluster analysis methodology and the analysis of child-classroom interactions using cluster assignments was something of a departure from previous research. An obvious question is, therefore, How do the results obtained with this approach compare with those using the more usual individual variable approach, represented in this research by the dimension-dimension analyses. Because the two approaches group the data differently, a simple and direct comparison of their results is not possible. Many occasions have been pointed out, however, when the results obtained by one approach were consistent with, or in general agreement with, those obtained by the other, while some occasions have also been noted when they appeared not to be in agreement. Furthermore, comparisons of the results obtained with the different approaches seemed useful in coming to a general understanding of the processes involved. Comparing dimension results with cluster results could suggest which of the cluster components was more critical in producing a particular effect; comparing cluster results with dimension results could indicate how the individual dimensions functioned with respect to particular effects when combined into groups. Thus, the present results do not appear to offer evidence for the superiority of one approach over the other. What they do seem to show is that it is very useful to have both methods applied to the same data, so that the two can be compared and generalizations developed which take both sets of results into account.

IMPLICATIONS

Practical Implications

The plan for this research was originally framed with reference to issues concerning "paired" or "alternate" schools or programs. In situations which allow a choice between several identifiable educational programs (either within one school or in different schools), knowledge about the performance of different types of children in different types of programs or settings could be used in making recommendations about the optimal placement for a particular child.

There are, however, some limitations on the degree to which the findings of this research can be generalized and applied. Since the research was limited to a single grade level, extensions to other levels should be done, if at all, with great caution. Strictly speaking, one should also be somewhat cautious about applying the results even at the fourth grade level until they have clearly been replicated in additional research. This is not to say, however, that applications should not be made. Tentative as these results may be (as the results of any single study must be), they still represent a large portion of the evidence currently available concerning the performance of different types of children in different types of classrooms. Therefore, it seems appropriate to consider these data as sources for hypotheses and for the identification of factors which should be considered in attempts to match students with classrooms or programs.

Several types of applications of these results can be envisaged. The most direct application would be in situations in which parents, children, or both, are being counseled regarding a choice between alternative programs. It is suggested that where alternative programs are being offered, data describing these programs should be routinely collected, either using instruments such as those developed for this research or shorter variants adapted from them. If this should not prove feasible, it might still be possible to characterize programs in terms similar to the classroom types identified in this research and in terms of their relative positions with respect to the various classroom dimensions. Even the simplest means of characterizing programs would require that some form of questionnaire be given to teachers or principals (or, possibly, to students). In cases where choices are being made with respect to programs which are being planned but are not yet in existence, these plans could possibly be characterized in terms of the same clusters and dimensions.

The relevant characteristics of the children involved in such alternative choices would also have to be assessed in some way before placement recommendations could be made. While the optimal way would be to use a fairly extensive battery of instruments, some briefer assessment procedures, involving teacher ratings and less extensive child questionnaires, could also be developed. It might be possible, for example, for teachers to rate children in terms of the various "types" and "dimensions." Preliminary research validating these abbreviated assessment procedures, however, would first be required.

When counselors had obtained the relevant information about the individual children concerned, they would be able to make some general recommendations about the kind of program in which a given child would be likely to make the best progress. It could then be determined which of the available alternative programs most closely approximated the suggested optimal program for any child. It would be important to emphasize that this would be considered a provisional placement, subject to continual reevaluation and to revision if it did not seem to be working out. It would also be important to periodically reevaluate a child's needs with respect to the different programs. For example, some of the results suggest that an open, permissive program may be beneficial for poorly motivated, low-achieving children, and that a controlled and orderly program (with some opportunity for self-direction) appears best for more proficient and more highly motivated children. If a poorly motivated child were placed in an open, permissive program which had the result, after a period of time, of improving that child's proficiency and motivation, it might be recommended that a more controlled program would then be in order.

This research also has possible implications for program planning and teacher selection. Once it has been established that certain programs produce optimal effects for certain types of children, and if it were known what the distribution of these types of children were (it is, of course, known within the context of the sample in this research), the relative frequency of some programs could be increased, and that of others decreased, so as to best match the needs of the general child population. Teacher recruitment and in-service training could in similar ways take the relative matching of program distributions and child-type distributions into account in determining what kinds of teacher-orientations and practices to emphasize and encourage at any particular time.

Although this research (and most other ATI research) has implicitly assumed that the "treatment," or the "educational environment," is essentially the same for all students within it, there may be many instances in which this is not the case. Teachers may have more contact with some students than with others, may be more lenient with some than others, or may respond more favorably to the contributions and productions of some than others. To the extent that this is true, different "environments" are being experienced by different children. The classroom experience of different students also varies according to their proximity to, and contacts with, particular subgroups of other students. Research which takes this into account and investigates attribute-treatment interaction according to the treatment received (or environment experienced) by each individual child would be a welcome addition to this area of investigation. By the same token, there would seem to be no inherent reason to limit potential applications of ATI findings such as those in the present research to the selection of homogeneous groupings of students in global and relatively undifferentiated environments. In fact, since the results of the present study were derived from classrooms composed of combinations of children with different sets of characteristics, they are most clearly applicable to similarly heterogeneous classrooms. Whether similar effects would occur in classrooms that are more homogeneous with respect to such student characteristics cannot be known without additional research. There are, however, alternatives to the creation of completely homogeneous classes. To the extent that this and similar research is successful in identifying optimal pairings of student characteristics and treatments (much more research will be required before this will be definitely established), it should be possible to design individualized settings in which particular sequences (or, in some instances, even a total class or course) can be presented to individual students or subgroups of students in ways that conform to their particular patterns of needs, interests, and abilities. (For instance, greater structure might be provided to those students for whom it is particularly beneficial.) Other approaches which would allow teachers to capitalize on the findings of ATI research without setting up distinct and homogeneous courses or sections are undoubtedly also possible.

Theoretical Implications

This study falls into the general framework of research on "attribute-treatment interaction." The general assumption of this expanding body of research—that educational treatments' effects are differentiated according to individual characteristics of the students— has been under attack. While it is a logical and attractive idea, it has not yet been definitively demonstrated with empirical findings. Goldberg (1969) suggested that much of the research in this area may have failed to find consistent evidence of such interactions because the measures of individual characteristics used had been originally developed to be cross-situationally general (to be relatively impervious to situational influences and effects). He suggested that new measures should be constructed, for the purposes of research of this type, which attempt to maximize situational effects. Some of the preference and orientation measures developed for the present research were fashioned with this intent (for example, structured role orientation, locus of instigation, class characteristics preferences); others were selected with this criterion in mind (bureaucratic orientation, locus of control). Although the particular set of individual measures used in this research may not have been the best possible, they did produce a large number of significant interactions (in their various groupings and combinations).

The present results constitute fairly substantial evidence that child-classroom interactions do exist and represent an important influence on academic outcomes. While the impact of such interactions is less than that of individual child characteristics considered by themselves, it is far from negligible and can add to general understanding of the educational process. For example, there are few instances in which initially high-achieving children will not outperform initially low-achieving children. But across class types, it is possible to identify those in which high-achieving children do their best and those in which low-achieving children do their best; these are usually not the same types of class. When such differences are identifiable, they are important to know and have obvious potential for application and for the refinement of theories of instruction.

The present research can also be considered within the context of the approaches to "interactionism" and "person-environment interaction" described in Chapter 1. The various interactions obtained in this study constitute evidence concerning several of the assumptions common to those approaches to the study of human behavior: that interactions between persons and environments do exist and exert relatively important influence on behavioral outcomes; that the effects of individual dispositions tend not to be uniform across situational variations, but rather interact with those variations; that, similarly, situational or environmental effects are not uniform but rather are dependent on interactions with relevant individual characteristics. As it was noted in Chapter 1, much of the interactionist work to date has focused on the investigation of these and related assumptions. Less has been devoted to identifying and developing specific interactional constructs or describing the mechanisms which can account for or predict specific interactions between variables representing person constructs and those representing environment constructs. The present research was guided by a general interactional orientation, but not a specific interactional theory. Its results, however, refer to specific interactions between specific groups of variables. These results, when combined and integrated with those of other parallel investigations, could contribute to the development of specific interactional theories of relevance to education in particular and social science in general. Some of the preceding discussion can be considered an initial step toward the end of developing such theories.

APPENDIX A
Analyses of Cluster-Dimension Interactions and of Interactions Involving Prior Achievement Levels

INVESTIGATIONS OF CLUSTER-BY-DIMENSION INTERACTIONS

In addition to analyses of the effects of interactions between child clusters and classroom clusters, and between child and classroom dimensions, it was decided to investigate "crossovers" between these ways of grouping the data. This made it possible to determine (1) how children characterized by particular attributes would perform in the different identified classroom "types" and (2) how well each of the three "types" of children would perform in classrooms identified by positions on each of the six classroom dimensions.

Interactions between Child Factors and Classroom Clusters

Table A.1 presents the significant two-way interactions obtained between the child factors and the classroom clusters (limited to those which reached the .05 level of significance or better).

Socioeconomic status was involved in two of these interactions, relating to self-esteem and to value on equality. Although neither of these showed significant differentiation between class types for the low-SES children, their self-esteem scores were highest in class cluster 1, the cluster combining extreme permissiveness, variety and self-initiation of activities, and moderate warmth. Children in the medium SES range showed highest self-esteem scores in the classroom cluster which combined warmth and friendliness with an emphasis on student expressiveness (5), while those in the high SES range scored highest on self-esteem in cluster 4, combining warmth with substantial control and orderliness. It will be noted that all three of these classroom clusters were characterized by fairly substantial degrees of warmth; apparently, warmth (which also showed a significant main effect by itself) is an important determinant of gains in self-esteem. But children at the different SES levels are influenced by warmth in different combinations; low-SES children, perhaps benefiting from the opportunity to learn that they can be effectively

TABLE A.1

Means for Significant Two-Way Interactions between Child Factors
and Classroom Clusters

Dependent Variable	Child Factor	Level	Classroom Cluster						$F_{(10, 88)}$*	Between-Mean Diff. Req. for Signif. (p < .05)
			1	2	3	4	5	6		
Self-Esteem	SES	Low	-.16	-1.27	-1.22	-.80	-.51	-.82	2.35	1.50
		Med	-1.32	-.35	.50	.41	1.72	-.31		
		High	.75	.84	.89	1.54	-1.21	.03		
Value on Equality	Achievement Motivation	Low	.02	-.03	.02	-.17	.08	-.14	1.94	.23
		Med	.00	.23	-.15	.08	.14	-.09		
		High	-.04	-.02	.09	.18	-.19	-.04		
Value on Equality	SES	Low	.00	-.13	.02	-.02	.00	-.09	1.94	.19
		Med	.00	.14	-.11	.01	.04	.11		
		High	-.07	.17	.01	.13	-.08	-.24		

(continued)

Table A.1 (continued)

Dependent Variable	Child Factor	Level	Classroom Cluster						F (10, 88)*	Between-Mean Diff. Req. for Signif. (p < .05)
			1	2	3	4	5	6		
Concern for Others	Personal Control, Intrinsic Motivation	Low	.07	-.20	-.12	-.22	.07	-.19	2.20	.18
		Med	-.05	.08	-.04	-.04	-.03	-.09		
		High	.06	.14	.13	.21	.11	.29		
Concern for Others	Achievement Motivation	Low	-.02	.04	-.17	-.32	.20	-.19	2.47	.19
		Med	.11	-.05	-.11	.07	.02	.03		
		High	.04	.11	.08	.19	.14	.20		
Value on Self-Direction	Preference for Class with Autonomy	Low	.05	-.12	.00	-.04	-.04	.04	2.25	.20
		Med	.05	-.16	.14	-.08	-.04	-.13		
		High	.12	.28	-.13	.10	.07	.19		

*p < .05 for all values.
Source: Compiled by the authors.

260

self-directing, come to think best of themselves when given the greatest autonomy; high–SES children, perhaps appreciating a serious approach to academic tasks, show highest self-esteem in orderly, disciplined classrooms which deemphasize student expression. Perhaps the most puzzling group shown in this interaction is the middle SES group, which does best with a strong emphasis on student expression. While this is not surprising in itself, the discrepancy between the results for this group and those for the two SES extremes is difficult to explain.

With respect to value on equality, both the medium and the high SES groups scored highest in class cluster 2, while low–SES children obtained their lowest mean score in the same cluster. Cluster 2 contains both teacher control and student self-initiation of activities, a combination which may amount in many of these classes to an effective sharing of control between teacher and students—a kind of equality of role. Students may be reflecting this role equality in their high gain scores for value on equality. The absence of this effect for the low-SES children may indicate that they prefer a clearer or simpler role structure, emphasizing either one or the other type of control rather than a combination.

Children's achievement motivation was also involved in two of the interactions shown in Table A.1, relating to value on equality and concern for others. Although the results for the moderate achievement motivation group were different in these two interactions (with highest scores in cluster 2 for value on equality and in cluster 1 for concern for others), they were similar across the two for the low- and high-motivation groups. Children with low achievement motivation scored highest in both instances in class cluster 5 (the warm and expressive class type), while those with a high achievement motivation obtained high scores in class cluster 4 (warm, controlled, orderly). As suggested earlier, it may be that children with low achievement motivation acquire an external substitute for their low degree of internal motivation in a classroom which provides for open expression of a variety of personal interests in a warm and friendly setting, while children who are already motivated prefer a situation which allows them to apply their motivation in an orderly way.

Concern for others was also influenced by an interaction involving children's personal control/intrinsic motivation. As in the interaction with achievement motivation, the low group of children scored high in class cluster 5 (but also did so in cluster 1). Children with moderate personal-control scores showed greatest concern for others in cluster 2 (combining the two types of classroom control mentioned above); while for those with high personal-control scores, the highest concern for others obtained in cluster 6, the class type which combined individualization of teacher-student interaction with encouragement of verbal (academic) participation.

The last interaction shown in Table A.1 represents the joint effect of children's preference for class with autonomy and classroom cluster on value on self-direction. Children lowest in autonomy preference obtained their highest self-direction scores in class cluster 1; since these children were not themselves inclined toward self-direction, it may be that the classes most strongly oriented in this direction (combining student autonomy and freedom from control with student self-initiation of tasks and activities) helped them to overcome their initial disinclination. (They also, however, performed about the same in cluster 6—individualized and academic.) The moderate autonomy group obtained highest self-direction scores in class cluster 3, which tended toward permissiveness and some student autonomy, but not self-initiation of tasks. Children with the strongest preference for autonomy stated the highest value on self-direction in the cluster 2 classrooms, which combined control and orderliness with student initiation of varied activities. Each of the preference levels, then, showed high self-direction scores in classrooms which provided for at least some type of student autonomy.

Three-way interactions involving the child factors (plus SES), the classroom clusters, and sex are shown in Table A.2. Four significant interactions were obtained, two of them involving preference for class with autonomy. The first of these, relating to children's achievement-test performance, shows generally highest scores for class cluster 4 (warm and controlled). Exceptions to this trend are found for boys with moderate preference for autonomy (who did well in clusters 2 and 5), and low-preference girls (who excelled in cluster 2). Moderate-preference girls also did well in cluster 5 classrooms. The highest mean scores in the significant main effect obtained with achievement-test performance were found in clusters 2 and 4; the present results necessitate the qualification of this finding according to the child's degree of preference for autonomy. Thus, it is the girls with low scores for this preference, and the boys with moderate scores, who apparently benefited from a cluster 2 class situation—in which they were expected to provide at least some of their own directions (but still in a controlled and orderly context).

The interaction affecting class disruptiveness (also with preference for class with autonomy as an independent variable) similarly shows results consistent with the obtained main effect, with the exception of two groups—high autonomy-preference boys and moderate autonomy-preference girls. These two groups perceive the most disruptiveness in the most permissive classrooms (cluster 1) while the other groups of students perceive it in the most hostile and unfriendly classrooms (cluster 3).

Inquiry skill shows a significant effect in Table A.2, with socioeconomic status as the interacting child variable. As with

TABLE A.2

Means for Significant Three–Way Interactions among Child Factors, Sex, and Classroom Clusters

Dependent Variable	Child Factor	Sex, Level	Classroom Cluster						F (10, 88)	Between–Mean Diff. Req. for Signif. (p < .05)
			1	2	3	4	5	6		
Achievement Test Performance	Preference for Class with Autonomy	Boys							2.38*	.09
		Low	-.01	-.07	.00	.20	-.06	-.01		
		Med	-.10	.22	-.16	-.06	.18	-.11		
		High	-.24	.01	-.01	.13	.04	-.03		
		Girls								
		Low	-.01	.17	.07	.13	.03	.01		
		Med	-.20	.13	-.03	.20	.18	.00		
		High	.16	.15	-.05	.23	-.05	-.10		
Inquiry Skill	SES	Boys							2.19*	.20
		Low	-.05	-.05	-.32	-.01	-.38	-.22		
		Med	-.29	.08	-.01	.13	.12	-.09		
		High	-.25	.17	-.08	.10	.40	.24		
		Girls								
		Low	-.59	-.05	.04	.16	.11	-.14		
		Med	.08	.02	.10	.46	-.33	.19		
		High	.13	.06	-.04	.33	-.13	-.06		

(continued)

263

Table A.2 (continued)

Dependent Variable	Child Factor	Sex, Level	Classroom Cluster						F (10, 88)	Between-Mean Diff. Req. for Signif. (p < .05)
			1	2	3	4	5	6		
Perceived Class Disruptiveness	Prefer-ence for Class with Autonomy	**Boys**								
		Low	-.02	.01	.16	-.22	-.37	-.03	2.08*	.12
		Med	-.23	.02	.21	-.01	-.08	.12		
		High	.11	.02	-.02	-.10	-.31	-.03		
		Girls								
		Low	-.06	-.12	.19	-.13	-.15	-.16		
		Med	.11	-.08	.07	-.09	.00	-.05		
		High	-.06	-.26	.26	-.14	-.17	.29		
Persever-ance, Social Maturity	Achieve-ment Motivation	**Boys**								
		Low	-.15	-.13	-.65	-.08	.50	-.46	3.21†	.21
		Med	-.14	-.21	-.16	.08	.17	-.45		
		High	-.57	-.19	-.38	-.04	-.29	.14		
		Girls								
		Low	.14	.20	-.04	.00	-.28	.04		
		Med	.46	.17	.07	.39	.81	.24		
		High	.39	.43	.34	.54	.74	-.01		

*p < .05.
†p < .01.

Source: Compiled by the authors.

achievement-test performance, inquiry-skill scores were generally highest in the warm, controlled, and orderly classrooms (cluster 4), with the exception of high-SES boys, who did best in the warm and expressive classrooms (cluster 5). The warm and expressive classrooms also generally produced the greatest perseverance in the children as shown in the interaction involving achievement motivation. Striving behavior was apparently stimulated by this combination of characteristics, particularly for boys with low achievement motivation (where it was perhaps providing an external substitute for motivation) and for girls with moderate or high achievement motivation (where it perhaps increased already high motivation with an additive-type effect). The exceptions occurred for highly achievement-motivated boys, who persevered most in the classrooms which combined individualized interaction with an emphasis on verbal (academic) participation and for girls with low achievement motivation, who persevered most in the most controlled and orderly classrooms (but also did fairly well in the cluster 1 classrooms).

Interactions between Child Clusters
and Classroom Factors

Table A.3 presents the means and significance levels for those child cluster by classroom factor interactions which achieved the .05 level of significance or better. Only two classroom factors were involved in these effects—control/orderliness and emphasis on student expressiveness. Classroom control/orderliness is involved in two interactions, influencing activity/curiosity and creativity. Children in cluster 1 (low in prior achievement, cognitive skills, and self-esteem, high in compliance) scored their highest on both these outcome measures in the most permissive classrooms (significantly so only for activity, however), perhaps because they felt more at ease and stimulated in classrooms which were relatively undemanding, were highly active, and required students to be self-directing. The high-achieving and motivated children of cluster 2 performed best with respect to both variables in the most controlled, orderly, and organized classrooms (but significantly so only for creativity). It is suggested that, in contrast to the cluster 1 children who were perhaps supplied with missing motivation by classroom permissiveness, these children, already well motivated, may have appreciated and been helped by the orderliness and discipline provided by the more controlled classrooms. They were enabled to advance from an already high level of creativity by a structured and orderly approach to tasks which gave more emphasis to development of content than to stimulation of students. The cluster 3 children, who

TABLE A.3

Means for Significant Two-Way Interactions between Child Clusters and Classroom Factors

Dependent Variable	Classroom Factor	Child Cluster	Levels of Class Var.			Between-Class-Level t-Values			F (4, 94 df)
			Low	Med	High	L vs. M	L vs. H	M vs. H	
Activity/ Curiosity	Control	1	.01	−.38	−.45	4.19*	5.04*	NS	3.38†
		2	.20	.20	.25	NS	NS	NS	
		3	.31	.10	−.09	2.35†	4.33*	1.98†	
Creativity	Control	1	−.09	−.20	−.13	NS	NS	NS	6.14*
		2	−.08	.16	.26	2.30†	3.23*	NS	
		3	−.36	.12	.47	4.58*	7.93*	3.35*	
Perceived Disruptive- ness	Emph. on S.-Expr- ness.	1	.02	.00	.12	NS	NS	1.66‡	3.00†
		2	.02	.02	−.18	NS	NS	2.92*	
		3	−.05	.13	−.01	2.55†	2.90*	1.95‡	
Creativity	Emph. on S.-Expr- ness.	1	−.26	−.09	−.07	NS	1.69‡	NS	3.38†
		2	.11	.05	.16	NS	NS	NS	
		3	.29	−.23	.14	4.71*	NS	3.37*	
Self- Esteem	Emph. on S.-Expr- ness.	1	−1.86	.16	−1.07	2.71*	NS	1.65‡	2.76†
		2	.62	.06	.84	NS	NS	NS	
		3	1.00	.31	−1.36	NS	3.18*	2.25†	

*p < .01.
†p < .05.
‡p < .10.

Source: Compiled by the authors.

were noncompliant and preferred autonomy and self-direction, were most active and curious in the classrooms which provided for the most autonomy, as would be expected; their creativity, however, was most benefited by the more controlled and orderly classrooms. As it was suggested earlier in a different context, it is possible that their inclination toward autonomy had to be tempered by a setting which supplied external structure and direction in order to achieve an optimal balance.

Classroom emphasis on student expressiveness participated in three interactions, shown in Table A.3, influencing creativity, self-esteem, and perceived class disruptiveness. The low-achieving (cluster 1) children were most creative, but also saw most disruptiveness, in the most expressive classrooms, perhaps again reflecting the provision of a motivating factor to those who need it. The high-achieving (cluster 2) children were not significantly differentiated across levels of class expressiveness for creativity or self-esteem, but saw most disruptiveness in the least expressive classes. The autonomous (cluster 3) children scored highest on creativity and self-esteem in the least expressive classrooms, although their creativity scores in the most expressive classrooms were also high (not significantly different from those in the least expressive). They saw the most disruptiveness in the moderately expressive classrooms. Included with the preference for autonomy of the cluster 3 children is a preference for situations which allow self-expression. One would therefore expect them to excel in the most expressive classrooms (and their creativity scores are quite high in these). Perhaps, however, the inclination toward self-expression, when combined with an expressive classroom, surpasses an optimal level of expressiveness for many of these children, who therefore are more creative and think better of themselves in situations where this individual inclination is counterbalanced by a class situation with an opposed emphasis.

Three-way interactions between the child clusters, classroom factors, and sex are presented in Table A.4. There were five significant interactions, involving four of the classroom factors. The first one shown in the table relates classroom control and orderliness, with the other independent variables, to children's value on self-direction. With the exception of those in cluster 1, for whom there was no significant differentiation, boys stated the highest residual values on self-direction in the classes which provided for the greatest amount of self-direction—those classes at the low end of the control/orderliness dimension. Low-achieving (cluster 1) girls also score high on self-direction in these classrooms, while those in cluster 2 show no significant differentiation and those in cluster 3 score highest in the most controlled classrooms. It is interesting that girls who are initially inclined toward self-direction show the greatest gains

TABLE A.4

Means for Significant Three-Way Interactions among Child Clusters, Sex, and Classroom Factors

Dependent Variable	Classroom Factor	Sex, Child Cluster	Levels of Class Var.			Between-Class-Level t-Values			F (4, 94 df)
			Low	Med	High	L vs. M	L vs. H	M vs. H	
Value on Self-Direction	Control, Orderliness	Boys							2.86*
		One	.01	-.02	.02	NS	NS	NS	
		Two	.17	-.02	.07	3.91†	1.98*	1.93‡	
		Three	.28	.10	.01	3.66†	5.57†	1.91‡	
		Girls							
		One	.07	-.15	-.14	4.63†	4.42†	NS	
		Two	-.01	-.01	-.07	NS	NS	NS	
		Three	.03	-.03	.24	NS	4.44†	5.63†	
Activity, Curiosity	Commonality Vs. Variety	Boys							2.96*
		One	-.07	.03	-.19	NS	1.99*	3.52†	
		Two	.26	.33	.50	NS	3.73†	2.65†	
		Three	.48	.34	.22	2.12*	4.01†	1.89*	
		Girls							
		One	-.53	-.65	-.22	1.97*	4.74†	6.71†	
		Two	.22	-.02	.02	3.76†	3.21†	NS	
		Three	-.16	-.23	-.03	NS	1.94‡	3.07†	
Writing Quality	Nonindividualized Interaction	Boys							2.47*
		One	-.22	-.80	-.43	5.92†	2.15*	3.77†	
		Two	-.03	-.04	-.01	NS	NS	NS	
		Three	.22	.31	.00	NS	2.24*	3.21†	

		Sex	Grade							
		Girls								
			One	.07	−.27	−.15	3.42†	2.23*	NS	2.54*
			Two	.75	.43	.24	3.29†	5.17†	1.88‡	
			Three	.39	−.16	.49	5.57†	NS	6.58†	
Value on Self-Direction	Nonindividualized Interaction	Boys								
			One	−.01	.08	−.05	1.92‡	NS	2.74†	
			Two	.18	.06	−.02	2.60*	4.16†	NS	
			Three	.09	.09	.20	NS	2.24*	2.12*	
		Girls								
			One	−.17	−.13	.08	NS	5.08†	4.37†	
			Two	.08	−.10	−.08	3.64†	3.25†	NS	
			Three	.12	.20	−.06	NS	3.66†	5.27†	
Value on Equality	Encouragement of Verbal (Academic) Participation	Boys								
			One	−.16	−.17	−.29	NS	2.40*	2.20*	2.60*
			Two	.00	.01	.07	NS	NS	NS	
			Three	.05	−.07	.01	2.12*	NS	NS	
		Girls								
			One	.09	−.25	.10	6.05†	NS	6.23†	
			Two	.28	.20	.11	NS	2.97†	NS	
			Three	.16	.32	.11	2.80†	NS	3.81†	

*p < .05.
†p < .01.
‡p < .10.
Source: Compiled by the authors.

in situations which do not provide for much of it, while boys with such inclinations gain most when given the opportunity to express and follow them.

The next significant interaction shown in Table A.4 included "commonality versus variety of class activities" as an independent variable; the effects in this analysis also appeared to be quite different between the sexes. Cluster 1 (low achieving) boys were most active and curious in moderately varied classrooms, while cluster 1 girls were in the least varied classrooms. Activity/curiosity scores were also at high points for high-achieving (cluster 2) boys and for autonomy-preferring (cluster 3) girls in the most common (least varied) classrooms, and for high-achieving girls and autonomy-preferring boys in the classrooms with the most student-initiated, varied activities. The results obtained here for the cluster 3 (non-compliant, autonomy-preferring, self-directing) children are somewhat similar to those obtained in the first analysis presented in Table A.4. Although the classroom factors are different, they both refer to aspects of student autonomy. In each case, the boys score highest on the dependent variable in the classes which provide for the greatest student autonomy while girls in this cluster do so in classes with the least.

The degree of individualization of teacher-student contacts constitutes the classroom variable involved in the next two interactions shown in Table A.4. In the first of these, affecting residual writing quality, scores are generally highest in the most individualized classes, with the exception of cluster 3 (autonomy preference) boys, whose scores are slightly (but nonsignificantly) higher in intermediate-level classrooms, and cluster 3 girls, whose scores are higher (also nonsignificantly) in the least individualized classrooms. In addition, no significant differentiation was obtained for the cluster 2 boys. The spreading out of the high means for the more autonomous children may indicate that this orientation represents, at least for some of them, a desire not to be given advice or direction. They may do relatively well in the less individualized classrooms because they are not given such advice and direction. At the same time, they also do well in the individualized classrooms because the teacher-student interaction observed in these classrooms was often initiated by the students. (This can be seen in the loadings for this factor, shown in Tables 5.4 and 5.9.)

The interaction in which individualization relates to value on self-direction shows a somewhat different pattern. The high-achieving (cluster 2) children score highest in the most individualized classrooms (similar to the effect for girls on writing quality). The autonomous (cluster 3) girls show the strongest value on self-direction in moderately or highly individualized classrooms, while the boys in the same cluster do so in the least individualized classrooms. It may be that boys who prefer autonomy feel most self-directing in situations which allow them to be "on their own," but that girls who prefer autonomy develop a value on self-direction if they have frequent feedback from, and consultation with, teachers concerning their activities. (Girls' greater social orientation has been frequently noted in previous research; this suggests that even the self-direction of those preferring autonomy may take a more social flavor for girls than for boys.) Low-achieving (cluster 1) girls show the greatest residual gains in value on self-direction in the least individualized classes (although their writing was best in individualized ones), a finding difficult to explain. The cluster 1 boys show greatest self-direction in moderately individualized classrooms.

The last interaction portrayed in Table A.4 is three-way and involves energetic encouragement of verbal (academic) participation, child cluster, and sex with the residual value on equality as the dependent variable. Low-achieving (cluster 1) boys show the greatest value on equality in classes low or moderate in verbal (academic) participation, possibly because these classes allow nonacademic objectives to assume importance. In fact, classrooms in the lowest verbal-academic emphasis category generally produced the highest value on equality scores; the major exceptions were autonomy-preferring girls (who scored higher in moderate-level classes) and low-achieving girls (who scored high scores at both extremes of the verbal-academic emphasis dimension).

SUMMARY OF CLUSTER-BY-DIMENSION INTERACTIONS

Child Dimension by Classroom Cluster Interactions

All of the child dimensions but "compliant orientation" were involved in interactions with the classroom clusters. Here are summarized what appear to be the major trends in these effects, focusing on differences between the highest and lowest scoring child groups for each dimension.

Children of low socioeconomic status did their best in terms of self-esteem in the more permissive classrooms, while high-SES children did so in the warm, controlled, and orderly cluster (4).

Children in the low achievement-motivation group generally obtained the highest outcome scores (value on equality, concern for others, perseverance) in class cluster 5, which combines warmth with an emphasis on expressiveness; those in the high achievement-motivation group obtained high scores (for the first two of these variables) in cluster 4 classrooms, which combined warmth with control and orderliness.

Personal control appeared in a single interaction; children with low personal-control scores showed the greatest concern for others in warm and expressive classrooms (cluster 5), while those with high scores did so in individualized and academic classrooms (cluster 6).

Children who stated a preference for structured situations obtained highest scores on self-direction in permissive or individualized settings and on achievement-test performance in class situations characterized by control and orderliness (as represented in clusters 2 and 4). The common element describing the class clusters in which children preferring autonomy generally did well for both of these outcomes was also control and orderliness.

It will be noted that for most of the child-dimension interactions just summarized, low scorers tended to do well in types of classes which provided activities and atmospheres perhaps functioning to engage the students' involvement, interest, and motivation (those including permissiveness, warmth, expressiveness, student initiation of varied activities), while high scorers tended to do best, in most instances, in classes whose most consistent characteristic was a controlled and orderly approach to tasks. The general explanation which has been used to account for these findings (as well as several others in earlier sections) is that the low-motivation children are being provided with an external substitute for the motivation which they lack internally, while the highly motivated children, not requiring additional motivation, are being provided with the structure and orderliness which helps them to progress from their initial level of accomplishment. While this explanation appears reasonable for the motivation factors and for SES (shown to be correlated with these factors in Table B.3), it fits less well the results obtained with the autonomy-preference factor. For these it was suggested that children may benefit from experiencing a type of situation which their inclinations would lead them to avoid.

Classroom Dimension by Child Cluster
Interactions

Processes similar to those just discussed were also evident in the interactions involving the classroom dimensions and the child clusters. Children in the first cluster, with low scores on measures of prior achievement and cognitive skills, low prior self-esteem, low personal control/intrinsic motivation, and high compliance-orientation scores, were more active and curious and more self-directing (girls only) in classes which were highly permissive and provided for student autonomy. They were also creative in classes which strongly emphasized student expressiveness (but also saw the most disruptiveness in these classes) and showed greatest self-esteem gains in the moderately expressive classes. Children in this cluster were also active and curious in classes characterized by moderate (for boys) or low (for girls) levels of student-initiated, varied activities and showed the best writing quality in classes with the most individualized teacher-student interaction. Results were more mixed with respect to encouragement of verbal (academic) participation. Boys' value on equality was highest in classes low or moderate on this dimension; girls' in those either high or low.

The cluster 2 children—highly motivated prior achievers with high scores on initial measures of self-esteem, cognitive skills, and preference for structure—scored highest in the most controlled and orderly classes on the residual measures of activity/curiosity and creativity (the boys were also most self-directing in the least controlled classes, however). They perceived the least disruptiveness in the classes which most strongly emphasized student expressiveness. Girls' self-direction and writing quality showed the highest scores in the most individualized classrooms. Results for "class commonality versus variety of activities" were mixed. Cluster 2 boys were most active in classes showing the most commonality of activities, girls in those showing the least. Cluster 2 girls also obtained the highest value on equality scores in classes with the least emphasis on verbal (academic) participation.

Children in cluster 3 were noncompliant, strongly preferred classes which allowed for autonomy and self-expression, had moderate scores on prior cognitive skills, and had moderate to low scores on the motivational measures. While a "matching" hypothesis would lead one to expect them to do well in classes which were permissive, emphasized expressiveness, and had many student-initiated activities, the results obtained, while showing some evidence of such effects, also showed the opposite in several instances. Thus, on one hand, cluster 3 children's activity/curiosity and boys' value on self-direction were highest in permissive classrooms, and boys' activity/curiosity was highest in the most varied classrooms; on the other hand, creativity and girls' self-direction were highest in the most controlled classrooms, creativity and self-esteem were greatest in the least expressive classrooms, and girls' activity/curiosity was strongest in the least varied classrooms. Several of these show a distinction between activity level (which is usually greatest when the classroom matches the predominant orientation of this child cluster) and creativity (maximized in classes which oppose the predominant cluster orientation). It may be suggested that, for these noncompliant children who prefer self-direction, a matching environment allows them to feel free to be active and to explore, but does not provide them with sufficient structure to develop this activity in productive directions. An environment which tempers or counteracts these inclinations by providing more structure and direction may promote greater development of cognitive skills (represented in these instances by creativity).

The remaining interactions produced more mixed results for the children in cluster 3. Boys' writing quality and girls' self-direction were greatest in highly or moderately individualized classrooms; girls' writing quality was greatest in classes at both extremes of individualization; boys' self-direction was greatest in the least individualized classes; boys' value on equality was greatest in classes with high or low emphasis on verbal (academic) participation, and girls' in those where it was moderate.

Thus, again there is evidence (1) that low-achieving, relatively unmotivated children benefit from class environments which provide them with external stimulation and encouragement, (2) that high-achieving, motivated children benefit from those which provide them with control, structure, and an orderly approach to tasks, and (3) that children preferring autonomy show the greatest cognitive benefits in classrooms which require them to experience relatively high levels of external control and structure.

INVESTIGATIONS OF INTERACTIONS INVOLVING CHILDREN'S INITIAL STATUS ON SELECTED ACHIEVEMENT-RELATED MEASURES

Another set of analyses explored the possibility that children at different initial levels of proficiency with regard to specific cognitive skills would show maximal gains in those skills in different types of classrooms. Seven cognitive skills measures were selected for these analyses: reading, mathematics concepts, mathematics problems, achievement-test performance, creativity, inquiry skill, and writing quality. The first three of these were achievement-test subscores, the next three factor scores, the last a summed rating across two items. The same repeated-measures analysis-of-variance procedure described in Chapter 8 was also used for these analyses. The independent variables for each analysis were a trichotomized prior-skill measure, a classroom variable, and sex; the dependent variable for each was the posttest score parallel to the pretest measure included in that analysis. For the three achievement-test subscores, the closest parallels were selected between the prior achievement test (ITBS) and the achievement test used for the final assessment (CAT). Cutting points used in trichotomizing the prior achievement test subscores are shown in Table B.4, Appendix B. Two groups of these analyses were run, one involving the classroom clusters, the other, the classroom dimensions. The .10 level was used as the minimal acceptable significance level for these analyses.

From the seven analyses involving the classroom clusters, only one significant prior status-by-cluster interaction was obtained. The means comprising this interaction are presented in Table A.5. It shows children's reading achievement to have benefited from different classroom environments differentially for children with different initial levels of reading skill. Although children from all starting points did relatively well in class cluster 2 (the cluster which combined control and orderliness with student self-initiation of varied tasks), initially poor readers showed the highest mean score in cluster 6, representing classes which were individualized and which strongly encouraged verbal (academic) participation; the initially proficient readers obtained mean scores nearly as high as that for cluster 2 in clusters 1 and 4 (all three being characterized by relatively high levels of student self-initiation of varied activities and two of them characterized by control and orderliness). The initially poor readers perhaps were stimulated and motivated by the individualized attention and the energetic and flamboyant teacher encouragement of participation characteristic of cluster 6, while the proficient readers, not requiring additional motivation, benefit from the opportunity to select topics and activities and from the provision of an orderly and structured approach to these activities.

The significant two-way interactions obtained with classroom dimensions as independent variables are presented in Table A.6. Both of these involved classroom control and orderliness as the classroom independent variable. The first, affecting reading comprehension (also shown in Figure A.1), shows a tendency somewhat similar to that suggested in the analysis involving the classroom clusters. The initially poor readers, although not significantly differentiated across levels of the class variable, show highest reading scores in the least controlled (most permissive) classrooms, but also show scores only slightly lower in the high-control classes. At the same time, the moderately and highly proficient readers clearly did best in the most controlled and orderly classrooms.

The second interaction shown in Table A.6 demonstrates the joint effect of class control/orderliness and prior inquiry skill on the final measure of inquiry skill. Although the most controlled and orderly classrooms show the highest inquiry scores for each of the initial status levels, the differentiation is not significant for those at the highest initial status. This does not add useful information beyond that shown by the significant main effect, in Table 9.2.

TABLE A.5

Fourth Grade Reading Comprehension Means for Interaction between Classroom Clusters and Prior Reading Level

Prior Reading Level	Classroom Cluster						$\underline{F}$ (10, 88)	Between-Mean Diff. Req. for Signif. (p < .05)
	1	2	3	4	5	6		
Low	18.47	19.76	18.38	19.00	19.30	20.86	2.11*	2.18
Med	24.41	25.80	24.02	24.40	22.63	21.47		
High	32.78	32.85	31.50	32.55	29.92	28.43		

*p < .05.
Source: Compiled by the authors.

TABLE A.6

Means for Significant Two-Way Interactions between Classroom Factors and Specific Prior Status Measures on Parallel Outcome Measures

Dependent Variable	Prior Status Variable	Pretest Level	Class Variable and Levels: Control, Order			Between-Class-Level t-Values			F (4, 94)
			Low	Med	High	L vs. M	L vs. H	M vs. H	
Reading Comprehension	Reading	Low	19.59	18.74	19.34	NS	NS	NS	2.78*
		Med	22.28	23.88	25.80	2.09*	4.58†	2.49*	
		High	29.79	31.82	33.12	2.64†	4.34†	1.70‡	
Inquiry Skill	Pretest Inquiry	Low	-.30	-.50	.00	2.08*	3.04†	5.12†	2.18‡
		Med	-.17	-.18	.14	NS	3.23†	3.35†	
		High	.26	.38	.40	NS	NS	NS	

*p < .05.
†p < .01.
‡p < .10.
Source: Compiled by the authors.

FIGURE A. 1

Interaction Effect of Prior Reading and Control-Orderliness on Reading Comprehension

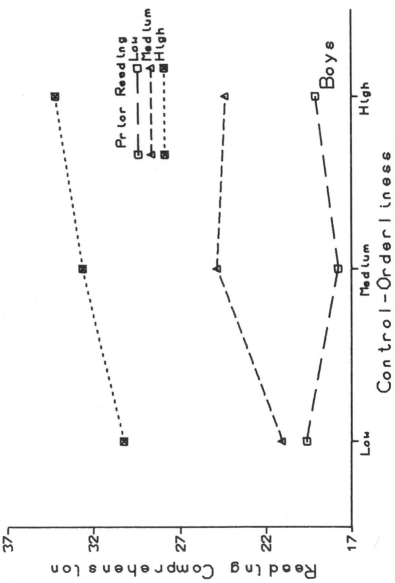

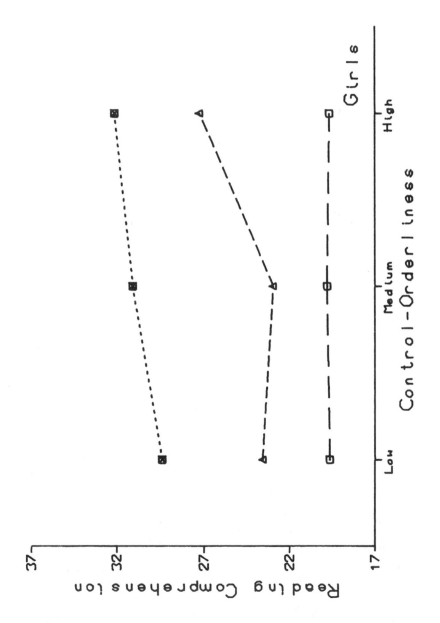

Girls

Control-Orderliness

Reading Comprehension

37   32   27   22   17

Low   Medium   High

Classroom orderliness and prior reading level, as independent variables, were involved in a three-way interaction affecting reading comprehension, shown in Table A.7. The tendency described above for the two-way interaction is here shown quite clearly for boys; those with initially low, medium, and high reading levels show the highest final reading comprehension scores in classrooms with low, medium, and high levels, respectively, of control and orderliness. The relationship for the low prior-status boys is also U-shaped, with only slightly lower scores for the high-control classes than for the low-control ones. The results for girls show no significant differentiation for the poor readers (but with the highest mean for the moderately controlled classes) and best reading scores in highly controlled classes for the moderately and highly proficient readers; thus the trend, although considerably weaker, suggests a similar direction of effect.

One additional interaction involving class control/orderliness is shown in Table A.7. Girls at each initial arithmetic concepts status level demonstrate the best posttest understanding of mathematics concepts in the most controlled and orderly classrooms. Boys in the high "pre-" status group also did well in the most controlled classrooms, while those in the low and medium pre- status groups scored the highest in the most permissive classrooms. The low status boys show a U-shaped trend (with relatively high scores at both extremes) quite similar to that shown with the reading scores.

Individualization of teacher-student interaction is involved in three of the interactions presented in Table A.7, influencing reading comprehension, mathematics concepts, and achievement-test performance. For the first two of these, boys of low initial status show high scores in classes at the two extremes of individualization. Moderate-status boys do relatively well in reading in nonindividualized classes, while high-status boys obtain high reading scores in classes at all levels of individualization. Moderate and high math-status boys obtain their highest final scores in, respectively, nonindividualized and moderately individualized classrooms. Low initial-status girls scored highest, with both of these outcomes, in nonindividualized classes; moderate-status girls did best in individualized classes; and high-status girls showed no significant differentiation. High and moderate initial-status boys showed a tendency to benefit from moderately individualized classes while lower-status boys did best in nonindividualized ones, with respect to overall achievement-test performance. The same was not found for girls. Thus, the general trend with regard to these classroom variables was for low-status boys to do well in classes at the two extremes of each (with a slight edge for the low control and nonindividualized levels), and for low-status girls to do well in classes which were

TABLE A.7

Means for Significant Three-Way Interactions among Classroom Factors, Sex, and Specific Prior Status Measures on Parallel Outcome Measures

Dependent Variable	Prior Status Variable	Sex, Pre-Level	Class Variable and Levels			Between-Class-Level t-Values			$F_{(4, 94)}$
			Low	Med	High	L vs. M	L vs. H	M vs. H	
Reading Comprehension	Pretest Reading		Control, Order						
		Boys							
		Low	19.58	17.74	19.04	3.51*	NS	2.49†	2.26‡
		Med	21.03	24.81	24.33	7.22*	6.29*	NS	
		High	30.22	32.57	34.13	4.48*	7.46*	2.98*	
		Girls							
		Low	19.60	19.75	19.63	NS	NS	NS	
		Med	23.54	22.96	27.26	NS	7.11*	8.21*	
		High	29.37	31.07	32.12	3.25*	5.25*	2.00†	
Mathematics Concepts	Pretest Arithmetic Concepts		Control, Order						
		Boys							
		Low	13.91	11.13	13.66	9.18*	NS	8.33*	2.40‡
		Med	15.93	15.55	15.32	NS	1.99†	NS	
		High	18.20	18.11	20.24	NS	6.72*	7.02*	
		Girls							
		Low	12.75	13.28	14.17	1.74‡	4.69*	2.91*	
		Med	16.31	17.17	17.88	2.85*	5.17*	2.32†	
		High	18.64	19.13	19.39	NS	2.46†	NS	

(continued)

281

Table A.7 (continued)

Dependent Variable	Prior Status Variable	Sex, Pre-Level	Class Variable and Levels			Between-Class-Level t-Values			F (4, 94)
			Low	Med	High	L vs. M	L vs. H	M vs. H	
Reading Compre-hension	Pretest Reading	_Nonindividualized_							
		Boys							
		Low	19.34	17.45	19.55	3.79*	NS	4.21*	4.80*
		Med	20.20	24.95	25.03	9.51*	9.67*	NS	
		High	32.31	32.15	32.42	NS	NS	NS	
		Girls							
		Low	17.93	18.87	22.13	1.88‡	8.41*	6.52*	
		Med	25.22	24.09	24.51	2.25†	NS	NS	
		High	30.80	30.73	31.02	NS	NS	NS	
Mathe-matics Concepts	Pretest Arith-metic Concepts	_Nonindividualized_							
		Boys							
		Low	13.12	11.87	13.75	4.13*	2.10†	6.24*	2.74†
		Med	14.67	15.82	16.32	3.80*	5.47*	1.67‡	
		High	18.79	19.55	18.30	2.50†	NS	4.14*	
		Girls							
		Low	12.84	13.68	13.71	2.78*	2.90*	NS	
		Med	17.36	17.10	16.89	NS	NS	NS	
		High	18.94	18.92	19.28	NS	NS	NS	

Nonindividualized

Overall Achievement-Test Performance	Prior Achievement								
	Boys	Low	-.89	-.96	-.77	NS	2.40†	3.97*	2.09‡
		Med	-.25	.06	.00	6.63*	5.25*	NS	
		High	.83	.87	.77	NS	NS	2.11†	
	Girls	Low	-.80	-.70	-.74	2.18†	NS	NS	
		Med	.19	.11	.19	1.72‡	NS	1.78‡	
		High	.87	.76	.88	2.44†	NS	2.62†	

Encour. S. Express.

Writing Quality	Pretest Writing Quality								
	Boys	Low	4.67	4.70	4.63	NS	NS	NS	2.11‡
		Med	5.56	5.06	5.94	4.06*	3.04*	7.10*	
		High	6.13	5.99	6.38	NS	2.03†	3.20*	
	Girls	Low	5.32	4.86	5.48	3.80*	NS	5.06*	
		Med	5.76	5.99	5.95	1.90‡	NS	NS	
		High	6.70	6.30	6.57	3.27*	NS	2.20†	

*p < .01.
†p < .05.
‡p < .10.
Source: Compiled by the authors.

relatively controlled and relatively nonindividualized; while higher-status children of both sexes did well in controlled classes, but showed mixed results regarding the optimal level of individualization (with a slight trend for higher-status children to do best with greater degrees of individualization).

The results involving control are similar to some of those which have been described in earlier chapters, showing unmotivated or unproficient children obtaining benefits relating to both extremes of the control dimension in different instances, while more highly motivated or proficient children generally benefited from classrooms with high levels of control and orderliness. It may be that, for some of the low initial-status children who lack motivation, a permissive and varied setting is optimal, while for others, who perhaps lack the ability to apply themselves to tasks in a disciplined and orderly way, an environment which provides for this lack may be best.

The results showing a similar U-shaped relationship with degree of individualization for low-status boys may also reflect relevance to different sets of needs. Those whose need is primarily motivational may benefit from the individual attention and student initiation of interaction characteristic of the individualized classes; and those whose need is more related to cognitive skills, may benefit from the nonindividualized setting, in which teachers make organized and structured presentations of the academic material.

The last interaction shown relates classroom encouragement of student expressiveness, prior writing quality, and sex to the post-test measure of writing quality. Although there are minor exceptions for low-status boys (who show no significant differentiation across class levels) and for middle-status girls (who show high scores for medium and high expressiveness classes), the results on the whole reflect the U-shaped relationship initially seen in the significant main effect, shown in Table 9.2, relating emphasis on expressiveness to writing quality. Children's writing was best in classes at both extremes of the expressiveness dimension, for the most part cutting across initial-status levels.

SUMMARY OF INTERACTIONS INVOLVING
CHILDREN'S PRIOR STATUS ON
COGNITIVE MEASURES

These analyses have examined the effects of different classroom settings on specific cognitive skills for children with different initial levels of proficiency with the same skills. The purpose of these analyses was to try to determine, for example, which type of class seemed to be optimal for the reading development of "poor

readers," and whether it was similar or different from the type of
class optimal for "good readers." The clearest trends were seen
with reading and mathematics concepts. Children with the lowest
initial reading scores showed the best final reading performance in
class cluster 6 (individualized, verbal-academic emphasis). Children
who were initially more proficient readers performed best in class
clusters 1, 2, and 4 (all characterized by varied, self-initiated
activities, and two of them by control and orderliness). Girls with
initially low reading and math scores did best in relatively controlled
and nonindividualized classrooms. Boys with low initial scores tended
to perform best in classes at the extreme poles of both the control
and individualization dimensions, while children of both sexes with
higher initial scores performed best in highly controlled and moderately or highly individualized classrooms.

　　Some of these results (particularly those for boys) reflected
trends seen repeatedly throughout these analyses, with less proficient
children benefiting from permissiveness and stimulation (but also
from discipline in some instances), and the more proficient children
from orderliness, discipline, and the opportunity for self-direction.
It was suggested that some low initial-status boys may have primarily
motivational deficiencies and, therefore, do best with reading and
mathematics in classes which are individualized and in those which
are permissive; while others may have more cognitive deficiencies
and, therefore, derive greatest benefit from the highly controlled
and the nonindividualized classes (in which teachers more frequently
made structured presentations of material).

APPENDIX B
Supplementary Tables

TABLE B.1

New Achievement Motivation Scales: Item–Total
and Interscale Correlations

Items in Scales	Scale 1 Total	Scale 2 Total	Scale 3 Total
Scale 1: Preference for Challenging Tasks Vs. Avoidance of Risk			
Preference for jobs "that I might not be able to do" (over those "I'm sure I can do")	.36	.01	.05
Liking for puzzle "that takes hard work to solve" (over one "easy to solve")	.50	.19	.08
Preference for helping at home with "things that are hard and I'm not sure I can do" (over "usual things I know I can do")	.47	-.01	.09
Preference for playing checkers against slightly better (rather than slightly worse) opponent	.52	.27	.15
Preference for working a hard, new (over an easy, familiar) puzzle	.48	.08	.04
Preference for getting model "like one I messed up last time" (rather than "one I did a good job on last time")	.42	.08	.05
Preference for solving "a hard problem without any hints" (rather than with hints)	.43	.12	.11
Preference for giving answer "even if it might be wrong" (rather than giving it "only if I'm sure it's right")	.43	.14	.06
Preference for working to improve "in a subject I'm not too good at" (rather than one "I'm pretty good at")	.51	.23	.06

Items in Scales	Scale 1 Total	Scale 2 Total	Scale 3 Total
Preference for playing a game "that is hard for me to win" (rather than one "that is easy for me to win")	.57	.18	.13
Scale 2: Preference for Interpersonally Equal Vs. Dominated Situations			
Preference for game "where everyone is about the same" (vs. one "where I'm better than anyone else")	.18	.57	.09
Predominant concern with "having fun" rather than with "winning" when playing game	.20	.63	.07
Preference for painting pictures when "everyone's work" vs. "only the best work" is displayed	.06	.59	.07
Preference for playing game when I am as good as my playmate" vs. "much better than my playmate"	.23	.67	.15
Preference for classes in which all students are about equally proficient vs. one in which "I (am) better than almost all the others"	.21	.65	.22
Scale 3: Academic Motivation			
Preference for learning "games where I would learn something" (vs. "fun games")	.11	.11	.61
"When I am sick, I would rather try to do my school work than rest and relax"	.09	.03	.63
"After summer vacation, I am glad" (rather than not glad) "to get back to school"	.11	.21	.62
"If I were getting better from a serious illness, I would like to spend my time learning how to do something" (rather than "relax")	.14	.14	.65
Scale 2 Total	.28		
Scale 3 Total	.18	.20	

Source: Compiled by the authors.

TABLE B.2

Class Preference Scales: Item-Total
and Interscale Correlations

Items in Scales	Scale 1 Total	Scale 2 Total	Scale 3 Total
Scale 1: Preference for Classes with **Freedom of Activity (vs. Restrictiveness)**			
Preference for class in which children get books and materials at will (vs. only at T direction)	.64	.39	.21
Preference for class in which children walk around at will (vs. only with T permission)	.60	.47	.30
Preference for class in which "things are very friendly" (vs. "main attention is on getting the work done right")	.52	.27	.11
Preference for class in which "work on any subject can start and end at any time" (vs. "regular starting and ending times")	.64	.33	.17
Preference for class in which "kids can talk whenever they want to" (vs. "only when the teacher calls on them")	.60	.38	.24
Preference for class with no (vs. much) testing	.50	.30	.16
Scale 2: Preference for Classes which **Allow Children Autonomy (vs. Teacher** **Control)**			
Preference for class in which children choose (vs. teacher plans) what they do	.47	.67	.24
Preference for class in which children (vs. teacher) decide who will work together on which things	.40	.59	.20
Preference for class in which children (vs. teacher) decide on rules and punishments	.42	.62	.26
Preference for class in which children (vs. teacher) decide what and how to learn	.11	.51	.20

Items in Scales	Scale 1 Total	Scale 2 Total	Scale 3 Total
Preference for class in which children (vs. teacher) decide on need for homework	.43	.70	.27
Preference for class in which "kids work on anything they want at any time" (vs. "teacher always decides what the kids should work on")	.50	.68	.28
Scale 3: Preference for Classes where Students are Involved in Teaching (vs. T Monopolization)			
Preference for class in which "kids spend a lot of time helping each other" (vs. "teacher gives kids any help they need")	.01	.06	.56
Preference for class in which "kids" (vs. only teacher) "always check and correct each others' work"	.18	.20	.62
Preference for class in which children "talk with each other about their work, mostly without the teacher" (vs. "only the teacher talks with the kids about their work")	.30	.29	.62
Preference for class in which "kids spend a lot of time teaching each other" (vs. "all the teaching is done by the teacher")	.34	.40	.69
Scale 2 Total	.60		
Scale 3 Total	.33	.39	

Source: Compiled by the authors.

289

TABLE B.3

Correlations between Individual-Level Factors, Outcome Residuals, and Miscellaneous Measures

		Orientation/Motive Factors				Prior Cognitive Skills and Self-Esteem				
		Pref. for Class with Autonomy	Compliant Conforming Orient.	Personal Control Intr. Motiv.	Achievement Motivation	Prior Achievement	Pre-Creativity	Pre-Inquiry Skill	Pre-Writing Quality	Pre-Self-Esteem
Orientation/Motive Factors										
Compliant Conforming Orient.	Boys	-.16*								
	Girls	-.09								
	Total	-.13*								
Personal Control Intrinsic Motivation	Boys	-.10	-.07							
	Girls	-.03	-.15*							
	Total	-.09	-.09*							
Achievement Motivation	Boys	-.22*	.09	.13						
	Girls	-.19*	.01	.26*						
	Total	-.21*	.05	.20*						
Prior Cognitive Skills and Self-Esteem										
Prior Achievement	Boys	.04	-.37*	.26*	-.11					
	Girls	-.06	-.35*	.35*	.16*					
	Total	-.02	-.34*	.31*	.03					
Pre-Creativity	Boys	-.06	-.14*	.10	-.07	.29*				
	Girls	-.03	-.15*	.16*	.06	.27*				
	Total	-.08	-.10*	.17*	.01	.29*				
Pre-Inquiry Skill	Boys	.05	-.26*	.19*	.01	.44*	.05			
	Girls	.02	-.31*	.20*	.14*	.37*	-.01			
	Total	.04	-.28*	.19*	.08	.40*	.02			
Pre-Writing Quality	Boys	.00	-.17*	.22*	-.02	.51*	.36*	.55*		
	Girls	-.09	-.17*	.22*	.10	.37*	.33*	.46*		
	Total	-.06	-.15*	.23*	.05	.45*	.37*	.50*		
Pre-Self-Esteem	Boys	-.04	.00	.36*	-.03	.23*	.11	.19*	.28*	
	Girls	-.03	.01	.21*	.08	.26*	.15*	.10	.21*	
	Total	-.04	.01	.29*	.02	.24*	.13*	.15*	.24*	

Prior Attitudes and Values

Pre-Self-Confidence	Boys	-.12	-.31*	.34*	.02	.38*	.20*	.25*	.31*	.48*
	Girls	-.13*	-.33*	.30*	.23*	.38*	.20*	.21*	.24*	.44*
	Total	-.14*	-.30*	.33*	.13*	.38*	.22*	.23*	.29*	.46*
Pre-Value on Equality	Boys	.17*	-.29*	.18*	.06	.21*	.10	.13*	.12	.10
	Girls	.12	-.31*	.16*	.11	.17*	.03	.20*	.11	.02
	Total	.15*	-.30*	.16*	.08	.19*	.05	.16*	.10*	.06
Pre-Concern for Others	Boys	.05	-.29*	.22*	.12	.28*	.14*	.18*	.23*	.05
	Girls	.04	-.39*	.26*	.26*	.30*	.16*	.26*	.21*	.03
	Total	.03	-.33*	.26*	.19*	.29*	.17*	.22*	.23*	.04
Pre-Value on Self-Direction	Boys	.30*	-.24*	-.06	-.04	.05	.01	.07	.01	-.04
	Girls	.13	-.14*	.02	.05	-.07	.00	.06	.03	-.08
	Total	.24*	-.20*	-.04	.00	-.01	-.03	.06	.00	-.06

Residuals: Cognitive Skills and Self-Esteem

Residual Achievement Test Performance	Boys	-.08	-.12	.15*	-.03	.05	.17*	.10	.24*	.17*
	Girls	-.01	.01	.09	-.02	-.08	.04	.03	.05	.12
	Total	-.06	-.04	.13*	-.02	.00	.12*	.07	.16*	.15*
Residual Creativity	Boys	-.04	-.13	.06	-.09	.23*	-.04	.15*	.11	.10
	Girls	-.06	-.13	.09	.04	.24*	-.04	.20*	.14*	.09
	Total	-.07	-.11*	.09	-.01	.24*	.00	.18*	.14*	.10*
Residual Inquiry Skill	Boys	-.11	-.13	.26*	.07	.27*	.23*	.06	.20*	.12
	Girls	-.03	-.15*	.18*	.06	.28*	.27*	-.06	.11	.13
	Total	-.08	-.13*	.22*	.07	.28*	.27*	.00	.17*	.12*
Residual Writing Quality	Boys	-.03	-.15*	.10	-.05	.36*	.14*	.13	.05	.10
	Girls	.02	-.16*	.17*	.03	.38*	.13	.04	-.10	.12
	Total	-.03	-.13*	.15*	.00	.37*	.17*	.09	.00	.11*
Residual Self-Esteem	Boys	-.02	-.02	.13	.03	.17*	.07	.07	.09	-.03
	Girls	.03	-.10	.18*	.08	.22*	.15*	.12	.16*	.05
	Total	.00	-.06	.15*	.05	.19*	.10*	.09	.12*	.01

(continued)

291

Table B.3 (continued)

		Prior Attitudes and Values				Residuals: Cognitive Skills and Self-Esteem			
		Pre-Self-Confidence	Pre-Value on Equality	Pre-Concern for Others	Pre-Value on Self-Dir.	Residual Ach. Test Performance	Residual Creativity	Residual Inquiry Skill	Residual Writing Quality
Prior Attitudes and Values									
Pre-Value on Equality	Boys	.16*							
	Girls	.22*							
	Total	.18*							
Pre-Concern for Others	Boys	.34*	.25*						
	Girls	.40*	.26*						
	Total	.38*	.25*						
Pre-Value on Self-Direction	Boys	.06	.13	.00					
	Girls	.08	.14*	.11					
	Total	.05	.14*	.04					
Residuals: Cognitive Skills and Self-Esteem									
Residual Achievement Test Performance	Boys	.16*	.08	.07	−.03				
	Girls	.06	−.05	−.02	−.01				
	Total	.12*	.02	.03	−.03				
Residual Creativity	Boys	.18*	.04	.02	.00	.16*			
	Girls	.11	.09	.09	−.07	.09			
	Total	.15*	.06	.07	−.05	.13*			
Residual Inquiry Skill	Boys	.22*	.14*	.18*	−.11	.20*	−.12		
	Girls	.13	.04	.11	−.05	.03	−.11		
	Total	.18*	.09	.15*	−.09	.12*	−.10		
Residual Writing Quality	Boys	.16*	.09	.06	−.02	.21*	.20*	.36*	
	Girls	.13*	.02	.07	−.07	.16*	.27*	.37*	
	Total	.16*	.04	.08	−.06	.20*	.25*	.37*	
Residual Self-Esteem	Boys	.06*	.07	.06	−.05	.19*	.09	.14*	.17*
	Girls	.11	.02	.05	−.02	.18*	.03	.12	.16*
	Total	.08	.05	.06	−.03	.19*	.06	.13*	.16*

		Orientation/Motive Factors				Prior Cognitive Skills and Self-Esteem				
		Pref. for Class with Autonomy	Compliant, Conforming Orient.	Personal Control, Intr. Mot.	Achievement Motivation	Prior Achievement	Pre-Creativity	Pre-Inquiry Skill	Pre-Writing Quality	Pre-Self-Esteem
Residuals: Attitudes and Values										
Residual Self-Confidence	Boys	-.06	-.07	.20*	.12	.16*	.09	.09	.09	.04
	Girls	-.02	-.13*	.16*	.09	.20*	.09	.18*	.13*	.07
	Total	-.05	-.09	.19*	.11*	.18*	.11*	.13*	.12*	.05
Residual Value on Equality	Boys	.02	-.15*	.07	.09	.08	.00	.09	.05	-.04
	Girls	.02	-.13	.18*	.08	.10	.09	.03	.04	.05
	Total	.00	-.12*	.14*	.09	.10	.08	.06	.07	.00
Residual Concern for Others	Boys	-.11	-.12	.19*	.12	.17*	.07	.12	.12	.13
	Girls	.01	-.15*	.25*	.22*	.26*	.08	.16*	.06	.04
	Total	-.07	-.11*	.24*	.17*	.22*	.11*	.14*	.11*	.09
Residual Value on Self-Direction	Boys	.14*	-.14*	.06	-.03	.06	.01	.02	-.01	.03
	Girls	.08	-.23*	.09	-.02	.10	.06	.15*	.09	.04
	Total	.12*	-.19*	.06	-.03	.07	.02	.08	.03	.03
Students' Ratings										
Enjoyment of Class	Boys	-.16*	.16*	.14*	.13*	.00	.00	.03	.05	.12
	Girls	-.06	.16*	.12	.20*	.08	.02	-.01	.00	.12
	Total	-.14*	.18*	.16*	.17*	.05	.06	-.01	.06	.12*
Friends in Class	Boys	.02	.08	.08	.09	-.09	-.02	-.03	.04	.02
	Girls	.00	.04	.05	.09	-.05	.04	-.05	-.03	.04
	Total	.00	.06	.07	.09	-.07	.02	-.04	.01	.03
Perceived Class Disruptiveness	Boys	.05	.03	-.08	-.01	-.06	-.10	-.05	-.03	-.05
	Girls	.06	.13	-.15*	-.05	-.12	-.02	-.07	-.08	-.09
	Total	.06	.08	-.12*	-.03	-.09	-.06	-.06	-.05	-.07

(continued)

293

Table B.3 (continued)

Residuals: Attitudes and Values

| | | Prior Attitudes and Values | | | | Residuals: Cognitive Skills and Self-Esteem | | | | |
		Pre-Self Confidence	Pre-Value on Equality	Pre-Concern for Others	Pre-Value on Self-Dir.	Res. Ach. Test Performance	Residual Creativity	Residual Inquiry Skill	Residual Writing Quality	Residual Self-Esteem
Residual Self-Confidence	Boys	.01	.12	.05	-.06	.18*	.11	.19*	.16*	.43*
	Girls	-.02	.08	.09	-.11	.08	.06	.07	.11	.40*
	Total	.01	.10*	.08	-.10*	.14*	.10*	.14*	.15*	.42*
Residual Value on Equality	Boys	.13	-.02	.18*	.01	.05	.09	.09	.03	.04
	Girls	.08	.03	.18*	-.05	.03	.02	.05	.06	.03
	Total	.11*	.00	.19*	-.03	.05	.07	.08	.07	.03
Residual Concern for Others	Boys	.19*	.13	-.08	-.09	.05	.14*	.13	.05	.01
	Girls	.06	.09	.04	-.13	-.03	.11	.10	.14*	-.03
	Total	.14*	.10*	-.01	-.12*	-.03	.14*	.12*	.12*	-.01
Residual Value on Self-Dir.	Boys	.04	.05	-.01	.02	-.05	-.08	.08	-.04	-.04
	Girls	.05	.09	.03	-.04	-.04	.08	.04	-.04	-.02
	Total	.04	.07	.01	.00	-.05	.00	.05	-.01	-.03
Students' Ratings										
Enjoyment of Class	Boys	.10	-.07	.03	-.13*	.12	.02	.05	.10	.23*
	Girls	.05	-.02	.01	-.06	.06	.00	.09	.07	.13*
	Total	.09*	-.06	.04	-.12*	.11*	.03	.08	.12*	.18*
Friends in Class	Boys	-.01	-.01	.01	-.03	.06	.05	.01	-.04	.25*
	Girls	.03	-.05	.06	-.01	-.04	-.03	-.01	-.07	.11
	Total	.02	-.03	.04	-.02	.02	.01	.01	-.05	.18*
Perceived Class Disruptiveness	Boys	-.10	-.04	-.15*	.03	-.14*	-.06	-.04	.00	-.08
	Girls	-.10	-.04	-.09	-.01	-.06	-.06	-.09	-.10	-.07
	Total	-.10*	-.04	-.12*	.01	-.10*	-.06	-.07	-.05	-.08

		Residuals: Attitudes and Values				Students' Ratings	
		Residual Self-Confidence	Residual Value on Equality	Residual Concern for Others	Residual Value on Self-Direction	Enjoyment of Class	Friends in Class
Residuals: Attitudes and Values							
Residual Value on Equality	Boys	.17*					
	Girls	.10					
	Total	.15*					
Residual Concern for Others	Boys	.22*	.17*				
	Girls	.18*	.19*				
	Total	.21*	.20*				
Residual Value on Self-Direction	Boys	.05	.15*	-.11			
	Girls	.16*	.14*	.03			
	Total	.10*	.14*	-.05			
Students' Ratings							
Enjoyment of Class	Boys	.20*	.02	.12	-.21*		
	Girls	.15*	-.03	.03	-.14*		
	Total	.19*	.03	.10*	-.19*		
Friends in Class	Boys	.08	.05	.09	-.12	.16*	
	Girls	.01	.05	-.03	-.04	.11	
	Total	.05	.06	.04	-.08	.14*	
Perceived Class Disruptiveness	Boys	-.05	.07	-.02	.12	-.13	-.08
	Girls	.02	-.14*	-.12	-.01	-.04	.01
	Total	-.02	-.03	-.07	.06	-.09	-.04

	Orientation/Motive Factors				Prior Cognitive Skills and Self-Esteem				
	Pref. for Class with Autonomy	Compliant, Conforming Orient.	Personal Control Intr. Mot.	Achievement Motivation	Prior Achievement	Pre-Creativity	Pre-Inquiry Skill	Pre-Writing Quality	Pre-Self-Esteem
Teachers' Ratings of Students									
Perseverance, Social Maturity									
Boys	-.14*	-.14*	.26*	-.03	.45*	.23*	.22*	.34*	.23*
Girls	-.06	-.10	.22*	.13*	.45*	.19*	.17*	.20*	.29*
Total	-.13*	-.09	.27*	.06	.45*	.27*	.19*	.30*	.25*
Activity Level, Curiosity									
Boys	.03	-.15*	.14*	.13	.27*	.06	.12	.18*	.14*
Girls	-.04	-.22*	.20*	.15*	.37*	.20*	.19*	.23*	.11
Total	.02	-.20*	.14*	.13*	.29*	.06	.15*	.16*	.12*
Miscellaneous Measures									
SES									
Boys	.01	-.20*	.19*	.04	.37*	.14*	.21*	.22*	.24*
Girls	.03	-.21*	.18*	.05	.30*	.13*	.20*	.14*	.14*
Total	.02	-.20*	.18*	.05	.33*	.13*	.20*	.18*	.19*
Sex									
Total	-.12*	.11*	.14*	.04	.09	.29*	.00	.17*	.01

		Prior Attitudes and Values				Residuals: Cognitive Skills and Self-Esteem				
		Pre-Self-Confidence	Pre-Value on Equality	Pre-Concern for Others	Pre-Value on Self-Dir.	Res. Ach. Test Performance	Residual Creativity	Residual Inquiry Skill	Residual Writing Quality	Residual Self-Esteem
Teachers' Ratings of Students										
Perseverance, Social Maturity	Boys	.30*	.08	.14*	-.02	.22*	.12	.24*	.24*	.17*
	Girls	.27*	.03	.08	-.04	.18*	.06	.20*	.22*	.32*
	Total	.30*	.04	.13*	-.06	.21*	.11*	.23*	.26*	.23*
Activity Level/Curiosity	Boys	.17*	.11	.10	.03	.12	.09	.11	.11	.09
	Girls	.21*	.09	.26*	-.01	-.03	.01	.11	.11	.17*
	Total	.16*	.11*	.15*	.04	.03	.02	.09	.06	.13*
Miscellaneous Measures										
SES	Boys	.24*	.17*	.16*	.04	.11	.10	.16*	.08	.09
	Girls	.17*	.16*	.17*	-.02	.12	.17*	.08	.12	.15*
	Total	.21*	.17*	.17*	.01	.12*	.13*	.12*	.10*	.12*
Sex	Total	.10*	-.05	.11*	-.12*	.08	.13*	.09	.17*	-.02

| | | Residual Self-Confidence | Residuals: Attitudes and Values | | | Students' Ratings | | |
			Residual Value on Equality	Residual Concern for Others	Residual Value on Self-Direction	Enjoyment of Class	Friends in Class	Perceived Class Dis- ruptiveness
Teachers' Ratings of Students								
Perseverance, Social Maturity	Boys	.14*	.00	.18*	-.10	.19*	.00	-.13*
	Girls	.17*	.05	.11	.06	.19*	-.06	-.07
	Total	.17*	.05	.17*	-.04	.23*	-.02	-.10*
Activity Level, Curiosity	Boys	.10	.01	.13	.06	.03	.12	-.03
	Girls	.15*	.03	.17*	.01	.10	.02	-.07
	Total	.10*	-.02	.11*	.05	.02	.06	-.05
Miscellaneous Measures								
SES	Boys	.10	.00	.13	.06	.03	-.05	-.13*
	Girls	.13	.06	.12	.10	.02	-.05	-.12
	Total	.12*	.03	.12*	.08	.02	-.05	-.13*
Sex	Total	.10*	.13*	.13*	-.06	.19*	.03	.00

| | | Teachers' Ratings | | Misc. Meas. |
		Perseverance, Social Maturity	Activity Level/ Curiosity	SES
Teachers' Ratings of Students				
Activity Level/Curiosity	Boys	.08		
	Girls	.20*		
	Total	.08		
Miscellaneous Measures				
SES	Boys	.21*	.18*	
	Girls	.17*	.11	
	Total	.18*	.14*	
Sex	Total	.24*	-.22*	.01

*p < .001.

<u>Note</u>: N (boys) = 500–645; N (girls) = 520–650; N (total) = 1035–1298.

<u>Source</u>: Compiled by the authors.

TABLE B.4

Cutting Points for Trichotomized Variables Used in Analyses of Variance
(Other than Factors)

Variable	Lower Cutting Point	Upper Cutting Point
SES	3.5	4.5
Pre-Reading (Percentile)	48.0	77.5
Pre-Arithmetic Concepts (Percentile)	54.0	81.5
Pre-Arithmetic Problems (Percentile)	47.5	82.0
Pre-Writing Quality	4.5	5.5

Note: Although several sets of factor scores were also trichotomized and used in analyses of variance (including classroom factors, person factors, pre-creativity and pre-inquiry), the cutting points are not presented here because these factor scores were standardized relative to the range of values obtained with this sample; knowing these points would not aid in comparing these groups with any others.

Source: Compiled by the authors.

BIBLIOGRAPHY

Abt Associates. 1977. Education as Experimentation: A Planned Variation Model. Cambridge, Mass.: Abt Associates, Inc.

Allender, J. S. 1968. "The Teaching of Inquiry Skills to Elementary School Children" (final report, United States Office of Education [USOE] Project, duplicated). Miami University, Oxford, Ohio.

Allport, G. W. 1967. Pattern and Growth in Personality. New York: Holt, Rinehart and Winston.

Anderberg, M. R. 1973. Cluster Analysis for Applications. New York: Academic Press.

Anderson, G. J. and H. J. Walberg. 1974. "Learning Environments." In H. J. Walberg, ed., Evaluating Educational Performance. Berkeley: McCutchan.

Arlin, M. 1975. "The Interaction of Locus of Control, Classroom Structure, and Pupil Satisfaction." Psychology in the Schools 12: 279-286.

Baron, R. M. et al. 1974. "Interaction of Locus of Control and Type of Performance Feedback: Considerations of External Validity." Journal of Personality and Social Psychology 30:285-292.

Barr, A. S. (ed.). 1961. "Wisconsin Studies of the Measurement and Prediction of Teacher Effectiveness." Journal of Experimental Education 30.

Bauer, R. A. 1964. "The Obstinate Audience: The Influence Process from the Point of View of Social Communication." American Psychologist 19:319-328.

Beach, L. R. 1960. "Sociability and Academic Achievement in Various Types of Learning Situations." Journal of Educational Psychology 51:208-212.

Bem, D. J. and A. Allen. 1974. "On Predicting Some of the People Some of the Time: The Search for Cross-Situational Consistencies in Behavior." Psychological Review 81:506-520.

Bennett, N. 1976. Teaching Styles and Pupil Progress. Cambridge, Mass.: Harvard University Press.

Berliner, D. C. and L. S. Cahen. 1973. "Trait-Treatment Interaction and Learning." In F. N. Kerlinger, ed., Review of Research in Education, 1, Itasca, Ill.: F. E. Peacock.

Blackie, J. 1971. Inside the Primary School. New York: Schocken.

Blashfield, R. 1976. "Mixture Model Tests of Cluster Analysis: Accuracy of Four Hierarchical Agglomerative Methods." Psychological Bulletin 83:377-388.

Bowers, K. S. 1975. "Situationism in Psychology: An Analysis and a Critique." Psychological Review 80:307-336.

Bracht, G. H. 1970. "Experimental Factors Related to Aptitude-Treatment Interactions." Review of Educational Research 40: 627-645.

Brophy, J. E. and C. M. Evertson. 1976. Learning from Teaching: A Developmental Perspective. Boston: Allyn & Bacon.

Brunswik, E. 1956. Perception and the Representative Design of Psychological Experiments. Berkeley: University of California Press.

Burton, R. V. 1963. "Generality of Honesty Reconsidered." Psychological Review 70: 481-499.

Buss, A. R. 1977. "The Trait-Situation Controversy and the Concept of Interaction." Personality and Social Psychology Bulletin 3:196-201.

Bussis, A. M. and E. A. Chittenden. 1970. Analysis of an Approach to Open Education. Princeton, N.J.: Educational Testing Service.

Calvin, A. D., F. K. Hoffman, and E. L. Harden. 1951. "The Effect of Intelligence and Social Atmosphere on Group Problem-Solving Behavior." Journal of Social Psychology 45:61-74.

Campus, N. 1974. "Trans-Situational Consistency as a Dimension of Personality." Journal of Personality and Social Psychology 29:593-600.

Cantrell, R. P., A. J. Stenner, and W. G. Katzenmeyer. 1977. "Teacher Knowledge, Attitudes, and Classroom Teaching Correlates of Student Achievement." Journal of Educational Psychology 69:172-179.

Cartwright, D. S. 1975. "Trait and Other Sources of Variance in the S-R Inventory of Anxiousness." Journal of Personality and Social Psychology 32:408-414.

Cattell, R. B. 1966. "The Meaning and Strategic Use of Factor Analysis." In R. B. Cattell, ed., Handbook of Multivariate Experimental Psychology. Chicago: Rand McNally, pp. 174-243.

Coutu, W. 1949. Emergent Human Nature. New York: Knopf.

Crandall, V. C. 1965. "Parents' Influences on Children's Achievement Behavior" (progress report, United States Public Health Service [USPHS] grant no. MH-02238, duplicated). Fels Institute, Yellow Springs, Ohio.

_____ and E. S. Battle. 1970. "The Antecedents and Adult Correlates of Academic and Intellectual Achievement Effort." In J. P. Hill, ed., Minnesota Symposia on Child Psychology, vol. 4. Minneapolis: University of Minnesota Press.

_____, V. J. Crandall, and W. Katkovsky. 1965a. "A Children's Social Desirability Questionnaire." Journal of Consulting Psychology 29:27-36.

_____, W. Katkovsky, and V. J. Crandall. 1965b. "Children's Belief in Their Own Control of Reinforcements in Intellectual-Academic Situations." Child Development 36:91-109.

Cronbach, L. J. 1957. "The Two Disciplines of Scientific Psychology. American Psychologist 12:671-684.

_____ and R. E. Snow. 1977. Aptitudes and Instructional Methods. New York: Irvington.

Cunningham, W. G. 1975. "The Impact of Student-Teacher Pairings on Teacher Effectiveness." American Educational Research Journal 12:169-189.

Daniels, R. L. and J. P. Stevens. 1976. "The Interaction Between the Internal-External Locus of Control and Two Methods of College Instruction." American Educational Research Journal 13:103-113.

Davidson, H. H. and J. W. Greenberg. 1967. School Achievers from a Deprived Background. New York: Associated Educational Services Corp.

Domino, G. 1971. "Interactive Effects of Achievement Orientation and Teaching Style on Academic Achievement." Journal of Educational Psychology 62:427-431.

Dowaliby, F. J. and H. Schumer. 1973. "Teacher-Centered Versus Student-Centered Mode of College Classroom Instruction as Related to Manifest Anxiety." Journal of Educational Psychology 64:125-132.

Doyle, W. 1978. "Paradigms for Research on Teacher Effectiveness." In L. S. Schulman, ed., Review of Research in Education, 5. Itasca, Ill.: F. E. Peacock.

____ and G. A. Ponder. 1975. "Classroom Ecology: Some Concerns About a Neglected Dimension of Research on Teaching." Contemporary Education 46:183-188.

Dunkin, M. J. and B. J. Biddle. 1974. The Study of Teaching. New York: Holt, Rinehart and Winston.

Ekehammar, B. 1974. "Interactionism in Personality from a Historical Perspective." Psychological Bulletin 81:1026-1048.

Emmer, E. T. and R. F. Peck. 1973. "Dimensions of Classroom Behavior." Journal of Educational Psychology 64:223-240.

Endler, N. S. and J. McV. Hunt. 1968. "S-R Inventories of Hostility and Comparisons of the Proportions of Variance from Persons, Responses, and Situations for Hostility and Anxiousness." Journal of Personality and Social Psychology 9:309-315.

____ and J. McV. Hunt. 1969. "Generalizability of Contributions from Sources of Variance in the S-R Inventories of Anxiousness." Journal of Personality 37:1-24.

____ and D. Magnusson, eds. 1976a. Interactional Psychology and Personality. Washington: Hemisphere.

____ and D. Magnusson. 1976b. "Toward an Interactional Psychology of Personality." Psychological Bulletin 83:956-974.

Epstein, J. L., and J. M. McPartland. 1975. "The Effects of Open School Organization on Student Outcomes" (report No. 194). Baltimore: Center for Social Organization of Schools, The Johns Hopkins University.

Featherstone, J. 1971. Schools Where Children Learn. New York: Liveright.

Flanders, N. 1970. Analyzing Teaching Behavior. Reading, Mass.: Addison-Wesley.

Forman, S. G. and J. D. McKinney. 1978. "Creativity and Achievement of Second Graders in Open and Traditional Classrooms. Journal of Educational Psychology 70:101-107.

Franks, D. D. and S. Dillon. 1975. "The Effects of Open Schools On Children: An Evaluation" (mimeographed). University of Denver.

Fredericksen, N. 1972. "Toward a Taxonomy of Situations." American Psychologist 27:114-123.

French, J. R. P., Jr., W. L. Rodgers, and S. Cobb. 1974. "Adjustment as Person-Environment Fit. In G. Coelho, D. A. Hamburg, and J. E. Adams, eds., Coping and Adaptation. New York: Basic Books.

Gage, N. L. 1972. Teacher Effectiveness and Teacher Education: The Search for a Scientific Basis. Palo Alto: Pacific Books.

____, et al. 1978. "An Experiment on Teacher Effectiveness and Parent-Assisted Instruction in the Third Grade" (duplicated). Stanford, Calif.: Center for Educational Research, Stanford University.

Goldberg, L. R. 1969. Student Personality Characteristics and Optimal College Learning Conditions (ORI Research Monograph, Vol. 9, No. 1). Oregon Research Institute.

Good, T. L. and C. N. Power. 1976. "Designing Successful Class-room Environments for Different Types of Students." Curriculum Studies 8:45-60.

Gordon, L. V. 1968. School Environment Preference Schedule. Albany: State University of New York.

_____. 1975. The Measurement of Interpersonal Values. Chicago: Science Research Associates.

Grimes, J. W. and W. Allinsmith. 1961. "Compulsivity, Anxiety, and School Achievement." Merrill-Palmer Quarterly 7:247-271.

Groobman, D. E., J. R. Forward, and C. Peterson. 1976. "Attitudes, Self-Esteem, and Learning in Formal and Informal Schools." Journal of Educational Psychology 68:32-35.

Guilford, J. P. 1956. Fundamental Statistics in Psychology and Education. New York: McGraw-Hill.

Haddon, F. A. and H. Lytton. 1968. "Teaching Approach and the Development of Divergent Thinking Abilities in Primary Schools." British Journal of Educational Psychology 38:171-180.

_____ and H. Lytton. 1971. "Primary Education and Divergent Thinking Abilities: Four Years On." British Journal of Educational Psychology 41:136-147.

Haigh, G. V. and W. Schmidt. 1956. "The Learning of Subject Matter in Teacher-Centered and Group-Centered Classes." Journal of Educational Psychology 47:295-301.

Hammond, K. R. 1954. "Representative vs. Systematic Design in Clinical Psychology." Psychological Bulletin 51:150-159.

Harckham, L. D. and D. V. Erger. 1972. "The Effect of Informal and Formal British Infant Schools on Reading Achievement." Paper presented at American Educational Research Association Convention.

Harman, H. 1960. Modern Factor Analysis. Chicago: University of Chicago Press.

Hartshorne, H. and M. A. May. 1928. Studies in the Nature of Character. Vol. 1: Studies in Deceit. New York: Macmillan.

Hassett, J. D. and A. Weisberg. 1972. Open Education: Alternatives Within our Tradition. Englewood Cliffs, N.J.: Prentice-Hall.

Hunt, D. E. 1971. Matching Models in Education. Toronto: The Ontario Institute for Studies in Education.

____. 1975. "Person-Environment Interaction: A Challenge Found Wanting Before It Was Tried." Review of Educational Research 45:209-230.

____ and E. V. Sullivan. 1974. Between Psychology and Education. Hinsdale: Dryden, 1974.

Inman, W. C. 1977. "Classroom Practices and Basic Skills. Kindergarten and Third Grade" (duplicated). Division of Research, North Carolina State Department of Public Instruction.

Judd, D. E. 1974. "The Relationship of Locus of Control as a Personality Variable to Student Attitude in the Open School Environment." Ph.D. diss., University of Maryland.

Kelley, G. A. 1955. The Psychology of Personal Constructs. New York: Norton.

Kennedy, M. M. 1978. "Findings from the Follow Through Planned Variation Study." Educational Researcher 7:3-11.

Kirschner Associates. 1977. Study Findings: Final Report of the Instructional Dimensions Study. 1976-1977. Washington, D.C.: Kirschner Associates.

Klaff, F. R. and E. M. Docherty. 1975. "Children's Self-Concept and Attitudes Toward School in Open and Traditional Classrooms." Journal of School Psychology 13:97-103.

Klein, P. S. 1975. "Effects of Open vs. Structured Teacher-Student Interaction on Creativity of Children with Different Levels of Anxiety." Psychology in the Schools 12:286-288.

Kohl, H. 1969. The Open Classroom. New York: Random House.

Kohlberg, L. 1966. "Moral Education in the Schools: A Developmental View." School Review 74:1-30.

Kulka, R. A. 1974. "Adjustment to High School: B = f (P, E) ?" Paper presented at meeting of American Psychological Association.

Levinson, D. J. 1959. "Role, Personality, and Social Structure in the Organizational Setting." Journal of Abnormal and Social Psychology 58: 170–180.

Lewin, K. 1955. Dynamic Theory of Personality. New York: McGraw-Hill.

____. 1951. Field Theory in Social Science. New York: Harper.

____, R. Lippitt, and R. K. White. 1939. "Patterns of Aggressive Behavior in Experimentally Created 'Social Climates'." Journal of Social Psychology 10: 271–299.

Lorr, M. and B. K. Radhakrishnan. 1967. "A Comparison of Two Methods of Cluster Analysis." Educational and Psychological Measurement 27: 47–53.

Maccoby, E. 1966. The Development of Sex Differences. Stanford: Stanford University Press.

Magnusson, D. and N. S. Endler, eds. 1977. Personality at the Crossroads: Current Issues in Interactional Psychology. Hillsdale, N.J.: Lawrence Erlbaum.

Marshall, H. H. 1976. "Dimensions of Classroom Structure and Functioning Project: Final Report" (duplicated). Instructional Laboratories, School of Education, University of California, Berkeley, California.

McDonald, F. J. 1976. "Beginning Teacher Evaluation Study, Phase II. 1973–74. Executive Summary Report" (duplicated). Educational Testing Service, Princeton, N.J.

____, and P. Elias. 1976. "Beginning Teacher Evaluation Study, Phase II. 1973–74. Final Report" (duplicated). Educational Testing Service, Princeton, N.J.

McKeachie, W. J. 1961. "Motivation, Teaching Methods, and College Learning." In M. R. Jones, ed., Current Theory and Research in Motivation. Lincoln: University of Nebraska Press.

____. 1963. "Research on Teaching at the College and University Level." In N. L. Gage, ed., Handbook of Research on Teaching. Chicago: Rand McNally.

____, R. L. Isaacson, J. E. Milholland, and Y. G. Lin. 1968. "Student Achievement Motives, Achievement Cues, and Academic Achievement." Journal of Consulting and Clinical Psychology 32: 26-29.

____, Y. G. Lin, J. E. Milholland, and R. L. Isaacson. 1966. "Student Affiliation Motives, Teacher Warmth, and Academic Achievement." Journal of Personality and Social Psychology 4: 457-461.

McPartland, J. M. and J. L. Epstein. 1977. "Open Schools and Achievement: Extended Tests of a Finding of No Relationship." Sociology of Education 42: 133-144.

McQuitty, L. L. 1957. "Elementary Linkage Analysis for Isolating Orthogonal and Oblique Types and Typal Relevancies." Educational and Psychological Measurement 17: 207-229.

Medley, D. M. 1977. Teacher Competence and Teacher Effectiveness: A Review of Process-Product Research. Washington, D.C.: American Association of Colleges of Teacher Education.

____, and H. E. Mitzel. 1963. "Measuring Classroom Behavior By Systematic Observation." In N. L. Gage, ed., Handbook of Research on Teaching. Chicago: Rand McNally.

Mischel, W. 1968. Personality and Assessment. New York: Wiley.

____. 1973. "Toward a Cognitive Social Learning Reconceptualization of Personality." Psychological Review 80: 252-283.

____, E. B. Ebbesen, and A. R. Zeiss. 1973. "Selective Attention to the Self." Journal of Personality and Social Psychology 27: 129-142.

Moos, R. H. 1978. "A Typology of Junior High and High School Classrooms." American Educational Research Journal 15: 53-66.

Murray, H. A. 1938. Exploration in Personality. New York: Oxford University Press.

Nelson, E. A., R. E. Grinder, and M. L. Mutterer. 1969. "Sources of Variance in Behavioral Measures of Honesty in Temptation Situations: Methodological Analyses." Developmental Psychology 1: 265-279.

Newcomb, T. M. 1929. Consistency of Certain Extrovert-Introvert Behavior Patterns in 51 Problem Boys. New York: Columbia University, Teachers College, Bureau of Publications.

Nie, N. H. et al. 1975. SPSS: Statistical Package for the Social Sciences. New York: McGraw-Hill.

Nunnally, J. C. 1967. Psychometric Theory. New York: McGraw-Hill.

Oberlander, M. and D. Solomon. 1973. "The Effects of Multi-Age Multi-Grade Programming on Students' Verbal and Non-Verbal Creative Functioning." Paper presented at annual meeting of the American Educational Research Association.

Overall, J. E. and C. J. Klett. 1972. Applied Multivariate Analysis. New York: McGraw-Hill.

Owen, S. V., R. D. Froman, and D. M. Calchera. 1974. "Effect of Open Education on Selected Cognitive and Affective Measures." Paper presented at annual meeting of the American Educational Research Association.

Page, E. B. 1975. "Statistically Recapturing the Richness Within the Classroom." Psychology in the Schools 12: 339-344.

Papay, J. P., R. J. Costello, J. J. Hedl, Jr., and C. D. Spielberger. 1975. "Effects of Trait and State Anxiety on the Performance of Elementary School Children in Traditional and Individualized Multiage Classrooms." Journal of Educational Psychology 67: 840-846.

Parent, J., J. Forward, R. Canter, and J. Mohling. 1975. "Interactive Effects of Teaching Strategy and Personal Locus of Control on Student Performance and Satisfaction." Journal of Educational Psychology 67: 764-769.

Pervin, L. A. 1968. "Performance and Satisfaction as a Function of Individual-Environment Fit." Psychological Bulletin 69: 56-68.

Peterson, P. L. 1977. "Interactive Effects of Student Anxiety, Achievement Orientation, and Teacher Behavior on Student Achievement and Attitude." Journal of Educational Psychology 69: 779-792.

Plowden, Lady B. et al. 1967. "Children and Their Primary Schools: A Report of the Central Advisory Council for Education." London: Her Majesty's Stationery Office.

Price, R. H. and D. L. Bouffard. 1974. "Behavioral Appropriateness and Situational Constraint as Dimensions of Social Behavior." Journal of Personality and Social Psychology 30: 579-586.

Ramey, C. T. and V. Piper. 1974. "Creativity in Open and Traditional Classrooms." Child Development 45: 557-560.

Rentfrow, R. K. and J. C. Larson. 1975. Correlates of school achievement in open and traditional settings in a sample of low-income children. Paper presented at annual meeting of Society for Research in Child Development.

Reiss, S. and N. Dyhdalo. 1975. "Persistence, Achievement, and Open-Space Environments." Journal of Educational Psychology 67: 506-513.

Rosenshine, B. 1976a. "Classroom Instruction." In N. L. Gage, ed., The Psychology of Teaching Methods (Part I, Seventy-fifth Yearbook of the National Society for the Study of Education). Chicago: NSSE.

____. "Recent Research on Teaching Behaviors and Student Achievement." Journal of Teacher Education 27: 61-64.

____, and N. Furst. 1973. "The Use of Direct Observation to Study Teaching." In R. M. W. Travers, ed., Second Handbook of Research on Teaching. Chicago: Rand McNally.

Rotter, J. B. 1954. Social Learning and Clinical Psychology. Englewood Cliffs, N.J.: Prentice-Hall.

____. 1955. "The Role of the Psychological Situation in Determining the Direction of Human Behavior. In M. R. Jones, ed., Nebraska Symposium on Motivation. Lincoln: University of Nebraska Press. of Nebraska Press.

Ruedi, J. and C. K. West. 1973. "Pupil Self-Concept in an 'Open' School and in a 'Traditional' School." Psychology in the Schools 10:48-53.

Ryans, D. G. 1960. Characteristics of Teachers. Washington: American Council on Education.

St. John, N. 1971. "Thirty-six Teachers: Their Characteristics and Outcomes for Black and White Pupils." American Educational Research Journal 8:635-648.

Salomon, G. 1972. "Heuristic Models for the Generation of Aptitude-Treatment Interaction Hypotheses." Review of Educational Research 42:327-343.

Samph, T., and White, S. n.d. "A Second-Order Factor Analysis of Selected Classroom Observation Systems" (mimeographed). National Board of Medical Examiners and Pennsylvania State University.

Schnee, R. G. 1975. "Effects of Open Spacing and Team Teaching on Reading and Arithmetic Growth in the Elementary School" (mimeographed). Oklahoma City Public Schools.

Selvin, H. 1960. The Effects of Leadership. Glencoe, Ill.: The Free Press.

Sermat, V. 1970. "Is Game Behavior Related to Behavior in Other Interpersonal Situations? Journal of Personality and Social Psychology 16:92-109.

Serow, R. and D. Solomon. 1978. "Classroom Conditions and Intergroup Behavior in Desegregated School Settings" (duplicated). North Carolina State University, Raleigh, N.C.

Shulman, L. S. 1970. "Reconstruction of Educational Research." Review of Educational Research 40:371-396.

Silberman, C. E. 1970. Crisis in the Classroom. New York: Random House.

Slovic, P. 1972. "Information Processing, Situation Specificity, and the Generality of Risk-Taking Behavior." Journal of Personality and Social Psychology 22:128-134.

Snow, R. E. 1974. "Representative and Quasi-Representative Designs for Research on Teaching. Review of Educational Research 44:265-292.

Snyder, M. and T. C. Monson. 1975. "Persons, Situations, and the Control of Social Behavior." Journal of Personality and Social Psychology 32:637-644.

Soar, R. S. 1972. "Teacher Behavior Related to Pupil Growth." International Review of Education 18:508-528.

____ and R. M. Soar. 1972. "An Empirical Analysis of Selected Follow Through Programs: An Example of a Process Approach to Evaluation." In I. J. Gordon, ed., Early Childhood Education. Chicago: National Society for the Study of Education.

____, R. M. Soar, and M. Ragosta. 1971. "Florida Climate and Control System. Observer's Manual" (duplicated). Gainesville: Institute for Development of Human Resources, University of Florida.

Solomon, D. 1963. "Influences on the Decisions of Adolescents." Human Relations 16:45-60.

____. 1966a. "Teacher Behavior Dimensions, Course Characteristics, and Student Evaluations of Teachers." American Educational Research Journal 3:34-47.

____. 1966b. "The Judgment of Appropriateness as an Intervening Variable." IJR Research Bulletin (Institute for Juvenile Research) 4, 1 (entire).

____. 1969. "The Generality of Children's Achievement-Related Behavior." Journal of Genetic Psychology 114:109-125.

____. 1977. "Perceptions of Similarity Between Striving Tasks and the Generality of Task Preferences." Motivation and Emotion 1:181-192.

____, W. E. Bezdek, and L. Rosenberg. 1963. Teaching Styles and Learning. Chicago: Center for the Study of Liberal Education for Adults.

____ et al. 1972. "The Development of Democratic Values and Behavior among Mexican-American Children." Child Development 43:625-638.

_____ and A. J. Kendall. 1974. "Progress Report. Individual Characteristics and Children's Performance in Varied Educational Settings" (duplicated). Montgomery County, Maryland, Public Schools.

_____ and A. J. Kendall. 1975. "Teachers' Perceptions of, and Reactions to, 'Misbehavior' in Traditional and Open Classrooms." Journal of Educational Psychology 67:528-530.

_____ and A. J. Kendall. 1976. "Individual Characteristics and Children's Performance in 'Traditional' and 'Open' Classroom Settings." Journal of Educational Psychology 68:613-625.

_____ and A. J. Kendall. 1977. "Dimensions of Children's Classroom Behavior, as Perceived by Teachers." American Educational Research Journal 14:411-421.

_____ and M. I. Oberlander. 1974. "Locus of Control in the Classroom." In R. H. Coop and K. White, eds., Psychological Concepts in the Classroom. New York: Harper & Row.

_____, R. J. Parelius, and T. V. Busse. 1969. "Dimensions of Achievement-Related Behavior among Lower-Class Negro Parents." Genetic Psychology Monographs 79:163-190.

Stallings, J. and D. Kaskowitz. 1974. "Follow Through Classroom Observation Evaluation. 1972-1973" (duplicated). Menlo Park, California: Stanford Research Institute.

Stern, G. G. 1971. People in Context: Measuring Person-Environment Congruence in Business and Industry. New York: Wiley.

_____ and W. J. Walker. 1971. Classroom Environment Index. Syracuse University.

Stevenson, H. W. and R. D. Odom. 1965. "Interrelationships in Children's Learning." Child Development 36:7-19.

Tallmadge, G. K. and J. W. Shearer. 1971. "Interactive Relationships Among Learner Characteristics, Types of Learning, Instructional Methods, and Subject Matter Variables." Journal of Educational Psychology 62:31-38.

Terhune, K. W. 1968. "Motives, Situation, and Interpersonal Conflict Within Prisoners' Dilemma." Journal of Personal and Social Psychology Monograph Supplement 8, 3: Pt. 2.

Thistlethwaite, D. L. 1960. "College Press and Changes in Study Plans of Talented Students." Journal of Educational Psychology 51: 222-234.

Tobias, S. 1976. "Achievement-Treatment Interactions." Review of Educational Research 46: 61-74.

Traub, R. E., J. Weiss, and C. W. Fisher. 1974. "Studying Openness in Education: An Ontario Example." Journal of Research and Development in Education 8: 47-59.

____ et al. 1972. "Closure on Openness: Describing and Quantifying Open Education." Interchange 3: 69-84.

Trickett, E. J. and R. H. Moos. 1973. "Social Environment of Junior High and High School Classrooms." Journal of Educational Psychology 65: 93-102.

Tuckman, B. W., D. W. Cochran, and E. J. Travers. 1974. "Evaluating Open Classrooms." Journal of Research and Development in Education 8: 14-19.

Walberg, H. and G. J. Anderson. 1968. "Classroom Climate and Individual Learning." Journal of Educational Psychology 59: 414-419.

____, J. Sorensen, and T. Fischbach. 1972. "Ecological Correlates of Ambience in the Learning Environment." American Educational Research Journal 9: 139-148.

____ and S. C. Thomas. 1971. Characteristics of Open Education: Toward an Operational Definition. Newton, Mass.: TDR Associates.

Wallach, M. A. and N. Kogan. 1965. Modes of Thinking in Young Children. New York: Holt, Rinehart and Winston.

Ward, J. H., Jr. 1963. "Hierarchical Grouping to Optimize an Objective Function." Journal of the American Statistical Association 58: 236-244.

Ward, W. D. and P. R. Barcher. 1975. "Reading Achievement and Creativity as Related to Open Classroom Experience." Journal of Educational Psychology 67: 683–691.

Weiner, B. and A. Kukla. 1970. "An Attributional Analysis of Achievement Motivation." Journal of Personality and Social Psychology 15: 1–20.

Wellisch, J. B. et al. 1977. An In-Depth Study of Emergency School Aid Act (ESAA) Schools. Santa Monica, Calif.: Systems Development Corp.

White, K. and J. L. Howard. 1970. "The Relationship of Achievement Responsibility to Instructional Treatments. Journal of Experimental Education 39: 78–82.

Williams, C. L. 1973. "Effects of Training on Rating Reliability, as Estimated by ANOVA Procedures, for Fluency Tests of Creativity." Paper presented at meeting of National Council on Measurement in Education.

Wilson, F. S., T. Stuckey, and R. Langevin. 1972. "Are pupils in the Open Plan School Different?" Journal of Educational Research 66: 115–118.

Wilson, J. P. 1976. "Motivation, Modeling, and Altruism: A Person-Situation Analysis." Journal of Personality and Social Psychology 34: 1078–1086.

Winer, B. J. 1971. Statistical Principles in Experimental Design. New York: McGraw-Hill.

Wright, R. J. "The Affective and Cognitive Consequences of an Open Education Elementary School." American Educational Research Journal 12: 449–468.

Wrong, D. H. 1961. "The Oversocialized Conception of Man in Modern Sociology." American Sociological Review 26: 183–192.

ABOUT THE AUTHORS

DANIEL SOLOMON is a Social Research Manager with Census Use Research in the United States Bureau of the Census. From 1971 to 1978 he was on the staff of the Montgomery County, Maryland, Public Schools, first in the Division of Psychological Services (where the study described in this book was undertaken), later in the departments of Research and Evaluation and of Educational Accountability. Before coming to Maryland, Dr. Solomon conducted research on a variety of social psychological and educational topics at the Center for the Study of Liberal Education for Adults and at the Institute for Juvenile Research, both in Chicago.

Dr. Solomon has published extensively in psychological, social psychological, and educational research journals, including the Journal of Educational Psychology, American Educational Research Journal, Developmental Psychology, and the Journal of Social Psychology.

Dr. Solomon received a BA from Antioch College, and an MA and a Ph.D. from the University of Michigan.

ARTHUR J. KENDALL is a partner in Social Research Consultants in Washington, D.C. He is also associated with Census Use Research, U.S. Bureau of the Census.

Dr. Kendall consults in many behavioral and social science areas. He has presented papers at conventions of the American Psychological Association and other professional associations, and has published in the Journal of Educational Psychology and the American Educational Research Journal.

Dr. Kendall recently received a doctorate in social psychology from the Catholic University of America.